CUTTING EDGE

THIRD EDITION

UPPER INTERMEDIATE

STUDENTS' BOOK

WITH DVD-ROM

SARAH CUNNINGHAM PETER MOOR
AND JONATHAN BYGRAVE

CONTENTS

Pronunciation	Task	World culture/ Language live	Study, Practice & Remember
Auxiliary verbs Sounding sympathetic	Keep a conversation going **Preparation:** Reading and listening **Task:** Speaking	**Language live** **Speaking:** Responding to how people feel **Writing:** Planning and drafting a biography	Study & Practice 1, page 131 Study & Practice 2, page 132 Remember these words, page 133
Noun suffixes	Do a class survey **Preparation:** Listening **Task:** Speaking	**World culture:** The happiness formula	Study & Practice 1, page 134 Study & Practice 2, page 135 Remember these words, page 136
Sounding calm or angry	Tell a story from two points of view **Preparation:** Listening **Task:** Speaking	**Language live** **Speaking:** Dealing with unexpected problems **Writing:** A narrative	Study & Practice 1, page 137 Study & Practice 2, page 138 Remember these words, page 139
Word stress	Choose people to go on a space mission **Preparation:** Reading **Task:** Speaking	**World culture:** Nature or nurture?	Study & Practice 1, page 140 Study & Practice 2, page 141 Remember these words, page 142
Intonation of statements and questions	Plan a fantasy dinner party **Preparation:** Listening **Task:** Speaking	**Language live** **Speaking:** Dealing with problems on the telephone **Writing:** Types of message	Study & Practice 1, page 143 Study & Practice 2, page 144 Remember these words, page 145
Weak and strong forms in questions	Present an idea for a TV programme **Preparation:** Listening **Task:** Speaking	**World culture:** Unsung heroes	Study & Practice 1, page 146 Study & Practice 2, page 147 Remember these words, page 148

CONTENTS

4

Pronunciation	Task	World culture/ Language live	Study, Practice & Remember
Sounding polite	Present ideas for an event **Preparation:** Reading and vocabulary **Task:** Speaking	**Language live** **Writing:** A review of an event **Speaking:** Awkward social situations	Study & Practice 1, page 149 Study & Practice 2, page 150 Remember these words, page 151
The weak form of *have*	Discuss two mysteries **Preparation:** Reading and vocabulary **Task:** Speaking	**World culture:** The Bermuda Triangle	Study & Practice 1, page 152 Study & Practice 2, page 153 Remember these words, page 154
Using stress for emphasis	Collect and present tips **Preparation:** Reading **Task:** Speaking	**Language live:** **Speaking:** Suggestions and advice **Writing:** A speculative covering letter	Study & Practice 1, page 155 Study & Practice 2, page 156 Remember these words, page 157
Reporting what people said	Discuss an article **Preparation:** Reading and vocabulary **Task:** Speaking	**World culture:** The science of film	Study & Practice 1, page 158 Study & Practice 2, page 159 Remember these words, page 160
Word stress and vowel sounds	Discuss a controversial issue **Preparation:** Listening **Task:** Speaking	**Language live:** **Speaking:** Reporting opinions **Writing:** A 'for and against' essay	Study & Practice 1, page 161 Study & Practice 2, page 162 Remember these words, page 163
Sentence stress	Hold the floor! **Preparation:** Listening and speaking **Task:** Speaking	**World culture:** Changing lives in Malawi	Study & Practice 1, page 164 Study & Practice 2, page 165 Remember these words, page 166

01

GETTING ON

IN THIS UNIT

- **Grammar: Past and present verb forms; Uses of auxiliary verbs**

- **Vocabulary: Relationships; Friendships; *Get***

- **Task: Keep a conversation going**

- **Language live: Responding to how people feel; Planning and drafting a biography**

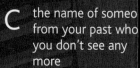

A a place that was important in your childhood

B something you remember about the first house/flat you ever lived in

C the name of someo from your past who you don't see any more

D the name of someone you have met recently

E something important that has happened in your family recently

F your least favourite day of the week or time of day

Speaking and listening
Your past and present

1a Read A–F above. Think of at least two things to say about each one.

b Work in pairs. Tell your partner about the things you have written. Your partner can ask you questions.

2a 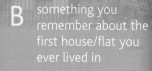 1.1 Listen to six speakers. Which item from exercise 1a does each speaker talk about?

b Listen again. Which speaker mentions the topics in the box? What do they say about them?

a farm	a coincidence	a baby
a pond	working on a film	an awful boss

3 1.2 Listen and complete the extracts from the recording.

1 We _____ there every summer for our holidays. I _____ it.
2 Normally it's fine because _____ on programmes _____ late ... But at the moment _____ a film.
3 It was my first job, but I think Kathy _____ different jobs before that.
4 I _____ three or four years.
5 Somehow _____ touch.
6 I think we _____ about five years.
7 We were _____ to each other and we just _____ .
8 It _____ sweet in the photo on Facebook.

6

Language focus 1
Past and present verb forms

1 Work in pairs and do the quiz. Then find another example from exercise 3 to go under each heading.

So you think you know about English grammar? Do the quiz and find out.

1 **Present simple and continuous**

Which sentence below describes something which is generally true? Which describes a temporary situation?

a *I'm a hairdresser and I do a lot of work for TV.*
b *At the moment, I'm getting up at about 5 a.m.*

2 **Past simple and Past continuous**

Which verb form in the sentence below describes a single action in the past? Which describes an action in progress at that time?

*I **met** Kathy when we **were** both **working** for this really awful boss.*

3 **State and action verbs**

Choose the correct verb in the sentences below. Why isn't the other verb possible?

a *I **don't remember** / **'m not remembering** its name.*
b *My uncle **owned** / **was owning** a farm when I was a child.*

4 *Used to*

Look at the example sentences below and choose the correct options in the rule.

*My aunt and uncle **used to** own a farm.*
*I **used to** spend hours staring at the fish.*

used to describes *habits / states / single actions* in the *past / present*

5 **Present perfect and Past simple**
Match examples 1–4 to descriptions a–d below.

*1 I**'ve known** Emma for six months.*

*2 Kathy and I **were** really good friends for a couple of years.*

*3 My cousin and his wife **have had** a baby.*

*4 We **moved** in about 1993.*

a Something that continued for a period of time in the past.
b Something that started in the past and continues to the present.
c Something that happened in the past and is important now. We don't know exactly when it happened.
d Something that happened at a finished time in the past.

6 **Past perfect**
Look at the sentences below. Which action in bold happened first?

*The house where I **was born** was quite small. My parents **had bought** it from an old man.*

PRACTICE

1 🎧 **1.3** Choose the correct verbs to complete the article below. Listen and check.

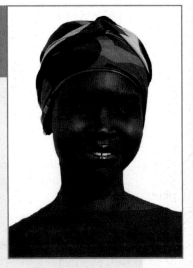

Alek Wek
Past and present

Alek Wek is one of the world's most popular models. She [1]*has appeared / appeared* in catwalk shows, high profile advertising campaigns and on the cover of *Vogue* magazine. Her life, however, [2]*hasn't been / hadn't been* easy.

Alek [3]*has been born / was born* into a poor family in Sudan in 1977, the seventh of nine children. In 1983, civil war [4]*broke out / had broken* out. Alek [5]*was playing / used to play* out in the streets, but it [6]*has got / got* too dangerous to go out. In the end, Alek's family [7]*have decided / decided* to leave their town and walk south. Eventually, the family ended up in Khartoum, the capital of Sudan. Unfortunately, in Khartoum, Alek's father died. Many years before, he [8]*had / had had* an operation on his hip, and during their long walks it [9]*was getting / got* badly infected.

In 1991, Alek and her younger sister moved to the UK. Their older sister [10]*was moving / had moved* there three years earlier, and later their mother [11]*joined / used to join* them.

In 1995, Alek [12]*shopped / was shopping* at a market in London when a modelling scout [13]*approached / was approaching* her, and against her mother's advice, 18-year-old Alek [14]*has decided / decided* to become a model.

It was the right decision. She [15]*is / has been* a top model for over 15 years. She [16]*also designs / is also designing* handbags, and [17]*writes / has written* an autobiography called *Alek*. However, these days she [18]*spends / is spending* more and more time working with charities which help Africa, like the Refugee Council.

In the 1990s, Alek Wek [19]*changed / was changing* the stereotype of how a model should look. Now she [20]*changes / is changing* the stereotype of how a model should behave.

Unit 1, Study & Practice 1, page 131

Reading

1 Work in pairs and discuss the questions below that are relevant to you.

- Would you like to have a brother or sister? Why?
- What are the advantages of being an only child?
- How close is your relationship with your sibling(s)?
- Are you similar to each other? In what ways?
- Are you closer to one sibling than the other(s)? Which one and why?
- Are you competitive with your sibling(s)? If yes, give examples.

2 Work in pairs and look at the photos. What do you know (or can you guess) about the people?

3 Read the article and answer the questions.

Which famous siblings ...
1 are friends despite their rivalry?
2 have continued their rivalry into old age?
3 have taken legal action against each other?
4 caused problems in their local community because of their rivalry?
5 often competed against each other in important competitions?
6 often criticise each other in the media?

4 Read the article again. Complete the sentences below.

1 The author of the article felt competitive towards her sister because ...
2 In her autobiography, Joan Fontaine boasted that she had ...
3 A lot of people were watching when Olivia de Havilland ...
4 Noel Gallagher once attacked his brother because ...
5 The Dassler brothers started separate companies because ...
6 Some people in Herzogenaurach refused to socialise with each other because ...
7 The Williams sisters are best friends despite the fact that ...
8 We know the author of the article is still competitive towards her sister because ...

5 Work in groups and discuss the questions below.

- Which case of sibling rivalry do you think is the most extreme? Why?
- Which siblings' achievements are the most impressive?
- Do you know any other examples of serious sibling rivalry?

IT'S A FACT!
Sibling rivalry in nature! Black eagles lay two eggs, but the first chick to hatch kills the other one!

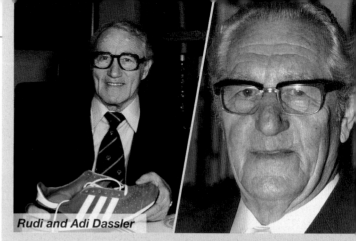

Rudi and Adi Dassler

Venus and Serena Williams

GREAT SIBLING

Sancha Ford reports

For most people, the longest relationship they will have is with their sibling. It's a shame, then, that we can't choose them. As children, my younger sister and I were always competing with each other. I was jealous of her looks and she felt threatened by my academic success. But our rivalry was nothing compared to that of some famous siblings.

Take 1940s movie stars Olivia de Havilland and Joan Fontaine. The competitive relationship between these sisters is the stuff of Hollywood legend. 'I married first, won the Oscar before Olivia did. And if I die first, she'll undoubtedly be livid because I beat her to it,' Joan wrote in her autobiography. Their rivalry became very public in 1946 when Olivia won an Oscar. Joan was asked to present the award but Olivia refused to even shake her hand. 'They just don't have much in common,' commented one person at the time. Now in their 90s, the sisters apparently still loathe each other!

More recently, the rivalry between rock stars Noel and Liam Gallagher has hit the news. As part of the band Oasis, they created some memorable music, but whenever they are interviewed, the brothers cannot resist putting each other down. 'There are only two things wrong with Liam,' Noel once said, 'everything he says and everything he does.' While the brothers were working on their second album, Liam invited some friends to the studio for a party. Noel was trying to work and ended up attacking Liam with a cricket bat. By 2011, the brothers had stopped working together and were suing each other – a sorry situation for any brothers to be in.

Noel and Liam Gallagher

Olivia de Havilland and Joan Fontaine

RIVALRIES

But it's not just in show business where siblings fall out. Entrepreneurs Rudolf and Adolf Dassler started making sports shoes in the small German town of Herzogenaurach in the 1920s. Their factory south of the river became very successful but they were always very different. Adolf, or Adi, was a quiet craftsman while Rudolf was "a loud-mouthed salesman". Eventually, in 1948, the brothers fell out permanently. Rudolf moved across the river and set up a rival sports-shoe company, which he called Puma. In response, Adi used the first letters of his name and surname to create his brand – Adidas.

The brothers never spoke to each other again and their rivalry divided the town. The residents wore either Adidas or Puma and would sometimes refuse to mix with each other. It became a place where you always looked at the shoes someone was wearing before starting a conversation. The brothers died in the 1970s and were buried in the same cemetery – at opposite ends.

But not all successful siblings hate each other. Top tennis players Serena and Venus Williams have played each other in over 20 major tennis tournament finals, but have always remained best friends. They played doubles together, lived together, and even had breakfast together before these big matches. 'We leave everything on the court,' Serena once said. 'We're sisters the moment we shake hands at the net.'

So, now that we're adults, have my sister and I learnt to be more like the Williams sisters and less like the Gallaghers? Well, I'd love to say "yes" but the truthful answer is "not always". I still hate seeing photos of us together because I still feel inferior to her. But our rivalry is not as bad as it used to be, and if I feel really jealous, I remind myself: beauty fades but a sister is for life!

Vocabulary
Relationships

1a Can you remember which siblings in the article (including the author) the sentences below describe? Try to complete the phrases in bold.

1 She **is jealous** _of_ her sister's appearance. *the author*
2 They are always **competing** ___ **each other**.
3 She **feels threatened** ___ her sister's academic abilities.
4 They **don't** ___ **a lot in common**.
5 They **loathe** ___ **other**.
6 They are always **putting each other** ___ .
7 They **fell** ___ permanently.
8 She **feels inferior** ___ her sister.

b Check your answers in the article. Use the context to check that you understand what the phrases in bold mean.

2 Which set(s) of siblings in the article could the sentences below describe?

1 They're very **close to** each other.
2 They don't **get on with** each other.
3 They're sometimes **violent towards** each other.
4 They're **loyal to** each other.
5 They don't **respect** each other.
6 Their relationship seems very **destructive**.
7 They are **supportive of** each other.

3a Complete the list with phrases in exercises 1a and 2.

• good relationships: *be close to each other* ...
• bad relationships: *loathe each other* ...

b Think of opposites to the phrases in exercise 3a. Add them to your list.

loathe each other – adore each other

4a Choose at least two relationships from the list below. Think about how to describe them, using phrases in exercises 1a and 2.

Your relationship with ...
• one of your siblings.
• someone who used to be a friend but isn't now.
The relationship between ...
• two siblings in your family.
• famous siblings from your country.
• a famous couple.
• a couple you know well.

b Work in groups. Take turns to describe the relationships and ask and answer questions about them.

> I'm really close to my brother, Idris.
> We get on well, but ...

Listening and vocabulary
Friendship

1a Work in pairs. Which characteristics below do <u>not</u> describe the behaviour of a good friend?

1 You can **trust** them.
2 They always **tell** you **the truth.**
3 They sometimes **lie to** you.
4 They are **fun to be with.**
5 They **gossip** about you **behind your back.**
6 You can **confide in** them about your problems.
7 They always **keep** their **promises.**

b Work in groups. Think of two more characteristics of a good friend. Which do you think is the most important characteristic in a friend?

2a 🎧 1.4 Work in pairs. You are going to listen to three conversations. Listen to Maz confiding in Anna, and answer the questions.

1 Who is Ben?
2 What problem does Maz have?
3 What do we learn about Maz and Ben as people?
4 What does Anna promise at the end of the conversation?

b 🎧 1.5 Listen to Joe talking to one of the women from the previous conversation, and answer the questions.

1 Who is Joe talking to?
2 What are they discussing?
3 What is their attitude towards the situation?
4 What does Joe promise at the end?

c 🎧 1.6 Listen to Joe talking to someone else, and answer the questions.

1 Who is Joe talking to?
2 What is the surprise that is mentioned?
3 What does Joe try to do in the conversation and why?
4 How does the other person respond?

3 Listen to all three conversations again. Summarise the situation between the four friends.

4 Work in pairs and discuss the questions.

- Do you have sympathy for Ben or Maz?
- Are Anna and Joe good friends to Ben and Maz?
- Should they say or do anything?
- What do you think will happen between Ben and Maz?

Language focus 2
Uses of auxiliary verbs

1 Complete sentences 1–7 from the conversations with the endings or responses in the box.

He says he is.   will you?   I know she will.
isn't it?   Oh, are you?   Yes, I have actually.
we do have a good time together.

1 You don't think he's interested? *He says he is.*
2 I do love him, and _____
3 You won't say anything to anyone, _____
4 Have you seen Ben and Maz at all? _____
5 I'm planning a bit of a surprise for her. _____
6 It's going to cost you a fortune, _____
7 She'll like this, _____

2 🎧 1.7 Listen and check.

GRAMMAR

1 Underline the auxiliaries in the endings/responses in the box in exercise 1.

2 Which auxiliaries in exercise 1 are used to …
1 form tag questions?
2 add emphasis?
3 show interest?
4 form a short answer to questions?
5 avoid repeating words or sentences?

▶ **Read Study 2, page 132**

PRACTICE

1a 🎧 **1.8** Listen to the first part of eight conversations and tick the correct responses below.

1 a Of course I am! b Of course I do!
  c Of course I have!
2 a I am listening, darling. b I do listen, darling.
  c I did listen, darling.
3 a No, to be honest, it isn't. b No, to be honest, it didn't.
  c No, to be honest, it wasn't.
4 a Really, are they? b Really, have they?
  c Really, did they?
5 a Oh no, had you? b Oh no, have you?
  c Oh no, were you?
6 a I am believe you! b I do believe you!
  c I can believe you!
7 a No, I can't! b No, I don't! c No, I'm not!
8 a I did, didn't I? b b I was, wasn't I? c I do, don't I?

b 🎧 **1.9** Listen to the complete conversations and check.

> ### PRONUNCIATION
>
> 1 🎧 **1.10** In a full sentence, auxiliary verbs are not normally stressed. Often a weak form or a contraction is used. Listen and practise.
>
> /dʒə/   /jə/
> <u>Do</u> you want to hear it?   John, <u>you're</u> not listening to me.
>
> 2 🎧 **1.11** When the auxiliary is used for emphasis, or stands alone without a main verb, it is never weak. Often it is stressed. Listen and practise.
>
> Of course I <u>do</u>.   I <u>am</u> listening, darling.
>
> 3 Practise the conversations in exercise 1b, paying attention to the pronunciation of the auxiliaries.

2 Complete the sentences with an auxiliary verb.

1 I _____ like your shoes. Where did you get them?
2 Everyone else seemed to like it, but I _____ .
3 You don't care about what I want, _____ you?
4 Things have got worse round here, _____ they?
5 You _____ remember to lock the back door when you left the house, didn't you?
6 Thanks for a lovely evening, we really enjoyed it, _____ we George?
7 Alex can't come but everyone else _____ .
8 But you're feeling better now, _____ you?

3a Work in pairs. Choose three sentences from exercise 2 and develop each one into a short conversation of four to eight lines. Think about the following ideas.

• the context
• who is speaking to whom and how they feel
• what happens, if anything

b Practise your conversations, paying attention to the pronunciation of auxiliaries.

> **Unit 1, Study & Practice 2, page 132**

Wordspot
get

1 Match the meanings of *get* in the box with the examples in the diagram below.

become   arrive   catch
obtain/receive   understand

2 _____
*get what you
are saying*

1 <u>become</u>
get tired

3 _____
get a present

6 <u>phrasal
verbs</u>
*get on
well with
someone*

get

4 _____
get home

5 _____
get the bus

2 Add the phrases in the box below to the diagram.

get a better job	get better/worse
get an early flight	get $50,000 a year
get on with your work	get to work
get a cold	get over an illness
get angry	get stuck
get lost	get a joke
get a shock	

3 Work in pairs. Student A: Turn to page 126. Student B: Turn to page 128.

4a Find someone in the class who ...

1 got home late last night.
2 got stuck in bad traffic on their way to work/school.
3 gets a lot of colds.
4 doesn't get on very well with their next-door neighbours.
5 got lost the first time they came to this school.
6 is getting the bus home today.
7 often gets tired in the middle of the afternoon.
8 rarely gets angry.

b Report back to the class.

Task

Keep a conversation going

Take a break!

Who do you know that you have a lot in common with? **75**

Which person from your school days would you most like to meet again? **30**

What are the pros and cons of coming from a large family? **45**

Take a break!

Who is the kindest person you know? Why? **45**

What situations make you feel competitive? **45**

What do you look for in a partner? **45**

Who do you know that you really admire and why? **60**

1 2 3 4 5 6

What kind of people annoy you? **45**

What qualities do you look for in a friend? **75**

Is there such a thing as true love? **30**

Have you ever had a boss or a school teacher you didn't like? Why didn't you like them? **45**

Take a break!

What makes a good parent? **60**

What is the ideal age to get married and why? **45**

Who have you fallen out with in the past? Why did you fall out? **30**

Take a break!

Preparation Reading and listening

1 Work in pairs. Read the rules below for a game called *Keep talking*. Then check what you can remember.

2 🎧 1.12 Listen to three sets of people playing the game. Answer the questions.

1 Which square does the player land on in each game?
2 Which set of players followed the rules successfully?
3 What did the other players do wrong?

Task Speaking

1 You have five minutes to prepare for the game. Try to think of two things to say about the topic in each square.

2 Work in groups of three or four and play *Keep talking*.

> Useful language a–c

3 Work in groups. Discuss the questions below.

- Which square was the most difficult to answer? Which was the easiest?
- Did you find out anything surprising about each other?

USEFUL LANGUAGE

a Answering questions
Let me see …
The first person who comes to mind is …
The reason I admire/fell out with him is …
Personally I (don't) think …
But I suppose you could argue that …

b Asking follow-up questions
So what/why exactly (do you get on so well)?
Anything else you can think of?
Tell me more about (how you met).
Really did you? How did that happen?
And when was it?

c Playing the game
Whose go is it?
Ok, your/my go.
Well done! That's (30) seconds.
I'd like to pass on that one.
I've run out of things to say!
I think we're out of time.

Keep talking!

a game for 3–4 players

- Each player finds a counter (e.g. a coin) and puts it on one of the four corners of the board. Each player must choose a different coloured corner.
- The aim of the game is for each player to move around the board once in a clockwise direction.
- Players take it in turns to throw a dice or close their eyes and point to a number in the middle of the board and move that number of squares around the board.
- When a player lands on a square, he/she (Player A) asks the question in the square to the player on their right (Player B).
- The two players must keep the conversation going for the number of seconds given on the square. Player A must keep asking questions and Player B must give full answers.
- If Player A doesn't keep the conversation going (if there is a pause of more than three seconds), he/she moves back three squares.
- If Player B doesn't give full answers, he/she moves back two squares.
- The other players keep time and judge whether Players A and B are following the rules.

SHARE YOUR TASK

Choose a topic from the game that you can talk about for a minute. Spend a few minutes preparing and practising what you will say.

When you feel confident, record/film yourself speaking for a minute.

Share your film/recording with other students.

LANGUAGE LIVE

Never mind

Speaking
Responding to how people feel

1 Look at the photo. Work in pairs and discuss. Who do you turn to if you need a sympathetic listener? Why?

2 🎧 **1.13** Listen to three short conversations and answer the questions.

   1 What is the person's problem in each case?
   2 Is the listener very sympathetic, reasonably sympathetic or not very sympathetic?
   3 What suggestion(s) does he/she make?

3 Check you understand the phrases in the box. Then read situations 1–7 below and choose one or two appropriate responses in the box for each.

You must be really worried.	That sounds awful!
Don't take any notice of him/her.	How annoying!
Don't worry, it doesn't matter.	Cheer up!
Try not to worry about it.	Never mind.
Just ignore him/her/it/them.	Calm down!
There's no point in getting upset.	What a shame!

   1 A visitor to your house is embarrassed because he's spilled his drink.
   2 A child tells you that his best friend said something unkind to him.
   3 Your best friend phones because she's had a row with her boyfriend.
   4 Your friend is in tears at the end of a sad film.
   5 Your friend is worried because his mother is going into hospital.
   6 Everyone is laughing at your friend's new hairstyle.
   7 Your friend is too scared to go to the dentist by herself.

4 Are any of the phrases in the box in exercise 3 inappropriate for any of the situations? Give one or two examples, and explain why.

PRONUNCIATION

1 🎧 **1.14** Listen to five phrases said in two different ways. Which sounds more sympathetic, a or b?

2 🎧 **1.15** Listen to the phrases being said in a sympathetic way. Repeat the phrases from exercise 3, paying attention to the intonation.

5 Work in pairs. Choose one of the situations in exercise 3 and prepare a conversation similar to the ones you listened to.

6 Act out your conversation for the class. The others listen and say which situation you are acting out and whether or not the listener is sympathetic.

Writing
Planning and drafting a biography

1a Work in pairs and discuss. What steps do you go through when you write something in English, for example a biography of a famous person?

  b Turn to page 133 and read the 'Five steps to better writing'. Which ideas do you find useful?

2a Look at notes A and B. Which stages in the writing process do they show? What is the last stage?

b Which notes in A could go in each paragraph in B? Some notes could go in more than one.

A

a applied to study law – overslept for interview

b husband = Don Gummer since 1978. 4 kids

c 1977 = first film, 1978 = first Oscar nomination

d range of characters: **Mamma Mia!, Iron Lady, Kramer vs Kramer**

e won more awards than any actor in history

f 'I follow no doctrine … ,' etc.

g born 1949, New Jersey

h played violin six hours a day for eight weeks – **Music of the Heart**

i now in her 60s – still giving great performances

j first husband = John Cazale – died soon after filming **The Deer Hunter** with Streep

B **Paragraph 1:** why she is a legend
Paragraph 2: early life and career
Paragraph 3: commitment and talent
Paragraph 4: personal life

3a Who is the actress in the photo on the right? Name as many of her films as you can.

b Read the first draft of the biography. There are several mistakes including spelling (sp), punctuation (p), grammar (gr) and missing words (mw). Can you find two more examples of each mistake?

4a Choose one of the topics below to write a biography about.
- a musical/sporting/artistic/comic/film legend (you may need to do some online research first)
- someone you know who you think is 'a legend' in their own way

b Write a first draft, using the steps to better writing on page 133.

5a Check your first draft, paying attention to the verb forms you studied on page 7. Then work in pairs and check each other's drafts.

b Write a final draft.

A film legend

Meryl Streep is seen by many as the greatest <u>actor of</u> (mw) <u>generation</u>. The range of feelings and emotions that she can portray is astounding and she has won more acting awards than any actor in history. Now in her 60s, she is still throwing herself into every role and giving performances, that attract praise and admiration from audiences everywhere.

Born Mary Louise Streep in 1949 in New Jersey, she took singing lessons as a child and thought about a career as an opera singer. Later she applied to study law but changed mind when she overslept and missed the <u>interview</u> (p) her destiny, she decided, lay elsewhere. Instead, Streep enrolled in the Yale School of Drama and began her career in theatre in the late 1960s. Her first film role has been in 1977 and she won her first Oscar nomination a year latter in *The Deer Hunter*. Steep's husband and co-star in *The Deer Hunter*, John Cazale, died shortly after filming finished.

Streep has always prepared in detail for every role, sometimes going to extremes. In 1999 <u>she has</u> (gr) <u>practised</u> the violin for six hours a day for eight weeks in order to play a violin teacher in *Music of the Heart* a role originally planned for Madonna. This commitment has allowed her to play a wide variety of characters. In 2008, she starred in her successful film to date, *Mamma Mia!*. The film, based on the music of Swedish pop group ABBA, involved Streep not only acting but singing and dancing, too. Contrast this to *Sophie's Choice*, in which she played a concentration camp victim or *The Iron Lady*, in which she played British Prime Minister Margaret Thatcher, and you get an idea of her range and <u>abilitys</u> (sp).

Despite the extraordinary characters that she plays, Streep's home life is quite ordinary. She is married to sculptor Don Gummer since 1978. They live in Connecticut and have four children together. 'I follow no doctrine,' says Streep. 'I don't belong to a church or a temple or a synagogue or an ashram … but I do have a sense of trying to make things better.' That's certainly true of her films.

UPS AND DOWNS

FACT! More women than men feel bad-tempered in the morning: 85% of women say they sometimes feel grumpy when they get up, compared to only 75% of men.

FACT! Most parents say that spending time with their children is what makes them happiest. However, when they are actually with their children, the majority of parents report feeling stressed and frustrated!

Track your feelings

A psychologist has invented a phone app which he claims will make users more self-aware and able to make better-informed life choices. 'Track your feelings' bleeps users at random points in their day. Users say what they are doing and choose a word to describe how they feel, registering the strength of their feelings from one to five. The inventor stresses that the app must be used during the activity (or immediately afterwards), as he believes that we often recollect our feelings differently from how we felt at the time.

IN THIS UNIT

- **Grammar:** Forming adjectives; Forming nouns and gerunds

- **Vocabulary:** Describing how you feel; Things that make you feel good

- **Task:** Do a class survey

- **World culture:** The happiness formula

Vocabulary and speaking
Describing how you feel

1 Read the facts at the top of the page. Then work in groups and discuss. Do they surprise you? Can you think of any explanations for them?

2a Read the text above about a new phone app. Answer the questions.

   1 What does the inventor claim it will do?
   2 How does it work?
   3 Do you think an app like this would be useful to you?

b Work in pairs. Look at the adjectives below that are used in the app and check you understand them. Which of the adjectives do you rarely or never feel?

amused	depressed	impatient	relaxed
awkward	dissatisfied	insecure	sleepy
bored	enthusiastic	lonely	stressed
cheerful	excited	nervous	uncomfortable
confident	frustrated	panicky	unsociable
curious	grumpy	positive	upset

3a Tick the situations on the list below that are relevant to your life. Add three more situations that you often find yourself in.

- attending a meeting at work
- being late for an appointment
- attending a large family gathering
- having an evening at home alone
- being on a flight
- making 'small talk' at a party or social gathering
- commuting to and from work or college
- waiting for an exam to start
- going out with your partner for the evening
- preparing to speak or perform in public
- spending time with small children
- going for a long walk in the country
- being alone in a large crowd

b Choose two adjectives from the app to describe your feelings in the situations in exercise 3a (be honest!). Rate the strength of your feelings from 1 (weak) to 5 (strong).

> If I'm late for an appointment I feel stressed and panicky …. extremely panicky, I can't stand being late.

4 Work in groups and compare your answers.

Language focus 1
Forming adjectives

1 Look at the adjectives in the text and from the phone app on page 16. Underline five prefixes and five suffixes.

GRAMMAR

1 Match the adjectives you underlined to the prefixes and suffixes below.

Prefixes that mean 'the opposite of'
un-   in-   im-   dis-
unsociable

Prefixes that modify the meaning of the adjective
self-/good-/well-/better-/bad-/badly
self-aware

Suffixes that form adjectives
-able/-ible   -ful   -(i)ous   -(i)ent   -y
-ic   -ure   -ive   -ed   -ing
uncomfortable

2a Many adjectives have both an *-ed* and an *-ing* form. Choose the best adjectives in the sentences below.
  1 The meeting was very *frustrated / frustrating*.
  2 I felt very *frustrated / frustrating* during the meeting.

b Think of at least five more adjectives like this.

▶ Read Study 1, page 134

PRACTICE

1a Complete adjectives 1–14 below.

At Inspirations, we offer words of wisdom to help you through your daily life. Here are your favourites this week!
- Life is a ¹fascinat____ journey. But sometimes the journey is more ²excit____ than the destination.
- Those who constantly run around are not always the most ³effic____ . Sometimes it's more ⁴use____ to stop and reflect.
- Few people are ⁵success____ simply because they are ⁶talent____ . Most succeed because they are ⁷determin____ .
- Tell the truth, even when it hurts. It is better to be ⁸____popular than ⁹____honest.
- Life is a series of ¹⁰marvell____ opportunities, but many come disguised as ¹¹unsolv____ problems.
- People who are always ¹²pessimist____ have one advantage over those who are always ¹³optimist____ : they are rarely ¹⁴disappoint____ .

b Work in pairs and discuss. Which 'words of wisdom' do you like best?

2a Add adjectives from exercise 1a to the grammar box.

b Work in pairs. Write your own 'words of wisdom' for Inspirations.com. Use adjectives from the grammar box.

3a Complete adjectives 1–9 below with the prefixes in the box. Use the definition in brackets to help you.

anti-	non	over	pre-	post-
pro-	self-	under	mis	

1 _____ paid   (= paid too much)
2 _____ fed   (= not given enough food)
3 _____ stop   (= without stopping)
4 _____ war   (= after the war)
5 _____ arranged   (= arranged in advance)
6 _____ critical   (= critical of yourself)
7 _____ shaped   (= wrongly or badly shaped)
8 _____ government   (= favouring the government)
9 _____ war   (= against war)

b 🎧 2.1 Listen and write down an example of what you hear.

c Work in pairs and explain what you wrote.

> I wrote 'banker' because I think a lot of bankers are overpaid.

> Unit 2, Study & Practice 1, page 134

Reading and speaking

1 Read quotes 1–5 and choose the one you agree with most. Compare answers with the class.

> Happiness is the meaning and the purpose of life, the whole aim and end of human existence.
> *Aristotle*

> Happiness is like a butterfly; the more you chase it, the more it will escape you. But if you turn your attention to other things, it will come and sit softly on your shoulder.
> *Henry David Thoreau*

> If you want happiness for an hour, take a nap. If you want happiness for a day, go fishing. If you want happiness for a year, inherit a fortune. If you want happiness for a lifetime, help someone else.
> *Chinese proverb*

> The secret of happiness is not in seeking more, but in learning to enjoy less.
> *Socrates*

> Anyone who is happy all the time needs to see a psychiatrist.
> *Anonymous*

2a Read the statements below. Do you think they are true or false?

1 Spending money doesn't make you happier.
2 Living in a sunny climate makes you happier than living in a cold country.
3 Talking to strangers makes you feel better.
4 Daydreaming makes you happy.
5 People who live in cities are more miserable than those who live in the country.
6 The more you earn, the better you feel.
7 Men who do less housework are happier than men who do a lot.
8 Forcing yourself to smile makes you feel better.

b Work in groups and compare answers.

3 Work in pairs. Student A: read the article on this page. Student B: turn to page 127 and read the article. Discuss the questions below.

- Which topics from exercise 2a are mentioned?
- Did you predict correctly if the statements are true?

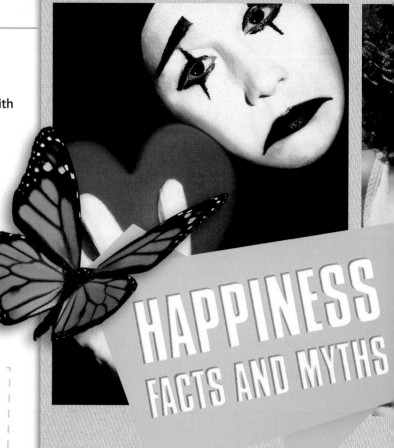

HAPPINESS FACTS AND MYTHS

HOW MUCH DOES HAPPINESS COST?

Do you want to earn more money? Do you think it will make you happier? If your answers are 'yes' and 'yes', then you are in for a surprise. Studies consistently show that how much we earn is actually less important to our happiness than how much other people earn. What we want most of all is to earn more than our friends and colleagues. This might explain why countries like China, South Korea and Chile have seen the average income more than double over the last 20 years, but have seen no increase in happiness. In the case of South Korea, 'life satisfaction' has actually fallen. However, this doesn't mean that we don't care about our income. According to Nobel Prize-winning psychologist Daniel Kahneman, money does not buy you happiness, 'but a lack of money certainly buys you misery'.

HAPPINESS AND THE CITY

Most people think that city folk are more stressed and less happy than country folk. Well, now it's officially true: cities are not only bad for your health with their pollution and overcrowding, they're also bad for your happiness. Using a special smartphone app, economist George MacKerron collected data on where, when and why people were happy. The results were clear: cities are the unhappiest places to live in. If you think of happiness as being on a scale from 1 to 100, cities reduce your well-being by between one and five points. And which places make people happiest? Mountains and forests!

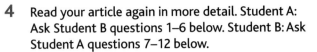

4 Read your article again in more detail. Student A: Ask Student B questions 1–6 below. Student B: Ask Student A questions 7–12 below.

Questions to ask Student B
1 What are the positive effects of talking to strangers?
2 What is the 'Talk to me' project? In what ways were the results positive and negative?
3 What sort of activities make us happy and why?
4 What type of father is more stressed?
5 Are fathers doing an increasing amount of housework? How do we know?
6 Does the Legatum Prosperity Index prove that we don't need sun?

Questions to ask Student A
7 According to the article, why might someone not be happy, even if their income goes up?
8 Is it true that money has no impact on our happiness? Why/Why not?
9 Where are people least happy and where are they happiest?
10 What experiment did Elizabeth Dunn carry out? What were the results?
11 What is pro-social spending?
12 Why is it a good idea to force yourself to smile sometimes?

5 Read your partner's article, then discuss one set of questions below.

Set 1
1 Why do you think ...
• men who do housework feel happier than those who don't?
• spending money on others makes people happier?
• daydreaming makes people less happy?
• cities make people unhappy?

2 Is there anything in the article that you don't really believe?

Set 2
1 Which of these things do/don't make people happy in your opinion?
• having lots of choices of what to buy
• spending a lot of time online
• living close to parents/relatives
• having a lot of friends
• spending time alone
• winning the lottery

2 Has the article made you feel that you should make any changes to your own lifestyle?

GIVE A LITTLE

Philosophers may tell us that money can't buy happiness, but is this reality or a myth? Psychologist Elizabeth Dunn from the University of British Columbia in Canada decided to find out. She gave one group of students $20 each to spend on themselves. She gave another group the same amount of money and asked them to spend it on other people. The next morning, the students were asked how happy they felt. Those who had spent the money on other people were overwhelmingly happier, proving that 'pro-social spending' as Dunn calls it, makes us happy. Newspapers tend to report on random acts of aggression or violence, but in reality, "random acts of kindness" make a bigger difference to society. Dunn's experiment shows that we can improve our own contentment, and other people's by giving more than we take. The problem is that very few people believe it!

HOLD A PENCIL BETWEEN YOUR TEETH

We all know that we smile when we're happy, but can it really be true that smiling itself can make us happy? Well, it turns out that this is no myth. Give it a go. Hold a pencil between your teeth – go on! What are you waiting for? Leave it there for a while. Are you feeling a bit happier yet? You should be. Holding the pencil between your teeth reminds your face muscles of what it feels like to smile, and smiling reminds you what it feels like to be happy. And even if you don't feel happy yet, at least everyone watching you is having a good laugh!

FIND OUT MORE Go online to find out more about happiness facts.

IT'S A FACT!
Denmark is offically the happiest nation in the world.

Listening and vocabulary
Things that make you feel good

1 A group of people were asked 'Which things in your life make you feel good and which make you feel bad?' Look at the most frequent answers below. Is anything important missing?

financial security

good friendships

a strong relationship/marriage

having variety and excitement in life

my hobbies and interests

lack of sleep/ exhaustion

being fit

criticism from others

being an employer, not an employee

being a non-conformist

lack of confidence

exam stress **paying taxes**

being unemployed

lack of money

doing something creative

2a Work in groups. Make lists with the ideas in exercise 1.

- things that make people feel good
- things that make people feel bad
- could be both

b Decide if the phrases in exercise 1 have an opposite. Add them to the list.

good friendships – lack of friends

criticism from others – support from others

3a Look at the three people in the photos. Can you guess which things in exercise 1 make them feel good and bad?

b 🎧 2.2 Listen and check your answers.

4a Listen again. Which things in the box below does each person mention? Are they good or bad things?

spending time with my family	anti-social behaviour
having an active social life	not having time to relax
watching my children grow up	intellectual stimulation

b Work in pairs and summarise the good and bad things about each person's life, giving as much detail as you can.

5a Work in pairs and discuss. Which things in exercises 1 and 4a do you think most affect the people below?

- teachers
- young people
- parents
- entrepreneurs
- athletes
- elderly people

Rudeness is a big problem for schoolteachers.

Young people worry about exam stress.

b Make a list of the things in life which make you feel good/ bad. Work in groups and compare your answers.

Language focus 2
Forming nouns and gerunds

1 Look again at the phrases in exercise 1 on page 20 and answer the questions.

1 Which are nouns and which are gerunds (verb + *-ing*)?

2 Make a list of the different noun suffixes you can find.

GRAMMAR

1a Look at the noun suffixes in the table below. Add at least one example of each noun suffix in exercise 1 and exercise 4a. Then add one example of your own for each suffix.

b Which three suffixes are usually used for people?

-ness *loneliness*	-ion/-sion/ -tion/-ation	-ity/-iety -y	-ment
-ance/-ence	-our/-iour	-ism	-age
-ship	-er	-ee	-ist

2 We often describe the opposite of nouns with *lack of* (*lack of money*, *lack of choice*, etc.). Find two more examples in exercise 1 and exercise 4a.

3 Many nouns are the same as the verb: *to interest/ an interest; to stress/some stress.* Which verb in the box below has a different noun form?

attack	cause	diet	exercise	increase
reduce	research	reward	risk	survey

4 Notice that gerunds (verb + *-ing*) are used in the same way as nouns and can be the subject or object of the sentence.

Spending time with family is important to most people.

Many young people worry about finding a job.

♦ **Read Study 2, page 135**

PRONUNCIATION

1 🎧 **2.3** Listen and write the nouns you hear. Mark the stress. Which suffixes, if any, are stressed?

2 Many of the unstressed syllables have schwa (/ə/) sounds. Mark where you think they are.

3 Listen again and check. Practise saying the words, paying attention to stress and weak forms.

PRACTICE

1 Work in pairs and have a race. Match definitions 1–12 below to nouns in the article on page 18. The words are in the same order in the article, and the ending of each noun is shown in brackets.

1 someone who studies the human mind: _____ (-ist)

2 harmful things in the air, earth or water: _____ (-ion)

3 the problem of too many people in one place: _____ (-ing)

4 a person who studies the economy: _____ (-ist)

5 the state of being happy and healthy: _____ (-ing)

6 the world as it actually is: _____ (-ity)

7 the use of money: _____ (-ing)

8 behaviour that is hostile or threatening: _____ (-ion)

9 using physical force: _____ (-ence)

10 the quality of being friendly and generous: _____ (-ness)

11 the opposite of similarity: _____ (-ence)

12 the state of happiness and satisfaction: _____ (-ment)

2 Complete the gaps in the text below with the noun or gerund form of the words in brackets. Use a dictionary to help you.

Finding the right balance

According to experts, the way you spend your free time is vital to your general [1]_____ (happy) and [2]_____ (healthy) and [3]_____ (get) the right balance is very important. It goes without saying that physical [4]_____ (fit) is the key, so everyone's leisure time should include some form of exercise, ideally something that you get [5]_____ (enjoy) from. Most people also gain [6]_____ (satisfied) from [7]_____ (do) something creative such as [8]_____ (paint), [9]_____ (cook) or [10]_____ (garden). [11]_____ (do) physical and creative activities is important then, but you should try to avoid [12]_____ (lonely). [13]_____ (companion) and [14]_____ (friend) will increase your sense of well-being. But you must find the right kind of social [15]_____ (interact). [16]_____ (be) a member of some groups, such as political parties, can simply lead to [17]_____ (stressful) and [18]_____ (frustrated). [19]_____ (join) a supportive social group like a choir or a dance class is likely to have more [20]_____ (beneficial).

> Unit 2, Study & Practice 2, page 135

Task

Do a class survey

Preparation Listening

1 Look at the photos and questions below. What can you see in each photo and which question do you think it relates to?

> What makes you happy?
>
> What makes you depressed?
>
> *What makes you giggle?*
>
> What annoys you or makes you angry?
>
> What makes you feel stressed?
>
> *What helps you to relax?*
>
> What scares you?
>
> What gives you the creeps?

2 🎧 2.4 Listen to five people answering one of the questions. Which question does the speaker answer? What reasons and examples do they give?

3 Listen again and tick the phrases you hear in the Useful language box.

Task Speaking

1a You are going to conduct a survey and talk about the questions in exercise 1. Read the questions again and think of at least one answer for each.

b Think about how to explain your answers. Make notes, using the prompts below. Ask your teacher for any words/phrases you need.

- Why do you feel like this? Are your feelings rational?
- Have you always felt this way?
- Have you had any experiences that have made you feel this way?

> Useful language a

2a Your teacher will give each student a question from exercise 1. You are going to carry out a class survey about this topic. First, think of some follow-up questions to ask.

> Useful language b

b Mingle with the class and ask your questions. If possible, interview six other students. Make notes about what they say.

3a Work alone or in pairs. Prepare to summarise your findings to the class. Think about the ideas below.

- any answers that came up more than once
- the strangest/most surprising answers you heard
- any funny stories you heard that are worth repeating

> Useful language c

b Take turns to summarise your findings to the class. Did you all have similar feelings or were there a wide variety of answers?

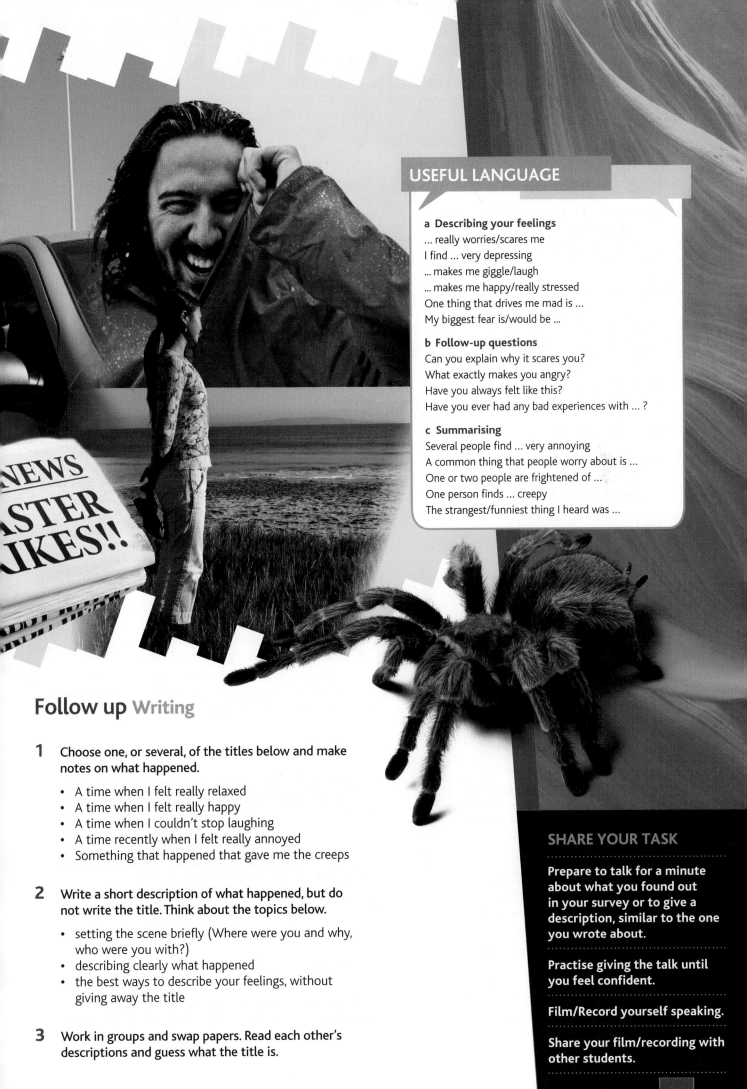

USEFUL LANGUAGE

a Describing your feelings

... really worries/scares me

I find ... very depressing

... makes me giggle/laugh

... makes me happy/really stressed

One thing that drives me mad is ...

My biggest fear is/would be ...

b Follow-up questions

Can you explain why it scares you?

What exactly makes you angry?

Have you always felt like this?

Have you ever had any bad experiences with ... ?

c Summarising

Several people find ... very annoying

A common thing that people worry about is ...

One or two people are frightened of ...

One person finds ... creepy

The strangest/funniest thing I heard was ...

Follow up Writing

1   Choose one, or several, of the titles below and make notes on what happened.

- A time when I felt really relaxed
- A time when I felt really happy
- A time when I couldn't stop laughing
- A time recently when I felt really annoyed
- Something that happened that gave me the creeps

2   Write a short description of what happened, but do not write the title. Think about the topics below.

- setting the scene briefly (Where were you and why, who were you with?)
- describing clearly what happened
- the best ways to describe your feelings, without giving away the title

3   Work in groups and swap papers. Read each other's descriptions and guess what the title is.

23

WORLD CULTURE

THE HAPPINESS FORMULA

Find out first

1a What are the best labour-saving devices and electronic gadgets that you own?

b Work in pairs. Do the Consumer technology quiz below.

Consumer technology

1 What percentage of Indian households own a television?
- **a** approximately 25%
- **b** approximately 50%
- **c** approximately 75%

2 What percentage of US households don't own a television?
- **a** approximately 10%
- **b** approximately 5%
- **c** approximately 1%

3 How many motor vehicles are there in the world today?
- **a** around 100 million
- **b** around one billion
- **c** around ten billion

4 How many mobile phones are in use in China?
- **a** ten million
- **b** 500 million
- **c** over one billion

c Go online to check your answers or ask your teacher.

Search: Indian/US households TV percentage / motor vehicles world / mobile phones in use China

View

2a You are going to watch a video about happiness. Look at the words and phrases below from the video. Do they have a positive (P) or negative (N) effect on happiness?

chores	drudgery	labour-saving devices
staring at a screen all day		technological utopia

b ⊳ Watch the video and answer the questions.

1 What does the science of happiness say about machines?
2 What have labour-saving devices failed to do?
3 What does technology push out of our lives?
4 What are the three ingredients of happiness?

3 Watch the video again and choose the correct answers (both answers may be correct).

1 Technology promises to bring us *drudgery* / *new possibilities*.
2 In a technological utopia, we would have more *free time* / *fun*.
3 Compared to 50 years ago, we now spend *less* / *more* time on household chores.
4 Because of technology, we now spend more time *alone* / *with other people*.
5 Online communities make us *more* / *less* social in the real world.
6 We now know *the key to* / *a recipe for* happiness.

4 Do you agree with the recipe for happiness in the video? What other 'ingredients' do you think are important for a happy life?

World view

5 ▶ Watch five people talking about technology and happiness. Complete the table.

	Technology mentioned	Effect on happiness	Reasons
Jurgen			
Audrey			
Guillem			
Helen			
Luis			

6 Work in pairs and discuss.

- Which speakers do/don't you agree with?
- Which items of technology in your life make you more or less happy?
- Do you think there will be new kinds of technology in the future which will increase our happiness? What will they be?

FIND OUT MORE

7a Look at the titles of global happiness surveys below. How do you think they measure people's happiness? Which countries do you think are the most/least happy?

The World Happiness Report
Better Life Index
The Happy Planet Index

b Go online and find out more about one of the global happiness surveys. Make notes about the following points:

- who produces the report/index
- how happiness is measured
- which places in the world are the happiest/ least happy
- which factors lead to happiness
- any other interesting conclusions

....

Search: World Happiness Report / Better Life Index / Happy Planet Index

....

Write up your research

8 Write one or two paragraphs about the report/index you researched. Use the prompts below to help you.

- The report is produced by ...
- It measures happiness by ...
- For example, it asks people ...
- According to the survey, one of the main factors leading to happiness is ...
- In conclusion ...

03

IT ALL WENT WRONG

Vocabulary
Mishaps

1   Look at the mishaps below and check you understand the words in bold. Think of more examples to add to the list.

- You **lose** your keys and **lock** yourself **out**.
- You **get stuck** in traffic and miss an appointment.
- You **slip** on some ice.
- You **trip** and **fall over**.
- You **get on the wrong train**.
- You **get confused** and make a mistake.
- Your car **breaks down**.
- You **bang** your head.
- You **get lost**.
- You **spill** paint on your clothes.
- You **run out of** petrol.
- You **oversleep** and **miss your train**.
- You **drop** something valuable and break it.
- You borrow something without asking and **damage** it.

2   Work in pairs. Which of the things in exercise 1 has happened to you? Take turns to say where and when.

> We ran out of petrol once when we were on holiday in France.

Language focus 1
Narrative tenses

1 🎧 **3.1** Listen to Clare, Luke and Rachel talking about mishaps. Answer the questions.

    1 Which mishap is each speaker describing?
    2 Who mentions the topics in the box below?

sugar	a spoonful of mashed potato
a first date	a great aunt and uncle
a station buffet	a remote part of Wales
a formal dinner	people wearing evening dress

2 Listen again and make notes. Work in pairs and briefly summarise each story.

3a Choose the best verb in the sentences below.

    1 I *talked* / *was talking* so much that I got confused and put sugar on my burger instead of salt.
    2 We did see each other again but I never admitted what *happened* / *had happened*.
    3 One day, after I *was working* / *had been working* at the hotel for a few weeks they had a big dinner event.
    4 They asked me to wait on the tables. But I *wasn't doing* / *hadn't done* any training as a waiter so I was very nervous.
    5 I *served* / *was serving* vegetables at a table when suddenly I tripped and fell.
    6 They *had travelled* / *had been travelling* for a while when the train stopped at a station.
    7 She got on another train which *was going* / *had gone* back to Wales.

b 🎧 **3.2** Listen and check.

GRAMMAR

1 Complete the table below with examples from exercise 3a. How is each tense formed?

Past simple	Past continuous
I put sugar on my burger.	
Past perfect	**Past perfect continuous**

2 Match explanations 1–4 to the tenses in the table.
    1 It describes actions in progress at the time of the main events in the story.
    2 It describes main events in the story.
    3 It describes actions that happened before the main events in the story.
    4 It describes actions that continued for a period of time before the main events in the story.

▶ Read Study 1, page 137

PRACTICE

1a Read two more stories about mishaps. Complete the gaps with the best verb forms (there may be more than one possibility).

A

It's not uncommon for people to fall asleep on trains, but snoring loudly in public is another matter. One day recently, I [1]_____ (read) my newspaper on the train when I [2]_____ (become) aware of a loud snoring sound coming from the man opposite me. As the train [3]_____ (come) into the last station on the line, I [4]_____ (give) the man a sharp poke with my umbrella to wake him up. Instead of being grateful, he [5]_____ (look) at me furiously. He [6]_____ (not be) asleep at all! The snoring [7]_____ (come) from the enormous dog who [8]_____ (lie) at his feet!

B

An Australian woman, travelling home from Melbourne, [9]_____ (drive) down a narrow road one dark evening when she [10]_____ (enter) a tunnel. Although a little surprised at this, as she [11]_____ (not notice) a tunnel on that route before, she [12]_____ (carry on). But after half an hour of twisting and turning, she [13]_____ (run out) of petrol. It [14]_____ (be) completely dark in the tunnel, so she [15]_____ (decide) to wait for help. She [16]_____ (only wait) for a few minutes when she [17]_____ (see) three men coming towards her. Rather surprisingly, the three men [18]_____ (wear) helmets with lamps on the front. The three men [19]_____ (seem) even more surprised to see her. It was then that the woman [20]_____ (realise) that she [21]_____ (drive) into a coal mine.

b 🎧 **3.3** Listen and check.

2a Think of a mishap which happened to you or someone you know. Think about the following topics.

    • When did this happen?
    • What were you doing at the time?
    • What happened?
    • Had you done/been doing anything just before the incident?
    • How did you feel?

b Write the story of the mishap, paying attention to the tenses you use. Then read your story to the class.

> Unit 3, Study & Practice 1, page 137

Task

Tell a story from two points of view

Preparation Listening

1a Look at the pictures. They show an incident that happened to Bill and Frank after they had been to a party. Match the words in the box to the pictures.

laugh your head off	thick ice
a police car	sway all over the place
break into a car	a police cell
a slippery road	be drunk
swear	a steep hill

b Work in groups. Can you guess what happened to Bill and his friend? Is there anything you don't understand from the pictures?

2 Work in groups.

Group A: 🎧 3.4 Listen to what Bill told his lawyer after the incident.

Group B: 🎧 3.5 Listen to what the old lady told the police. Listen as many times as necessary to be sure of the details. Make notes if necessary.

Task Speaking

1 Practise re-telling the story with students from the same group.

> Useful language a and b

2a Work in pairs, one person from Group A and one from Group B. Take turns to report what Bill and the old lady said.

b Make a list of differences between the two stories and any information that one person mentioned, but the other didn't. Compare your list with the class.

> Useful language c

3 Work in pairs. Discuss the questions below.

- Whose side of the story do you believe?
- Were the police right to arrest Bill and his friend?
- What further action do you think the police took?

B

USEFUL LANGUAGE

a Re-telling the story

He was just *-ing* when ...
All of a sudden/Suddenly ...
At that moment ...
She saw/heard them *-ing* ...
So then, he/she/they ...
In the end/Eventually, ...

b Telling an anecdote

Did I ever tell you about ... ?
For some reason, I ...
It was a nightmare!
As soon as I realised, I ...
I felt so (embarrassed/humiliated)!

c Comparing the two stories

According to (the old lady) ...
He said ..., whereas she said ...
He was absolutely certain that ...
She mentioned/didn't mention the fact that ...
He/She didn't mention anything about ...

D

F

G

SHARE YOUR TASK

Imagine you are Bill years later, or think of your own anecdote.

Practise telling the anecdote until you feel confident.

Film/Record yourself telling the anecdote.

Share your film/recording with other students.

29

Vocabulary
Crime and punishment

1 Work in pairs and have a race. In two minutes, list as many crimes as possible.

burglary, murder, …

2a Read the questionnaire and check the meaning of the words and phrases in bold.

b Work alone. Do the questionnaire.

3a Work in groups and compare your answers. Give reasons.

b Discuss the questions below.

- In which cases do you need to know more about the circumstances to make your decision?
- In what circumstances should a judge be very lenient/harsh?

4a Work in pairs and write two more situations for the quiz, with possible punishments.

b Work with another pair. Take turns to discuss your situations and possible punishments. Explain your choices.

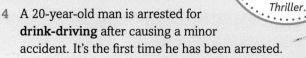

IT'S A FACT! In Cebu in the Philippines, prisoners are taught to dance to songs such as Michael Jackson's *Thriller*.

Are you harsh or lenient?

Tick the punishment you think is most appropriate for each crime.

1 A university student buys an essay online and submits it as her own. The university recognises the essay as **plagiarism**.
- She should **receive a warning**. □
- She should **be expelled**. □
- She should be prosecuted for **fraud**. □
- other (what?)

2 A 12-year-old girl consistently **plays truant** from school. The parents say that the child won't listen to them and they are powerless to help.
- She should **be suspended**. □
- She should be expelled. □
- Her parents should **be prosecuted**. □
- other (what?)

3 A family with eight children are living in a quiet street. They are very noisy and the neighbours complain of **anti-social behaviour**. They are renting their house.
- The family should **be evicted**. □
- The parents should be prosecuted. □
- The neighbours should learn to cope. □
- other (what?)

4 A 20-year-old man is arrested for **drink-driving** after causing a minor accident. It's the first time he has been arrested.
- He should be **let off with a warning**. □
- He should **lose his licence**. □
- He should **be given** 200 hours of **community service**. □
- other (what?)

5 A homeless man is arrested for **begging** in the city centre. The local laws do not allow begging and he has been arrested several times for the same crime.
- He should be let off with a warning. □
- He should be prosecuted. □
- He should **be fined**. □
- other (what?)

6 A student is arrested for writing political **graffiti** on a building.
- His parents should be called. □
- He should have to pay for the damage. □
- He should be prosecuted. □
- other (what?)

7 A mother of two young children is **charged with** the **possession of illegal drugs** and found guilty.
- She should be **sentenced** to six months **in jail**. □
- She should be given a **suspended sentence**. □
- Her children should be **taken into care**. □
- other (what?)

Language focus 2
Continuous aspect in other tenses

1 Choose the best answers to complete the cartoons.

GRAMMAR

1 Complete the table with verb forms from the cartoons.

Present perfect simple	Present perfect continuous
Future simple	Future continuous

2 Which form, simple or continuous, is used to show duration or repetition?

▶ Read Study 2, page 138

PRACTICE

1 Work in pairs. Choose the best answers to complete the conversations below. Give reasons.

1 **A:** What are the police doing outside?
   B: I called them. Our neighbours **have rowed** / **have been rowing** again.
2 **A:** Are you looking forward to leaving prison?
   B: I can't wait. This time next week I'll **lie** / **be lying** on the beach.
3 **A:** Have you **broken** / **been breaking** something?
   B: Yes, I've **dropped** / **been dropping** a glass.
4 **A:** I'll give you a ring over the weekend.
   B: OK, but don't call me on Sunday evening. I'll **do** / **be doing** my daughter's homework.
5 Don't drive so fast. You'll **lose** / **be losing** your licence if the police catch you.
6 **A:** I've **run out** / **been running out** of petrol. Maybe I can borrow Diana's car.
   B: You'll **get** / **be getting** into trouble.

2a 🎧 3.6 Listen to two people each answering the same questions. Can you guess what the questions are?

b 🎧 3.7 Listen to the questions and answers together. Write down the questions. Did you guess correctly?

c Work in pairs. If necessary, change the questions to make them more suitable for your partner. Then take turns to ask and answer the questions.

How long have you been learning ~~to drive~~ French?

> Unit 3, Study & Practice 2, page 138

1 I'm really upset. I paid for an 'A' but I've **lost** / **been losing** the receipt!

2 Five minutes from now, our friends on Facebook will **read** / **be reading** all about this.

3 I think you've **spelt** / **been spelling** her name wrong.

4 Stay away or you'll **break** / **be breaking** it.

5 No officer, I haven't **drunk** / **been drinking** but I think someone has **stolen** / **been stealing** my steering wheel.

Vocabulary

Headlines

1 Work in pairs. Read the newspaper headlines below and explain each story in your own words.

> Donald vows to return from injury

> **Heavy rain set to cause severe flooding**

> 82-year-old breaks leg on Everest climb

> **PM backs calls to tighten safety**

> Couple lost in maze call 999

> Restaurant to close after 65 years

> Death toll climbs in air crash

2a Find words in the headlines which have the same meaning as the words below.

1 supports *backs*
2 promises
3 is probably going to
4 the number of people who died
5 people's demands

b Why do you think the words in the headlines were used instead?

3 Work in pairs and discuss the questions about headlines in general.

1 Which tense is often used to talk about the past?
2 How do headlines usually refer to the future?
3 Which of the grammatical features below are commonly missing from headlines?
   - the verb *be*
   - articles (*a/an/the*)
   - relative pronouns
   - nouns and noun phrases
   - auxiliary verbs

Reading and listening

1 Work in pairs. Look at the newspaper headlines and introductions on page 33. Make two guesses about what is happening in each story.

I think the woman in the photo has won the lottery.

2a Choose the best word to complete the phrases below. Which article do you think each phrase comes from?

1 claim *a prize / a competition*
2 build a nuclear *engine / reactor*
3 violate someone's *happiness / privacy*
4 access someone's email *address / account*
5 reimburse a *debt / person*
6 go through a *wedding / divorce*
7 split an *atom / radiation*
8 buy radioactive *materials / stuff*
9 pay off a *debt / bank account*

b Read articles A–C quickly. Were your predictions correct?

3a Read articles A–C on page 33. Are statements 1–12 true (T) or false (F)? Which lines in the articles give you the information?

A
1 Amanda knew it was a winning ticket when she found it.
2 The Staceys spent all the money.
3 Dorothy had proof that it was her ticket.
4 Camelot thinks Dorothy should have been more careful.

B
5 The minimum punishment is five years in jail.
6 Leon and Clara were still living together.
7 Leon wasn't Clara's first husband.
8 Most people under 25 read their partner's emails.

C
9 Handl told the authorities what he was doing.
10 He publicised the fact he was doing the experiments.
11 He doesn't have the nuclear materials anymore.
12 He plans to do more experiments in the future.

b Work in pairs and check your answers.

4 Work in pairs. Discuss the questions below.

- The three articles are all true stories. Only one person was not charged. Who do you think it was?
- What do you think happened to the other people?

5a 🎧 3.8 Listen to three news stories which explain what happened in the end. Check your answers to exercise 4.

b Listen again and make notes on any other information you hear.

6 Work in groups. Discuss the questions below.

- Are you surprised by the outcome in any of these cases?
- Do you think the outcome of each case was fair? Why/Why not?
- Do you know of any recent legal cases that had a controversial outcome? What happened?

A

Couple arrested after finding winning lottery ticket

A couple from Swindon who found a winning lottery ticket on the floor of a shop and collected the £30,000 prize have been arrested.

34-year old mother, Amanda Stacey, found the ticket on the floor of the Coop supermarket in Swindon and took it home to her husband, Michael. They discovered that it was a winning ticket and claimed the prize immediately, using half the money to pay off their debts, buy new carpets and treat their children.

The ticket, however, had actually been bought by 61-year-old Dorothy McDonagh. As soon as Dorothy realised she had lost

the ticket, she alerted lottery organiser Camelot, who called the police. Fortunately for Dorothy, she had kept the receipt.

Police have now frozen the remaining £15,000 in the Staceys' account and have to decide whether to bring charges against the pair. Camelot has already said it will not reimburse Mrs McDonagh. 'We sympathise with her situation,' a spokesman said, 'which is why we remind players it is their responsibility to keep tickets safe.'

B

Leon Walker faces five years in jail

Michigan man faces hacking charges over wife's email

A husband who accessed his wife's email account while they were going through a divorce could be charged with hacking.

Leon Walker, a 33-year-old computer technician from Michigan, the USA, faces up to five years behind bars if the case goes to trial. According to reports, Leon accessed his wife Clara's email account without her consent or knowledge.

They were in the process of divorcing at the time but were still living under the same roof and sharing a computer.

Leon suspected that Clara was having an affair with her former husband, a fact the emails confirmed. The former husband had a history of violence and Leon claims that he was acting out of concern for his daughter.

When she found out about the incident, Clara called the police. 'He violated my privacy,' she told a local TV network, 'I was violated.' Leon, however, maintains that Clara kept her passwords in a book next to the computer and no hacking was involved.

Earlier this year, an online survey found that 38 percent of under-25s had spied on their partner's email.

C

Mr Handl posted photos of his home experiment on the internet

Swede confesses to 'crazy' home-made experiment

A Swedish man who tried to build a nuclear reactor in his kitchen at home has confessed that his plans were a bit 'crazy'. Richard Handl tried to split the atom at his flat in Angelholm, southern Sweden, but the results were not what he expected.

Sweden's radiation authority was first alerted to Handl's actions by Handl himself. He had emailed them to check if what he was doing was legal. It took the authority three weeks to read his email,

but when they finally did, they took immediate action. The police were called and Handl's computer and radioactive materials were confiscated.

Handl claims that his motivation was simple curiosity and says that he had the whole thing under control. He had bought the radioactive material entirely legally on the internet and not on the black market as some papers have reported. He had been working on the experiment for more than six months, posting regular updates on his blog.

It is not clear what will happen next in the police inquiry. Handl says that he expects a fine but he could be facing up to two years in prison. In the meantime, he has promised to stick to reading books about physics to satisfy his curiosity.

LANGUAGE LIVE

What?

Speaking
Dealing with unexpected problems

1a 🎧 **3.9** Listen to three short conversations. There is an unexpected problem in each. Answer the questions.

1 Where does the conversation take place?
2 What is the problem?

b Listen again and complete the extracts below.

Conversation 1
1 I _____ _____ **but** I couldn't buy a ticket.
2 **Can I** _____ **a** _____? **Why** _____ I buy a ticket now?
3 Look, **this is** _____ ! I'm not a criminal.

Conversation 2
4 Look, **there's been a** _____ . **We didn't** _____ **that** you wanted to be paid.
5 **I don't think** _____ _____ . You should have told us at the start.
6 No, **you** _____ _____ . We really aren't your customers.

Conversation 3
7 **What do you** _____ you've given it to someone else?
8 **It's not** _____ _____ we couldn't find a parking space.
9 I _____ _____ **that, but** this is very unfair.
Perhaps I _____ **to** _____ to the manager.

2 Work in pairs and discuss. How would you deal with each situation if it happened in your country?

> *I would pay the fine and make a complaint later.*

3a Read the situations below. What might you say in each situation? Use the phrases in bold in exercise 1b.

- You park your car and go shopping. When you come back, a traffic warden is writing you a ticket. You have overstayed the 30-minute limit.
- You buy some food in a shop but when you get outside, you realise that the shopkeeper gave you too little change. She refuses to give you the rest.
- You arrive at a hotel where you made a reservation for two nights. They have no record of your reservation and the hotel is full.
- You take a taxi. When you arrive, you realise that the taxi meter isn't working. You think the taxi driver is asking too much.
- You take your computer to a repair shop. When you pick it up, the man says he has spent two days trying to repair your computer, but it still doesn't work. He gives you a bill for €120.

b Work in pairs. Choose a situation and prepare a conversation. Try to use the phrases in exercise 1b.

c Act out the conversation for the class.

Writing
A narrative

1 Work in pairs. Read the story. Which of the titles below would you choose for it? Which other titles are suitable and why?

- The luckiest day of my life
- A day when everything went wrong
- The most frightening day of my life
- A day I'll never forget
- A nightmare journey

¹_____ , my husband and I were planning a holiday and ²_____ I went to the travel agency to pay for the tickets, taking our baby son. It was quite busy so I sat down to wait, feeling quite excited. I started playing with the baby and wasn't paying much attention to what was happening around me. ³_____ I noticed that a group of men had walked in. They were calm and quiet, but they moved very fast, speaking to each travel agent in turn. ⁴_____ everyone got up, emptied their pockets, put their bags on the floor and went into the bathroom at the back of the shop. I still didn't understand what was happening, but one of the men gestured to me to go with them, and ⁵_____ I realised that they were carrying guns. However, ⁶_____ , I wasn't asked to hand over anything, ⁷_____ because I had a baby. ⁸_____ , I had just drawn out all our savings for the holiday, and had $2,000 in my bag!

They locked us in, and ⁹_____ , we could hear them searching the place. There were about eight of us in a tiny bathroom, all trying to stay very quiet. I was terrified that my son would start crying and make the robbers angry. I remember one of the travel agents giving him her bracelets to play with, to distract him. ¹⁰_____ , we realised that the men had gone, and we all started shouting as loudly as we could for help. We seemed to be in there ¹¹_____ , but ¹²_____ someone heard us and called the police. ¹³_____ I was shaking and felt sick but ¹⁴_____ everyone, including my baby, was fine.

2 Work in pairs and answer the questions.

1 Where did the experience happen and what were the circumstances?
2 Who were the main people involved?
3 What were the main events?
4 How did the narrator feel?
5 What happened in the end?

3 Choose the correct adverbial phrases for gaps 1–14. Sometimes both answers are possible.

1 Several years ago / Once upon a time
2 it all happened when / one day
3 All of a sudden / Suddenly
4 Very quickly / Very slowly
5 at this point / fortunately
6 for some reason / amazingly
7 possibly / undoubtedly
8 Ironically / Luckily
9 for a while / for ages
10 Eventually / After a while
11 forever / for a short time
12 in the end / eventually
13 By this stage / At this point
14 fortunately / strangely

4a Think of an experience, either your own or of someone you know, that matches a title in exercise 1. Make notes on what happened.

b Write a first draft of your story. Use the checklist below.

- Check the list of questions in exercise 2. Does your narrative answer them? Could you improve the way you describe any of these things?
- Have you used narrative tenses correctly?
- Could you use the adverbial phrases in exercise 3 to make your story more interesting?
- Are the spelling, grammar and punctuation correct?

5 Work in pairs. Swap stories and suggest improvements. Use the checklist to help you.

6 Write a final draft. Read other students' stories. Which do you like best?

AFTER UNIT 3 YOU CAN ...

Talk about crimes and mishaps.

Talk in detail about past events and tell stories.

Use phrases that help you to deal with unexpected situations.

Write a detailed narrative.

YOUR MIND

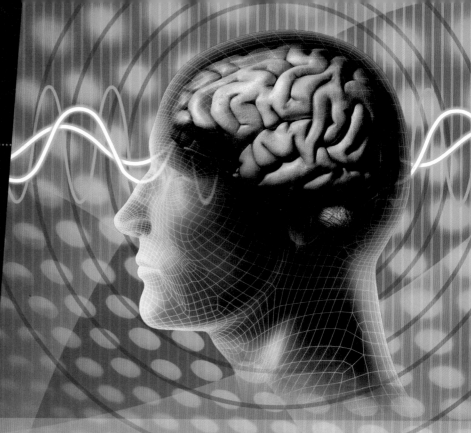

IN THIS UNIT

- Grammar: Use and non-use of the passive; Passive forms with *have* and *get*

- Vocabulary: Mental skills; *Mind*; Personal characteristics

- Task: Choose people to go on a space mission

- World culture: Nature or nurture?

What kind of mind have you got?

1 What is the missing number in this sequence?
96 95 92 87 ( ) 71

2 Turn to page 126 and study the 'things to buy/do in town' list for one minute. Then close your book and write down all the things you can remember.

3 How many sides does this figure have?

4 You are looking after some children for the day. One little girl, Anna, comes to you crying because the others won't play with her. What do you do?

  a Tell the other children off for being mean.

  b Tell Anna to sort it out herself.

  c Give Anna a biscuit to make her feel better.

  d Tell the children they can all have a biscuit if they promise to play with Anna.

  e other:

5 Write down as many possible uses for a newspaper as you can in two minutes.

6 You have a wolf, a goat and a cabbage which all have to be taken across a river. You have a small rowing boat in which you can only take one thing with you at a time. However, if the wolf and goat are left alone, the wolf will eat the goat. And if the goat and cabbage are left alone, the goat will eat the cabbage. How can you get across the river with the two animals and the cabbage?

7 How creative do you think you are?

  a very creative

  b creative

  c averagely creative

  d about as creative as a potato

Vocabulary and listening
Mental skills

1a Look at the mental skills in the box. Which are your strongest? Put them in order (1 = strongest, 9 = weakest).

musical ability	problem-solving skills
organisational skills	emotional intelligence
mathematical skills	visual/spatial intelligence
logic	creativity and imagination
memory	

b Work in pairs and compare answers.

2 Do the quiz. Which mental skills do you think each question tests?

3 🎧 4.1 Listen to the answers and an analysis of the quiz. Were you right about the purpose of the questions?

4 Work in pairs and discuss the questions.
- Which questions did you each find most interesting/easiest/most difficult?
- What do you think this shows about the type of people you both are?

Language focus 1
Use and non-use of the passive

1a Complete the sentences from the listening with the active or the passive form of the verbs in brackets

1 This question _____ (design) to test logic and mathematical skills, but the mathematical skills that _____ (require) are not very great.
2 The average number of items that people _____ (remember) was eight.
3 The best way to remember is if you _____ (group) all the similar items together.
4 The shape has to _____ (rotate) in the mind's eye.
5 Visual skills cannot _____ (teach easily)
6 According to experts, you _____ (should discuss) the situation with the child.
7 Children certainly _____ (should not bribe) with biscuits.
8 It _____ (show) in studies that if you think you are very creative, then you are very creative.
9 They _____ (say) that the strongest power we possess is self-belief.

b 🎧 4.2 Listen and check your answers.

2 Look again at the sentences in exercise 1a and find an example of a modal passive and a passive infinitive.

GRAMMAR

Use of the passive

1 Cross out the statement below that is not true.
1 We often use the passive in order to put the main topic at the beginning of the sentence.
2 In passive sentences, the 'doer' of the action (the agent) is not the main focus of the sentence.
3 In passive sentences, the agent is often obvious, unknown or 'people in general'.
4 The passive is mostly used in informal contexts.
5 The passive is often used in reports, academic writing and newspaper articles.

2 Passive sentences are often introduced with *it*. Find an example in exercise 1a.

3 Relative clauses with passives can be shortened. Look at the example. Then find a similar example in exercise 1a and shorten it in the same way.
These are the skills ~~that are~~ needed by architects.

Alternatives to the passive

4 We often use alternatives to the passive (especially in less formal contexts) by using *we, you, they, people, someone*, etc. Find three more examples in exercise 1a.
You should discuss the situation with the child.
(= The situation **should be discussed** with the child.)

▶ Read Study 1, page 140

PRACTICE

1 Choose the correct answers to complete the text Which relative clauses can be shortened.

- IQ (intelligence quotient) is one way in which a person's intelligence [1]**can measure / can be measured**, and it [2]**says / is said** that the average score is around 100.

- IQ tests [3]**had not invented / had not been invented** in the days of Mozart or Charles Darwin, but it [4]**thinks / is thought** that if they were alive today, these great geniuses [5]**would probably score / would probably be scored** around 160–170.

- The highest IQ that [6]**has ever recorded / has ever been recorded** was that of William James Sidis (1898–1944), who [7]**says / is said** to have had an IQ of 250–300, but IQ [8]**measured / was measured** differently in those days.

- Kim Ung-Yong, who [9]**generally regards / is generally regarded** as the cleverest person alive, has an IQ of 210. He [10]**made / was made** famous when he [11]**appeared / was appeared** on Japanese TV at the age of four, solving complex mathematical problems. He [12]**attended / was attended** university between the ages of four and seven, and at the age of of eight, he [13]**invited / was invited** to the USA to join NASA. At the age of 16, he [14]**chose / was chosen** to return to Korea, because he [15]**missed / was missed** his mother!

2 Do the exercise on page 126.

> Unit 4, Study & Practice 1, page 140

Reading and speaking

1a Work in pairs and discuss. What do you understand by the phrase 'nature or nurture'?

b Do sentences 1–4 below support the theory of nature or the theory of nurture?

1 Everything comes from our genes.
2 The roots of personality are in our upbringing.
3 We can't change who we are.
4 Our environment influences our personality.

2a Read the article. Which paragraphs do the pictures illustrate?

b Work in pairs and discuss. What did you learn about the things/people in the pictures?

3 Work in pairs. Check you understand the words in bold in the questions below. Then read the article again and answer the questions.

1 According to Hippocrates, what **personality traits** were **bile** and **blood** responsible for?
2 How long did the theory of the 'four humors' last?
3 Why do you think people consulted phrenologists about job applicants and marriage partners?
4 Explain in your own words what 'we are all born as **blank slates**' means. How does this relate to the quote from Skinner?
5 What is the connection between criminals who were **executed** in ancient China and children in the UK who **play truant**?
6 How does the Stanford Prison experiment support the nurture theory? Why do you think it has become 'infamous'?
7 According to nurture theory, should **identical twins** who grow up apart be similar? Why/Why not? What happens in practice?

4 Work in groups and discuss the questions.

- We blame our parents for our weaknesses but we don't thank them for our strengths. Do you agree?
- How would you describe your personality in terms of the 'big five' personality traits in the article?
- What has most influenced your personality?

PRONUNCIATION

1 🎧 4.3 Listen to the words below and mark the stress. Which look similar in your language but have a different pronunciation? Listen again and practise.

psychologist	scientist	environment
medicine	theory	ethics
genes	analysis	experience
neurotic	experiment	

What shapes our personality?

Is it the result of nature – what we are born with – or nurture – what we experience? We search for the answer.

It's definitely nature.

1 Two and a half thousand years ago, the ancient Greeks believed that your personality was the result of different fluids, or 'humors', in your body, like blood, phlegm and bile. According to Hippocrates, the 'father of modern medicine', black bile caused depression and irritability, while blood made you brave and hopeful. These ideas spread all over the world, and in the 18th century, people with mental illnesses were sometimes treated with leeches in order to restore the balance of their humors. It was only in the 19th century that scientists began to doubt the theory of humors, although patients may have noticed much earlier that they weren't getting any better!

2 By the late 19th century, personality had been correctly linked to the brain. This was a big advance, but some people took it too far and phrenology emerged as a new 'science'. Phrenologists believed that the brain affected the shape of the head, and so by feeling someone's head, they could discover the shape of their brain and therefore their personality – including, for example, how likely someone was to commit murder. At the height of its popularity, phrenologists were consulted about possible marriage partners or to give a background check on job applicants. Job interviews must have been interesting in those days!

3 More recently, scientists have looked to our genes as the source of personality. While there is certainly a link, it is far from simple. For a start, a single gene might be involved in many different aspects of our personality – and we have around 25,000 genes in our body. And when even a simple thing like the colour of your skin is the result of more than 100 different genes, imagine how many are involved in a character trait like being open, extrovert, agreeable, conscientious or neurotic (the 'big five' traits that psychologists nowadays use to describe human personality).

It's definitely nurture.

4 If it's hard to find the roots of personality in nature, then can we find them in nurture? The nurture theory says that we are all born as 'blank slates'.
Our personality develops as the result of our parents, our peers, our environment, and so on. As the famous psychologist BF Skinner once said, 'give me a child and I'll shape him into anything'.

5 Nurture theory has even been enforced by law. In Ancient China, if a young man committed a serious crime and was sentenced to death, then his parents might be executed, too – because they were responsible for the character of their son. Even in modern Britain, if a child plays truant from school, her parents can be prosecuted.

6 However, there's more to nurture than parents, there's environment, too. One shocking example of how easily environment can affect personality comes from the infamous 1971 Stanford Prison experiments. These experiments took 24 normal, healthy men and asked them to play the role of prisoners or guards in a pretend prison. The experiment had to be ended after just six days because the guards became very cruel, locking one prisoner in a cupboard and forcing the others to bang on the cupboard door.
In a new environment, it seems that 'normal' people can completely change their behaviour.

7 Some studies of twins, however, challenge the importance of nurture. According to nurture theory, identical twins (who have the same genes) should only have similar personalities if they grow up together, but different personalities if they grow up apart, due to different upbringing and experiences. However, studies show the same striking similarities in personality, whether these twins are brought up separately or together.

So do we have an answer?

Well, sort of. The consensus these days is that our personalities result from a complicated interaction between nature and nurture. Perhaps one day we will understand the exact recipe for personality but then again, we may never understand ourselves fully!

> **FIND OUT MORE**
> Go online to find out more about nature versus nurture.

Wordspot
mind

1 Replace the words and phrases in bold below with the correct form of a phrase from the diagram.

1 No, I won't tell you! ~~It doesn't concern you!~~
   Mind your own business
2 Try to be **unprejudiced** about Trudi's new boyfriend – don't **decide** about him before you've met him.
3 Although it was an easy question, suddenly **I couldn't remember**, and I was unable to answer.
4 Many people are afraid to **give their opinion** because of what others may think.
5 Is there **something worrying you**? Can I do anything to help?
6 **It's OK for me** if you're late as long as you phone.
7 'I'm sorry, I dropped a glass on the floor.'
   '**Don't worry about it**. I'll get a pan and brush.'
8 I've **changed my opinion** – I'll take it after all.
9 **Would it be possible to move** your car? It's blocking the entrance.
10 She is over 80 years old, so it's not surprising Anne's a bit **forgetful**.
11 **Be careful with your head**. The ceiling's very low.

2 *be careful*
   Mind your head

3 *(not) a problem*
   I don't mind.
   Never mind.

1 *deciding/opinions*
   speak your mind
   make up your mind
   change your mind

4 *thoughts*
   something on your mind

mind

5 *minded*
   open-minded
   absent-minded

8 *requests*
   Would you mind + -ing?

6 *forgetting/ remembering*
   my mind went blank

7 *spoken phrases*
   Mind your own business

2 🎧 4.4 Listen to three short conversations and choose a phrase with *mind* to replace each beep.

3 Work in pairs. Write three short conversations with a phrase with *mind* in each.

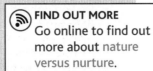

The future of your mind

...according to Hollywood.

Check out our top five mind-bending future possibilities from Hollywood films.

1. Get rid of bad memories
In *Eternal Sunshine of the Spotless Mind*, Clementine and Joel have their memories of each other erased by a doctor when they split up. But things get complicated when they meet again.

2. Plant ideas in other people's minds
Wouldn't it be incredible to plant an idea in someone's mind while they're asleep? Then, when they wake up, they believe it's their idea. That's all possible in the Christopher Nolan film *Inception*.

3. Learn to do anything - instantly
In the classic sci-fi film, *The Matrix*, the characters don't waste time actually learning new skills, they get them downloaded directly to their brains. How convenient!

4. Buy memories
Perhaps we won't have bad memories erased (see 1), but we'll have good ones implanted instead. We'll choose the ones we want, just like we choose clothes in a shop. Both the original version and the 2012 remake of *Total Recall* explore this idea, in typical Hollywood style.

5. Record and play back your experiences
Or, perhaps, we'll be able to record all our experiences so that we (or other people) can watch them again. This is the future reality in *Brainstorm*, a film from 1981.

Language focus 2
Passive forms with *have* and *get*

1 Read the text 'The future of your mind.' Then work in pairs and say which ideas you think will come true and when.

2 Work in pairs. Discuss the questions below.
- If your mind could be manipulated as suggested in the article, what skill would you download first?
- What idea would you plant, and in whose mind?
- Whose memories would you buy? Why?

GRAMMAR

1 Look at the examples and answer the questions.
*The characters **record** their experiences.*
*The characters **have** bad memories **erased**.*
1 Who records the memories in the first sentence?
2 Who erases them in the second sentence?

2 Find two other examples in the article with *have* + *something* + past participle and answer the questions.
1 What is the tense in each example?
2 How is this construction used in other tenses?

3 Look at the example below. Notice that we can also use *get* instead of *have* in this construction. It is more informal than *have* but the meaning is the same. Find an example with *get* + *something* + past participle in the article.
*We'll **get** our bad memories **erased**.*

▶ Read Study 2, page 141

PRACTICE

1 Use the prompts to write sentences about each picture.

1 read/palm
She's having her palm read.

2 read/horoscope

3 test/eyes

4 take/blood pressure

5 dye/hair

6 paint/nails

2 Work in pairs and discuss the questions.
- Which things in the pictures do/don't you do yourself?
- Do you or have you ever had anything like this done at the optician's, beautician's, etc.?

I sometimes dye my hair myself, but I never cut my own hair – I always have it cut at the hairdresser's.

3 Work in pairs. Look at the business cards and discuss. What can you have done in each of the places?

You can have applicants' handwriting analysed.

 Redland **Staff Services**

- We interview applicants for you.
- We do personality assessments and IQ tests.
- We analyse applicants' handwriting.

Ready Steady Go
personal training for people with busy lives!

- We design an exercise programme to fit in with your life.
- We monitor your progress on a weekly or twice-weekly basis.
- We plan your weekly menu and even deliver healthy meals to your door!

Discreet Professional Thorough

Porter's Private Investigation Agency

We trace long-lost relatives.
We monitor business competitors.
We follow family members.

4a 🎧 **4.5** Listen to someone phoning one of the businesses. Answer the questions.

1 Which business is the customer phoning?
2 Which service is he asking about?

b Work in pairs. Write two similar conversations about the other businesses.

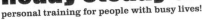 **> Unit 4, Study & Practice 2, page 141**

Listening and vocabulary
Personal characteristics

1 Work in pairs. Look at the photo of six men who spent nearly 18 months alone together in a space capsule. Discuss the questions.

- What do you think it was like?
- What do you think their biggest problems were?
- Do you think you could cope with this situation?

2 🎧 **4.6** You are going to listen to a radio programme about the Mars 500 mission. Listen and answer the questions below.

1 What was unusual about the Mars 500 mission?
2 Which countries did the crew come from?
3 What was the main point of the mission?
4 What personality traits do astronauts need, according to the programme?

3 Work in pairs and choose the correct alternative. Then listen again and check.

1 The mission lasted *almost / more than* 18 months.
2 The crew were *volunteers / professional astronauts*.
3 In general the men got on *well / badly* together.
4 They disagreed over who *was in charge / did what jobs*.
5 They all had *the same / different* amounts of contact with people back home.
6 If the crew on a space mission are fed up they normally blame *each other / their colleagues on the ground*.
7 On a space mission in 1982, the crewed *shouted at / avoided communicating with* each other.

4a On a mission like Mars 500, which characteristics in the box would be an advantage, a disadvantage or both?

argumentative	arrogant	attention-seeking
calm	extrovert	hot-tempered
humorous	humourless	individualistic
introvert	jealous	needy
rebellious	resilient	self-sufficient
talkative	good in a team	uncommunicative

b Work in groups and compare answers. Which other qualities do you think would be important on a mission like this?

Task

Choose people to go on a space mission

Mission 2050

Following the success of the Mars 500 mission, the International Space Agency (ISA) has decided to carry out a more extended simulated space mission. 'Mission 2050' will send seven volunteers to live for ten years at an isolated, top-secret desert location, known as 'Novaterra'.

Volunteers cannot leave the mission unless they are critically ill. They can only contact their families and friends every three months by email.

The climate and habitat of 'Novaterrra' will be adapted to reflect what is known about Mars and the mission will be closely monitored by scientists, doctors and psychologists researching how to set up real space colonies in the future. It will be promoted as an important symbol of international co-operation.

Its mission statement is to:

- involve people from a cross-section of nationalities, races and social backgrounds
- study how people of different sexes, ages, react under these conditions
- study the needs and behaviour of any children born into these conditions, etc.
- find out the most important characteristics that future space travellers need.

The ISA will provide food capsules for three years, but the volunteers should become self-sufficient after this. Water, emergency medical supplies, blankets and basic shelter will also be provided. The volunteers will attend a course covering survival skills, agriculture and first aid, but practical skills that volunteers can bring will of course be an advantage.

Preparation Reading

1a Read the article about Mission 2050 and summarise the main information.

b Work in pairs and discuss. What characteristics do you think will be most useful in Novaterra?

2a You have been accepted for Mission 2050! You have been asked who should go with you.
- Read about the other nine shortlisted candidates.
- Circle the factors that you think make them suitable and underline the factors that do not. (Unless stated above, all candidates are free of family ties, speak English and are healthy.)

b Decide which candidates you would and would not like to spend the next ten years with.

K. Mi Kyong, Korean, 36

- nurse
- does not speak English
- calm and self-sufficient and good team player
- tends to be introvert and uncommunicative

Paterno C., Filipino, 34

- professor of engineering
- gifted musician and singer
- friendly, but very intellectual and 'bookish'

Sabrina S., American, 24

- beautician married to Al (below)
- four months pregnant
- sociable and well-meaning but very talkative
- can be needy and attention-seeking

Carolina L., Colombian, 27

- artist
- very extrovert and humorous
- very individualistic, can be rebellious
- heavy smoker

Al S., American, 29

- five years in US army, now a builder
- married to Sabrina (above)
- strong physically, but has put on a lot of weight
- disciplined in army for aggressive behaviour, but now very religious

Alik B., Russian, 38

- primary school teacher
- former ballroom dancing champion
- friendly with very good people skills
- has suffered from depression

Task Speaking

1a Work individually. Make a preliminary selection of the five candidates that you would most like to go with you on Mission 2050.

b Think about how to explain your reasons. Ask your teacher for any words/phrases you need.

2 Work in pairs. Compare the candidates you have chosen and explain why. Reach an agreement on the five candidates you want to go with you.

> Useful language a and b

3 Work in groups. Present your shortlist of five candidates. Give reasons for your choice. Try to agree on a final shortlist of candidates.

> Useful language c

Follow up Writing

1 Imagine you have been on the mission for three months and are allowed to send your first email home. Write to friends or family on the topics below.

- the other volunteers and what you think of them
- what it is like living together
- the best/most difficult things about the mission
- how you feel about the mission now

Omar H., Egyptian, 21

- law student
- slightly disabled in left arm
- ex-member of Egyptian Paralympic football team
- highly intelligent, humorous, excellent communicator
- can be hot-tempered and argumentative

Bahar M., Turkish, 42

- agricultural expert who has worked a lot in developing countries
- widow and mother of two daughters, aged 17 and 18
- calm and resilient but rather humourless
- rather impatient with other people, not a team player

Giorgio M., Italian, 55

- doctor (general practitioner)
- good leadership, charming and good fun
- had heart attack four years ago, but health now good

SHARE YOUR TASK

You have to give a brief press conference to journalists. Prepare a short presentation explaining who has been chosen for Mission 2050 and why.

Practise the presentation until you feel confident.

Film/Record yourself giving your presentation.

Share your film/recording with other students.

WORLD CULTURE

NATURE OR NURTURE?

Find out first

1a Work in pairs. Read the information below about the differences between males and females and try to guess the correct answers.

Men **versus** Women

Various scientific studies over the last two decades have proved that there are differences between boys and girls at school in terms of how good they are at certain skills (although we don't know the reasons for those differences). For example, [1]*boys / girls* tend to be better at spatial skills, for example rotating an object in their mind, while [2]*boys / girls* are better at judging what people are feeling. When boys and girls grow up, we find that [3]*men / women* tend to make more money over the long terms when they invest in the stock market.

We also find that [4]*men / women* are more likely to have an accident while driving, despite being more able to see detail at a distance.

b Go online to check your answers or ask your teacher.

Search: boys versus girls spatial skills / judging feelings / men versus women stock market / driving accidents

View

2a You are going to watch a video about why boys and girls like different toys. What gender-stereotyped toys do you think the video will mention?

b ▶ Watch the video. Then work in pairs and answer the questions.

1 What does the experiment with toddlers prove?
2 What does the experiment with monkeys prove?
3 Why might males be attracted to vehicles like helicopters and cars?
4 What does the presenter conclude about the nature-nurture debate?

3 Watch the video again and tick the three sentences that are true. Correct the false sentences.

1 Before 15 months, boys and girls don't show a preference for particular toys.
2 The first experiment with toddlers is designed to test the nature argument.
3 The volunteers are tricked into believing the toddlers are the opposite sex.
4 The first experiment shows that nurture is probably important.
5 The second experiment is new and surprising.
6 Dr Hines chose monkeys because she couldn't find the right kind of children.
7 Dr Hines found that both male and female monkeys were more likely to play with cars, trucks and so on.
8 The classic scientifc view is still supported by recent research.

4 Work in pairs. Were you surprised by the outcome of the experiment? What are your views on the nature-nurture debate in terms of children and toys?

World view

5a ▶ Watch seven people answering the question 'Did your parents treat you/ your siblings in a gender-stereotyped way?'. Complete the first column in the table.

	Treated in a gender-stereotyped way?	Issues mentioned
Eben	yes	
Heather		
Fauzia		
Monica		
Elliot		
Louisa		
Luis		

b Watch again and complete the second column.

6 Work in groups and discuss.

- Whose experiences do you most relate to?
- Did the age of the speaker make a difference to the way they answered?
- Do you think the way parents treat boys and girls has changed much in your country in recent generations?

FIND OUT MORE

7a Look at the psychology experiments listed below. What do you think each one is about?

- Pavlov's dogs experiments
- Stanford prison experiment
- Milgram obedience experiment
- Asch conformity experiments

b Choose one of the experiments and go online to find out more about it. Make notes about the following points.

- when it was conducted
- who led it and who took part
- what the researchers/participants did
- what the findings were
- what the public reaction was at the time
- the impact of the experiment

....

Search: Pavlov's dogs experiments / Stanford prison experiment / Milgram obedience experiment / Asch conformity experiments

....

Write up your research

8 Write one or two paragraphs about the experiment you researched. Use the prompts below to help you.

- The experiment was carried out in …
- Each participant was asked to …
- As the experiment progressed …
- The study showed that …
- The surprising/shocking conclusion of the experiment was that …
- It changed the way people saw …

AFTER UNIT 4 YOU CAN …

Describe and discuss personal and mental characteristics.

Persuade other students of your point of view, giving detailed reasons.

Present decisions in public.

05

FACE TO FACE

IN THIS UNIT

- **Grammar:** Review of future forms; More complex question forms

- **Vocabulary:** Getting together; Colloquial language

- **Task:** Plan a fantasy dinner party

- **Language live:** Dealing with problems on the telephone; Types of message

Vocabulary
Getting together

1 Which of the people in A take part in the events in B?

Delegates and speakers attend conferences.

A	B
acquaintances	a blind date
business associates	a business meeting
clients	a celebration meal
delegates	a conference
ex-classmates	a dating website
friends	a dinner party
guests	a family get-together
neighbours	an online forum
political leaders	a housewarming party
speakers	a school reunion
relatives	a summit
people looking for a partner	a conference call
strangers	a social-networking site

2 Match the verbs below to the ways of meeting in exercise 1.

- have *a business meeting ...*
- make
- go on
- attend
- use

3a Choose three ways of meeting from exercise 1 that you have experienced recently. Make notes on the topics below.

- when and where it was held
- who was there
- whether you enjoyed it

b Work in groups. Take turns to briefly describe each event, but don't say what it was. The other students must guess.

Language focus 1
Review of future forms

1a Read the messages below. Answer the questions.

1 Which events in exercise 1 are they about?
2 What do you think is the relationship between the people involved?

b Choose the correct answers.

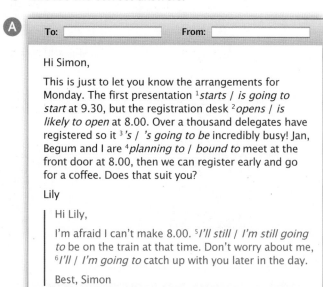

A

To: _____ From: _____

Hi Simon,

This is just to let you know the arrangements for Monday. The first presentation ¹*starts / is going to start* at 9.30, but the registration desk ²*opens / is likely to open* at 8.00. Over a thousand delegates have registered so it ³*'s / 's going to be* incredibly busy! Jan, Begum and I are ⁴*planning to / bound to* meet at the front door at 8.00, then we can register early and go for a coffee. Does that suit you?

Lily

Hi Lily,

I'm afraid I can't make 8.00. ⁵*I'll still / I'm still going to* be on the train at that time. Don't worry about me, ⁶*I'll / I'm going to* catch up with you later in the day.

Best, Simon

B

Comments 🗩

ANDY: Hey guess what! I just heard Laura's finally passed her driving test – third time lucky! We ¹*will / 're going to* take her out for a meal tomorrow night to celebrate. You can come, can't you? Any ideas where to go?

EMMA: She loves China Royal.

ANDY: OK. I ²*'m going to / 'll* call and book it for 8.00. Can you make it then?

EMMA: I think so. I ³*'ll be seeing / see* Rich at college later, shall I invite him along?

ANDY: If you really must.

C

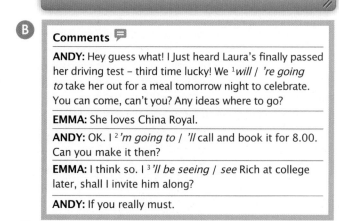

¹*Do you do / Are you doing* anything exciting this weekend?

Yes actually … well maybe. Stuart and his girlfriend Bella ²*will have / are having* this dinner party on Saturday night and he's invited this girl he thinks I ³*'ll like / 'm liking*.

Ooooh! Who is she?

Some friend of Bella's from uni, I don't know her name. She ⁴*probably won't / isn't going to* be my type … or I ⁵*won't / 'm not going to* be hers. ⁶*It'll probably / It's probably going to* be dreadful!

You've got to think positively – you never know!

Mmm … well ⁷*I'm keeping / I'll keep* you updated!

Yeah do, I can't wait!

GRAMMAR

1 Match the uses for future tenses 1–10 to examples in the conversations and emails. Complete uses 6 and 10 with your own ideas.

Plans and arrangements
1 a general intention
   *going to – We're **going** to take her out for a meal*
2 an arrangement that has been made
3 an arrangement that is officially fixed
4 a plan that is made at the moment of speaking
5 something that will happen anyway without any special plan
6 other phrases for describing plans and arrangements

Predictions
7 a prediction based on evidence
8 a prediction based on opinion
9 a future fact
10 other phrases for making predictions

▶ **Read Study 1, page 143**

PRACTICE

1 Complete the conversations below with the correct future form of the verbs in brackets. Sometimes there is more than one correct answer.

1 **A:** Is it five o'clock already? I'm afraid I've got to go, I _____ (cook) dinner for my mum tonight.
   B: OK, we _____ (finish) this tomorrow.
2 **A:** What are you up to this evening?
   B: My train _____ (leave) at five tomorrow morning, so I _____ (have) an early night.
3 **A:** I'm afraid we've run out of today's special.
   B: OK, never mind. I _____ (have) the pasta instead.
4 **A:** Do you want a lift? I _____ (pass) the end of your road.
   B: If you're sure you _____ (not go) out of your way.
5 **A:** Sayeed _____ (leave). His bags are packed and his taxi is waiting.
   B: _____ he _____ (fly) with Continental Airways?
6 **A:** Where _____ (go) for your holidays?
   B: Well, actually we _____ (stay) at home this year. We _____ (have) a family get-together instead.
7 **A:** Have you decided what to wear to the reunion?
   B: Yes, I _____ (wear) my new red dress.
8 **A:** That was a terrible foul. Ricardo _____ (be) lucky to stay on the pitch.
   B: The referee is now looking for his red card. He _____ (send) him off!

2a Turn to page 127. Choose three of the topics and prepare a 30-second talk on each. Think about which future forms to use.

b Work in pairs and take turns to talk about your topics.

> Unit 5, Study & Practice 1, page 143

Reading and speaking

1 Work in groups and discuss the questions below.

- How important are these things in your interaction with other people:
  - your phone
  - social-networking sites
  - other forms of online communication?
- In what ways do you use them?
- Have these things improved your social life? Why/Why not?

2 Read the introduction to the article. Predict what the writer will say about the questions in exercise 1.

3a Read the article and check your answers.

b Work in pairs and summarise how communication media affects the topic below.

- the author's daily routine
- social events like dinner parties and gigs
- his relationships with his friends and girlfriend

4 Find the words or sentences in the article that tell you the things below.

1 The author is always close to his phone and laptop. (para. 1)
My phone and laptop are within constant touching distance.

2 He receives news from his friends online throughout the day. (para. 2)

3 He has friends that he has known for years. (para. 2)

4 He is not the only person who feels lonely in this way. (para. 3)

5 His phone is not helping his relationship with his friends. (para. 3)

6 It's not easy for his girlfriend to get his attention. (para. 4)

7 He talks to friends online when he should be working. (para. 5)

8 His friend did not concentrate fully when he was watching Rihanna play. (para. 6)

9 He and his friends can't give up social media. (para. 7)

5 Work in groups. Read the facts at the end of the article and discuss the questions.

- Do you know anyone who is like the author of the article?
- Do you recognise any of the things he describes in your own life?
- What advice would you give to the author and people like him?
- Do you think social networking makes people feel anxious and inadequate?
- Do you think young people today are lonelier than they were in the past? Why/Why not?

'We may have 750 friend

He spends his life emailing, texting and tweeting. So why does Andy Jones feel so isolated?

1 Whatever I'm doing, wherever I am, I'll tell you about it. My phone and my laptop are within constant touching distance, whether I'm eating, drinking, in the shower, at a gig or watching the football. Before I get up every morning, I check my email, my texts and my Twitter feed. By the time I've got out of the shower, it's time to do it again.

2 I have a constant drip-drip of information from any of the 750 online friends and followers that I associate with. Yet I have never felt lonelier. How does a 28-year-old man get like this? I am a rational professional man with a beautiful girlfriend and long-standing mates.

3 I am not alone in feeling like an island. In a recent survey of young people, 60 percent said they found it difficult to make friends 'in real life' compared with online. I'm way beyond being an awkward teen, but I am wired up most of the day, as are most of my friends. I go to parties, pubs and dinners, but I am there only in spirit. Far from bringing me closer to people, my phone drives me further away. I can tell you how many followers I have on Twitter, but cannot remember the last time I saw my housemates from university.

4 Social networking and the internet has made me need to scroll through something constantly. I'll be due at the pub at 9 p.m. At 8:50 p.m. I'll still be sitting on my bed thumbing online. Then it's 9:30, then it's closing time and I'm still in my flat. Alone in the dark, I download albums, then another, but barely listen to them; the thrill is looking for things to listen to rather than the listening. When my long-suffering girlfriend comes round, she has to prise me from my phone or the internet. The moment she's gone, my mind wants the hyperactivity that the internet and social networking provide.

nline, but we're lonely'

5   I feel isolated. During work hours, I chatter away on social-networking sites, delaying tasks. I am in a constant state of distraction. Paradoxically, I no longer see the very people I want to see because I have been 'talking' to them all day.

6   Last weekend, I threw a dinner party. The moment that the food arrived, one best mate aged 26 got up to make a phone call. My other best mate, 27, sat through dinner checking Twitter for football scores. What's worse is that I didn't think either was being rude. Social networking dominates. At the V festival last year, we spent half a day looking for somewhere so that one of our party could charge his phone. Once charged, he spent all of Rihanna's headline set reading updates from Twitter about a gig that he was already at.

7   The terrifying thing is that none of us can go cold turkey. I dropped Facebook for six months last year, but came back because I was missing invitations. It was as if I didn't exist. If you're an alcoholic, you can avoid booze, but how do I avoid the internet or my phone? I need it to do my job, because my employers demand that they can contact me at any time.

8   That's the problem with social networking. You are hardwired in, but you are always the same cool distance apart.

Did you know...?

- A recent study in the journal Cyberpsychology, Behaviour and Social Networking found that the more time people spent on Facebook, the happier they perceived their friends to be, and the sadder they felt as a consequence.

- The phrase FOMO, or 'Fear Of Missing Out', has been coined to describe the feelings of anxiety and inadequacy that many people feel when they read about their friends' nights out on Facebook.

- 80% of under-18s say they feel lonely, compared to 68% of over-80s.

Vocabulary
Colloquial language

1   Choose the correct meaning of colloquial phrases 1–4 from the article. Check your answers in the article.

   1   mates (para. 2) = *friends / family members*
   2   way beyond (para. 3) = *a short way past / a long way past*
   3   go cold turkey (para. 7) = *something less / stop doing something completely*
   4   booze (para. 7) = *alcoholic drinks / soft drinks*

2   Work in pairs. Find at least seven colloquial words and phrases in the conversation below. Guess what they mean.

   A: All right, Mike?
   B: Hey Jamilla. What's up?
   A: I'm totally stressed out actually. Can I talk to you?
   B: Sure. Grab a chair.
   A: It's about Daniel. He's doing my head in, Mike. I mean, what's going on? You're his best friend. Tell me!!
   B: OK, OK, chill out.

3a 🎧 5.1 Listen and complete the rest of the conversation below.

   B: Here – this coffee's for you.
   A: Thanks, Mike.
   B: A fiver for two coffees! It's such a ¹_____ _____ here.
   A: I know. Here I'll pay for mine.
   B: Nah, don't be silly. Now, do you ²_____ tell me why you're stressed out about Daniel?
   A: The thing is, when we chat online or on the phone, he's really friendly. But then when we meet up he's like a different person.
   B: ³_____ _____ ?
   A: Well, he just seems really ⁴_____ _____ _____ . Like yesterday, we had a real laugh on the phone, he was ⁵_____ 'Hey, we're ⁶_____ have a great time at the party this evening, ⁷_____ _____ _____ ,' but then when we met up, he was just ... distant.
   B: The thing about Daniel is, he's just incredibly shy. I mean, he just can't help himself ...

b   Work in pairs. Do you know or can you guess from the context what the colloquial words and phrases in exercise 3a mean?

Listening and vocabulary
Online dating

1a Work in pairs and discuss the questions.

- How popular are online dating websites in your country?
- Do you think people who use them are always honest about themselves?

b Look at the online dating profile below. Can you guess which information is a lie or an exaggeration?

Age:	27
Height:	175 cm
Body shape:	athletic
Job:	film director

About me: Fun and lively man. Not into quiet nights in, and never boring! My PA calls me a 'party animal'. Fond of hanging out with my mates – some of them are celebrities. Keen on skydiving and paragliding.

Looking for: A partner-in-crime to join me on an adventure. Must be 20–25 years old, tall, blonde, chilled out and ready to fall in love!

2 🎧 5.2 Listen to some information about online dating and answer the questions.

1 What do men and women tend to lie about in their profile?
2 What are the clues that a profile is not accurate?
3 What are the arguments in favour of lying?

3 Listen again and complete the idioms in bold below. Can you guess their meaning?

1 The men hope, presumably, that women will **fall hopelessly in _____ with** them on the first date ...
2 So if you want to know whether a profile that you are reading is mostly lies, **keep an _____ out for** three things.
3 These can be a sign that someone is being _____ **with the truth.**
4 Most online daters know that they have to **take** what they read **with a pinch of _____.**
5 Telling **little _____ lies** online can also have a positive benefit.
6 It's best not to **stretch the _____** too far however.

4 Work in pairs and discuss the questions.

- What are the advantages and disadvantages of online dating websites?
- Has anyone you know ever used one? What were his/her experiences?

Blind date

Ursula Porter, 26, librarian, meets web designer Josh Franks, 28

Ursula on Josh

Hopes before the date?
Johnny Depp or Colin Farrell. He's neither of those.

First impressions?
Pretty chilled out and interesting. I was hoping he'd be wearing a suit, but he wasn't. His outfit was ... unusual.

Remind you of anyone?
My father.

Conversation topics?
Our education, career goals, favourite films, blah, blah, blah. Standard first date conversations.

Awkward moments?
There was a very embarrassing incident when a bit of the lobster he was eating landed on my dress.

Similarities between you?
Neither of us are motivated by money. I think that's a good thing.

Marks out of ten?
I'll be generous and give him a six.

Another meeting?
Probably not.

Language focus 2
More complex question forms

1 Work in pairs. Read the article about Ursula and Josh's blind date and discuss. What does the article describe? What does Ursula think of Josh?

2a 🎧 5.3 Josh is being interviewed about his opinion of the date. Listen and make notes on his answers. Who is kinder and who is crueller about the other, Ursula or Josh?

b Listen again and write the questions that the journalist asked.

Could you tell me what you were looking for?

PRACTICE

1a Write a question for each set of prompts in the box.

what/worry about	long/be single	who/vote for
who/most care about	like/talk about	often/cry
what/dream about	where/grow up	much/earn
have/plastic surgery	similar/are we	
jokes/make you laugh	happen/last relationship	
who/depend on	qualities/want in a partner	

What do you like talking about?

b Work in pairs and discuss. Which questions are suitable for a first date or to ask a classmate? Which are never suitable?

c Work in groups. Choose seven suitable questions from exercise 1a and take turns to ask and answer them, using indirect questions. Then ask follow-up questions.

Could you tell me where you grew up?

GRAMMAR

1a Choose the correct word to complete the rules below.

b Find another example of rules 1–5 in the questions you wrote in exercise 2b.

Compound questions

1 Use *What* and *Which* + **adjective / verb / noun**, or *How* + **adjective / verb / adverb** to form questions.

How similar are you and Ursula?

Questions with prepositions

2 When a verb or adjective takes a preposition, put the preposition at the **beginning / end** of the question. Do not omit the preposition.

What did you talk about?

Statements and negative questions

3 Statements can be used as questions, usually to express surprise or check information. This is shown through **intonation / word stress**.

She reminded you of your sister?

4 Negative questions also express surprise or check that information is correct.

Didn't you enjoy the date?

Indirect questions

5 When you use phrases like these ones below, use **affirmative / question** word order.

Could you tell me ... ?   *I wonder ...*

Do you know ... ?   *Tell me ...*

I wanted to know ...   *Can you remind me ... ?*

Could you tell me if there's a bank near here?

I wonder whether she enjoyed the date.

Remember!
Use *if* or *whether* for yes/no questions.

▶ **Read Study 2, page 144**

PRONUNCIATION

1a 🎧 **5.4** Listen to six pairs of sentences. Which sentence in each pair is a statement and which is a question? What is the difference in pronunciation?

→

Their date went really well?

→

Their date went really well.

b 🎧 **5.5** Listen to the questions again and practise.

2a Complete the sentences below with information about yourself (the more surprising the better).

- I'm very afraid of ...
- One day I hope to ...
- When I was a child I used to ...
- My favourite film/food/TV programme/book is ...

b Work in pairs and swap sentences. Read out the ones which surprise you. Ask for more information.

> You're very afraid of snakes?
> Have you ever seen one up close?

▶ Unit 5, Study & Practice 2, page 144

Task

Plan a fantasy dinner party

Preparation Listening

1   You are going to plan a fantasy dinner party with two other students. Read the information. Which aspects of planning do you think will be most difficult?

2   🎧 5.6 Listen to six people talking about who they would invite to dinner. For each suggested guest, make notes on the topics below.

   • reasons for inviting him/her
   • suitable subjects of conversation
   • questions to ask or things to say

3a   Listen again and tick the phrases in section a of the Useful language box that you hear.

b   Whose suggestion do you like best?

Your fantasy dinner party

There will be a total of eight guests: the students in your group and five other guests.

You can invite any person you like, living or dead. This is an opportunity to meet famous people who you have always longed to meet!

It is important that the evening is a success, so the guest list should work well as a whole. You may decide that you want a particular theme such as sport, politics or film, or you may prefer a mixture of people.

You should produce a seating plan, according to who you think will get on well together and have plenty to talk about. Include yourselves in the plan.

You will also need to think about what subjects of conversation to introduce and what questions you would like to ask your famous guests.

Task Speaking

1a Work individually. Think of five guests to suggest. Put them in order of preference. Make notes on the topics in exercise 2.

b Think about how to explain and justify your suggestions. Ask your teacher for any words/phrases you need.

> Useful language a

2a Work in groups of three. Compare your suggestions and try to agree on a guest list.

b Decide on a seating plan. Make a list of good conversation topics, topics that are best to avoid, and questions that you want to ask your guests.

> Useful language a and b

3a Work with students from other groups. Take turns to explain your guest lists and seating plans.

b Discuss the questions below.

- Were any guests chosen by more than one group?
- Who made the most interesting and original suggestion?
- Whose dinner party would you most like to attend?

Follow up Writing

1 Choose one of your fantasy dinner party guests and write a letter of invitation. Include the topics below.

- who you are and what the event is
- why you want to invite him/her
- who the other guests are

USEFUL LANGUAGE

a Explaining your suggestions
The reason I've chosen him is …
It's someone that's always fascinated me.
I've always wanted to meet …
I'd ask/talk to him about …
I could ask her about …
I'd love to ask her what she thinks about/why she …
It would be amazing to find out the truth about …

b Reaching agreement
I (don't) think it's a good idea to invite …
Do we all agree that we're (not) going to invite … ?
I (don't) think … will get on well with …
… and … will probably have a very interesting discussion about …
I think we should introduce/avoid the subject of …
Personally, I'd like to sit next to …

SHARE YOUR TASK

Prepare to talk for a minute about your favourite fantasy dinner guest.

Practise describing why you chose them and what you would talk about.

Film/Record yourself giving your description.

Share your film/recording with other students.

LANGUAGE LIVE

Speaking
Dealing with problems on the telephone

1 Work in groups. Discuss the questions below.

- Do you enjoy chatting on the phone or do you prefer to keep your calls short and to the point?
- Have you ever got annoyed or frustrated when making a phone call? Why?

2 🎧 5.7 Listen to three telephone conversations. Answer the questions below for each conversation.

1 Who is speaking to who?
2 What problem occurs?
3 How does the conversation end?

3a Listen again and complete the sentences.

1 Thanks for _____ back to me.
2 I _____ a message _____ .
3 Could you speak _____ a bit, please? Your voice is very _____ .
4 Sorry, you're _____ up.
5 Can I just _____ your name and _____ , please?
6 I'll have to _____ you _____ to another department.
7 If you'll just _____ with me ...
8 It's _____ your flights to Istanbul next week.
9 Am I _____ at a bad time?
10 When _____ be a _____ time to call?

b Look at audio script 5.7 on page 172 and underline other useful phrases for telephoning.

c 🎧 5.8 Listen to the sentences in exercise 3a and practise saying them.

4 Work in pairs. Turn to page 129 and use the prompts to prepare and practise a conversation.

Writing
Types of message

1a Look at messages A–E on page 55 and match them to descriptions 1–5 below.

1 an email giving details of travel arrangements for a business trip
2 a note to a family member or flatmate
3 a note pushed under someone's door
4 an informal email to a friend
5 a text message to a friend

b Put messages A–E in the order that they were sent.

1 B ... 5 D

c Complete messages A–E with the phrases in the box.

....

By the way,
We're both really delighted for you!!
Hope you had a good day at work
I'll be out of the office tomorrow (Fri)
Please be more considerate in future
Can't wait to see u both!
I have some news,
Can you let me know if these flights suit ASAP?
Best wishes,
Much love

....

2 Read messages A–E again. Find at least one example of the features below. Which message is formal?

1 words being missed out to make the message shorter
2 capital letters and exclamation marks for extra emphasis
3 simplified 'incorrect' spellings
4 use of abbreviations

A

New Message

Dear Sienna,

What great news! Congratulations! [1]_____
Let's celebrate when you're over in May – our treat.

[2]_____

Arlo and Giovanna

B

Dear Sienna,

We can now confirm available flights for your trip to Milan on 25th May.
The times closest to those you requested are:
Depart: LONDON LHR 06:10
Arrive: MILAN MALPENSA 09:15

Return 28th May
Depart: MILAN MALPENSA 10:15
Arrive: LONDON LHR 11:15

[3]_____ Either myself or Teresa Zanetti will be there to pick you up at the airport. [4]_____ but will be back on Monday if you wish to discuss any further details.

[5]_____ Pam Jones

C

Hey Gio, [6]_____ I'm pregnant! Can't believe it! V excited and v nervous. Can u let Arlo know? Coming to Italy for work next month. Fancy meeting up? [7]_____ Sienna x

D

While you were away this weekend your burglar alarm went off every hour during the night and kept the whole street awake. [8]_____ and leave a key with someone who can turn it off.

Ian Madison (no. 22)

E

Arlo,

[9]_____ . I'm at the gym. I'll pick up some food for dinner on the way home. Back about 8.
[10]_____ , don't forget Sienna is coming to stay tomorrow. We're taking her out for dinner.
Gio xx

3 Write an appropriate message for each situation below.

- Send a card congratulating an old friend and her partner, who have just had their first baby.
- Send an email suggesting possible travel details, from London to your city, for someone who is attending an international conference.
- Write a note to put under someone's door to complain about the loud music coming from their flat most evenings.
- Write a note for your flatmate or a member of your family explaining why you will be out when he/she gets home, when you'll be back and what the arrangements for the evening meal are.
- Write an informal email to a friend who you have just heard is going to get married.

4a Work in pairs. Swap messages and comment on your partner's messages, using the checklist bleow. Which message is clearest?

- Is your message formal or informal as appropriate?
- Is the purpose of your message clear?
- Have you included the features in exercise 2 in your informal messages?
- Have you used correct spelling and punctuation in your formal message?

b Redraft the message which was least clear. Try to improve it.

AFTER UNIT 5 YOU CAN ...

Describe different types of social events.

Guess the meaning of colloquial language.

Discuss and plan a social event.

Deal with problems on the telephone.

Write different types of messages.

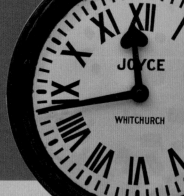

06

BIG IDEAS

IN THIS UNIT

- Grammar: Perfect tenses; More about the Present perfect simple and continuous

- Vocabulary: Human achievements; *First*

- Task: Present an idea for a TV programme

- World culture: Unsung heros

Five inventions that shape the way we live today

What inventions have had the greatest impact on the way we live? Most people would mention the wheel, the printing press, the internet, and so on. But pause for a moment and consider the following five contenders. They shape our lives in ways you may never have thought of!

Standard time

OK, so time has always existed, but 'standard time' hasn't. Imagine the world today, if our clocks weren't synchronised. In the 18th and 19th centuries, towns around the world used their own local time, which was different from town to town. This meant that a train could arrive in one town before it had officially left the previous one! In England, for example, it wasn't until 1880 that a law was passed creating a "standard time" for the whole country. Time zones across the world were only standardised at the beginning of the 20th century [1]_____ . The last country to adopt international time zones was Nepal, in 1986.

Running water

Around 4,000 years ago on the Greek island of Crete, a palace was built with hot and cold running water that flowed from taps made of silver and gold. The palace also housed the first known flushing toilet. As recently as the early 20th century, however, most houses in Europe didn't have their own toilet or running water. One or two toilets would be shared by a whole street, and water came from a communal pump. Disease and poor personal hygiene were common. These days, we feel it is only natural to take showers, flush our toilets and water our gardens. While [2]_____ , it has also caused its own problems, with even the UK frequently finding itself in danger of running out of water.

The light bulb

When the electric light bulb first appeared in the 19th century, it came with a warning sign to be placed on the wall next to the bulb: "Do not attempt to light with a match". Now, perhaps more than any other object in our lives, we take it for granted. Light bulbs illuminate our cities and roads at night, [3]_____ and they enable us to do much more with our free time. Imagine your evenings without electric lights!

Reading and speaking

1a Work in pairs and discuss. What do you think have been the most important five inventions of the last 200 years?

b Look at the photos and the headings in the article above. What impact do you think each invention has had?

2 Read the article and check your answers. Work in pairs and answer the questions about each invention.
   1 When was it invented?
   2 What problem did it solve?

Algorithms

You can't see them, you can't touch them, but they're everywhere and they control our lives. An algorithm is defined as "the steps that you follow to solve a problem or reach an answer". The first algorithms date back almost 4,000 years to the Babylonians, but the word itself comes from the 9th-century Persian mathematician, Al-Khwarizmi. Algorithms started to make a big impact in the 20th century. They are central to how computers process information and they decide everything from the search results you see when you Google a word, to the time you wait at traffic lights. 4_____ . Algorithms also control more than 70 percent of Wall Street's stock market trades. In fact, you could argue that we are living in the age of the algorithm. It's a shame so few of us understand them!

Shipping containers

First used in the 1950s, shipping containers are, in many ways, the symbol of our time. They have made globalisation possible. Before shipping containers, goods were loaded and unloaded by hand. Each package had to be carried onto the ship, tied down with ropes and then untied and carried out at the other end. Just unloading a single ship could take 20 men a week, making goods from abroad very expensive. Nowadays, three people operating three cranes can unload a ship in about ten hours. The largest modern ships are four football pitches long and can carry almost 15,000 containers. This has made shipping costs low, which 5_____ . So next time you buy a T-shirt, book, or an electronic gadget which was made in another country, remember that it's only possible because of those big metal boxes.

Your shout!

What do you think? Is there something missing from our list? Should we have chosen a different invention? Post your comment below and tell us what you think.

What about the credit card? It has made the online shopping revolution possible.
saltpeter

I think the mobile phone has to be on the list. It's led to huge changes in society.
janejones11

What about the bar code? It's on everything and it's affected the lives of shop workers everywhere.
simoncarly

3a Complete the article with the phrases below.

    a **has resulted in** cheaper goods all over the world and **has affected** all our lives **dramatically**
    b **enabling** international air travel and global business to take place
    c they **have led to** more flexible working hours
    d this **has transformed** public health
    e Basically, they **make** modern machines **possible**

  b Look at the phrases in bold in exercise 3a. Put them in pairs with similar meanings.

4 Work in pairs. Read the article again, then summarise what you remember about each invention.

5a Put the five inventions in order according to the impact they have had on our lives.

  b Work in groups and compare answers.

6a Work in pairs and discuss the questions.

    • Do you agree with the list in the article?
    • What would you add and what would you take away?

  b Write a comment for the 'Your shout' section.

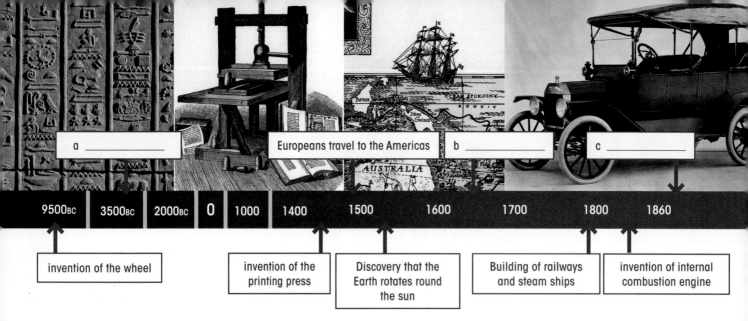

a _____ | Europeans travel to the Americas | b _____ | c _____

| 9500BC | 3500BC | 2000BC | 0 | 1000 | 1400 | 1500 | 1600 | 1700 | 1800 | 1860 |

invention of the wheel

invention of the printing press

Discovery that the Earth rotates round the sun

Building of railways and steam ships

invention of internal combustion engine

Listening
Important dates

1 How do you say the dates in the box? What approximate dates do the other time expressions refer to?

5000 BC	the 17th century
3200 BC	the mid 16th century
1600	the late 18th century
1850	the next decade or so
the 1860s	within 30 years
2050	the beginning of the
the 7th century AD	21st century

2 Work in pairs. Look at the timeline of human achievements, past and future. Say approximately when each happened/will happen, using the phrases in exercise 1.

The invention of the wheel happened in about 9500 BC.

3a Look at the past and future achievements below. Try to match them to boxes a–f on the timeline.
  1 the discovery that bacteria cause diseases
  2 a cure for the common cold
  3 the invention of writing
  4 human control of extreme weather events, like hurricanes
  5 the first manned mission to Mars
  6 the arrival of Europeans in Australia

  b 🎧 6.1 Listen and check your answers.

4 Listen again and make notes about what else you learnt. Work in pairs and compare answers.

Language focus 1
Perfect tenses

1a Work in pairs. Complete sentences 1–5 with an appropriate date or time phrase from exercise 1 above. Use the timeline to help you.

  1 By _____ , people in ancient Mesopotamia *had / have / will have* invented the wheel but they *hadn't / haven't / won't have* learnt how to write.
  2 By _____ , Europeans *had / have / will have* discovered how the solar system works, but they *hadn't / haven't / won't have* arrived in Australia.
  3 By _____ , the steam engine, railways and even the first combustion engine *had / have / will have* been invented, but scientists still *hadn't / haven't / won't have* discovered that bacteria causes diseases!
  4 Today, at _____ , we *had / have / will have* landed on the moon and invented the internet, but we still *hadn't / haven't / won't have* found a cure for the common cold!
  5 Scientists believe that within _____ , we *had / have / will have* sent a manned mission to Mars and found a cure for many serious illnesses, but we probably *hadn't / haven't / won't have* learnt how to control the weather.

  b Choose the correct verb forms in sentences 1–5.

> ### GRAMMAR
>
> **1** Find an example in exercise 1b of the Past perfect, the Present perfect and the Future perfect. How is each tense formed?
>
> **2** Look at the timeline and the sentences in exercise 1b. Choose the correct answers in the rules below and find an example of each one.
> 1 We use the Past perfect to describe events *before / at* a particular time in the past.
> 2 We use the Present perfect to describe events *'before now' / at the present moment*.
> 3 We use the Future perfect to describe events *before / at* a particular time in the future.
>
> ▶ **Read Study 1, page 146**

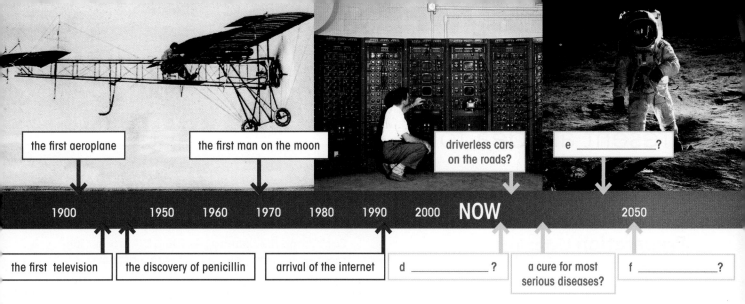

the first aeroplane | the first man on the moon | driverless cars on the roads? | e _____?

1900   1950   1960   1970   1980   1990   2000   **NOW**   2050

the first television | the discovery of penicillin | arrival of the internet | d _____? | a cure for most serious diseases? | f _____?

PRACTICE

1 Complete the sentences below with the correct form of the verbs in brackets (positive or negative). Use the timeline to help you.

1 By 2000BC, the Egyptians and Chinese _____ (invent) writing, but they _____ (learn) how to print books.
2 By 1900, the telephone _____ (be invent), but the Wright brothers _____ (yet make) their first flight.
3 Today, we _____ (discover) the cure for many diseases, but we _____ (find) a cure for the common cold.
4 By 2050, we _____ (probably find) a cure for the cold, but we _____ (discover) the cure for all serious diseases.
5 In 30 years' time, we _____ (probably learn) how to control the weather fully. However, we _____ (probably learn) how to influence it.

2a Write five more sentences about the past, present and future using information from the timeline, or your own ideas. Two sentences should be false.

b Work in pairs. Take turns to read your sentences. Guess which of your partner's sentences are false.

3 Complete the sentences below to make them true for you. Then work in groups and compare answers.

1 I hope I *'ll have learnt* (learn) *to drive* by the time I'm *21* .
2 I _____ (be) interested in _____ since I _____ .
3 I _____ never _____ until this year.
4 By the time I was _____ , I _____ (learn) how to _____ .
5 I'll probably have _____ by midnight tonight.
6 I haven't _____ recently.
7 By the end of today, I probably won't _____ .
8 When I was _____ , I had never _____ .
9 By nine o'clock this morning, I had already _____ .
10 By the time I'm _____ years old, I hope I _____ .

> Unit 6, Study & Practice 1, page 146

Vocabulary
Human achievements

1 Match verbs 1–13 to achievements a–m.

1 discover
2 invent/develop
3 explore
4 found
5 lead
6 raise/donate
7 set/break
8 win
9 defeat
10 write
11 inspire
12 become
13 give

a the first (man/woman/ Italian) to … /leader of …
b a planet/a cure for a disease
c an organisation/a new country
d great speeches
e others/future generations
f a political group/an army/ a country
g a symphony/play/poem/ novel/song
h space/a continent/a country
i a machine/theory/system
j money for/to charity
k an army/enemy/opponent
l a gold medal/the world cup/a Nobel prize
m a (new) world record

2a Work in pairs. Use the prompts below to describe the people's achievements. Use phrases from exercise 1.

1 Beethoven / some of the greatest / in history
Beethoven wrote some of the greatest symphonies in history.
2 Captain Cook / Australia and Antarctica
3 Federer / in the 2012 Wimbledon final
4 Marie Skłodowska-Curie / twice: once for physics and once for chemistry
5 Alexander Fleming / penicillin
6 Neil Armstrong / land on the moon
7 Aung San Suu Kyi / with her peaceful approach
8 Bill Gates / billions of dollars to help children in Africa
9 Usain Bolt / for the 100 metres
10 Mark Zuckerberg / Facebook

b 🎧 **6.2** Listen and check your answers.

Task

Present an idea for a TV programme

Preparation Listening

1 Read the advert about a TV series that is being planned. Summarise in your own words what the concept is.

2a Work in groups. Match the achievements below to the suggested categories on the ZooTV website.

1 the invention of the microchip
2 the building of the pyramids
3 the leadership of Mahatma Gandhi
4 the story of Scott of the Antarctic
5 the novels of Tolstoy
6 the career of Pelé
7 the music of Bob Dylan
8 the films of Steven Spielberg
9 the Theory of Evolution
10 the right to vote for women

b Think of other examples for the categories on the website. Then compare lists with the class.

3a 🎧 6.3 Listen to five people presenting an idea for the programme and make notes about the points below.

- the subject
- the category of achievement
- the arguments in favour

b Listen again and tick the phrases from the Useful language box you hear.

4 Work in groups and discuss the questions.

- Do you agree with what the speakers say? Can you add any more arguments to the ones they give?
- Which achievements do you find most amazing?

The top 50 achievements

Ever fancied the idea of making a TV programme?

ZooTV, one the country's leading TV production companies, is making a new series of short programmes called *The Top 50 human achievements*. Members of the public are invited to nominate topics for the programmes by submitting a three-minute video presentation, making the case for their choice.

The TV company will select the best 50 nominations and use each presentation as the basis for a ten-minute film. The films will be shown every weekday evening for ten weeks and at the end, the public will vote for their favourite human achievement.

Visit our website for more information and guidelines.

Task Speaking

1 You are going to present a nomination for the TV programme. First choose a topic, bearing the following in mind.

- The topic should interest and inspire you, but should also appeal to your classmates, who will vote at the end for their <u>favourite</u> achievement.
- If you cannot think of anything, you can choose a topic already mentioned in this unit.

2 Prepare what you will say. If possible, research facts online. Make notes about the points below. Ask your teacher for any words/phrases you need.

- the background to this achievement
- what happened
- the influence/impact it has had
- why you find it interesting/amazing

> Useful language a–c

a Introduction and background

I'd like to nominate (the leadership of Kemal Atatürk).
(Mozart) was (one of) the greatest composer(s) ever.
She was the first woman to (lead ...)
Before (the inventon of the wheel), people hadn't
been able to ...

b Telling the story

In the 1850s/in the early 20th century ...
Previously/before that, no one had ever ...
It took (him/her) ... years to ...
Eventually/finally, ...
It was only after his/her death that ...

c Describing the impact/influence

Without them...
(this invention) meant that/led to/resulted in ...
It's changed the way ...
... has made ... possible
It was an amazing achievement ...
Just imagine life if ... hadn't happened.
They changed the face of (music).
What she did really changed the world, because ...
It's incredible to think that ...
Their influence is still being felt today.

**Want to make a nomination, but not sure what is expected?
Here are some suggestions to get you thinking!**

- An extraordinary artistic/
musical/literary/scientific/
sporting/political
achievement or career.

- The discovery of an important
cure or medicine.

- An extraordinary building or
piece of engineering.

- The invention of an important
piece of technology.

- An idea or philosophy that
changed the world.

- An important human 'first'.

- A great step forward for
peace/human rights/
international relations.

- A great victory/struggle for
independence.

- Outstanding leadership at a
key point in history.

- An extraordinary example
of human courage/
determination.

- Any other human achievement
you find amazing!

3a Take turns to give your presentations to the class. Try to speak for about
three minutes.

b Listen to each other's presentations, and make notes similar to those in
exercise 3a on page 60. Think of two questions to ask at the end of each
presentation.

c Vote for your favourite achievement from the presentations you
listened to.

Follow up Writing

1 After each programme has been broadcast, a short summary is posted
on the ZooTV website to remind viewers of the nominees before they
vote. Write a summary of your nomination, giving the main reasons
why you think it should win.

SHARE YOUR TASK

Practise giving your
presentation until you feel
confident.

Film/Record yourself giving
your talk.

Share your film/recording with
other students.

Language focus 2
More about the Present perfect simple and continuous

1a Complete the world records in the fact file with the phrases in the box.

did it in nine minutes   did it underwater
used his nose   only used one arm
was carrying 300 kilos at the time

Fact file:
UNUSUAL WORLD RECORDS

1 In 2009, Agris Kazelniks ran 20 metres in 11.40 seconds. He …

2 Tom Sietas set a new world record when he swam 200 metres. Tom …

3 Paddy Doyle completed 1,868 press ups in one hour in 1993. He …

4 In 2004, Sonya Thomas ate 5 kilos of cheesecake. She …

5 In 2010, Andrew Dahl inflated 23 balloons in three minutes. He …

b Turn to page 128 and check your answers. Which record do you think is the most impressive/dangerous/ridiculous?

2 Look at pictures 1–5 on the right of more people who are attempting or hold unusual world records. Choose the sentence which best describes each picture.

GRAMMAR

1a Match the sentences in exercise 2 with the rules below.

1 If an action happens in a moment and is complete, we use the Present perfect *simple / continuous*.

2 If an action is not finished, we use the Present perfect *simple / continuous*.

3 If we want to emphasise that an action has lasted for a long time or is repeated, we use the Present perfect *simple / continuous*.

4 However, if we say how many times someone did something, we always use the Present perfect *simple / continuous*.

5 If we are describing a state (using verbs like *be, know*, etc.) we usually use the Present perfect *simple / continuous*.

b Choose the correct answers to complete the rules.

▶ Read Study 2, page 147

1a He's landed successfully and broken the world record for base jumping.

b He's been landing successfully and breaking the world record for base jumping.

2a He's headed the ball 2,377 times without dropping it.

b He's been heading the ball 2,377 times without dropping it.

3a She's grown her hair since 1973.

b She's been growing her hair since 1973.

4a He's been a gardener for 90 years.

b He's been being a gardener for 90 years.

5a He's eaten doughnuts for over two hours.

b He's been eating doughnuts for over two hours.

PRACTICE

1a You are going to find someone in the class who has done/been doing the things below. First, choose the best verb form for each sentence. Which sentences could have both forms?

Find someone who has …
1 *passed / been passing* an important exam this year.
2 *gone / been going* out a lot recently.
3 *felt / been feeling* tired this week.
4 *broken / been breaking* an arm or a leg.
5 *lost / been losing* some money recently.
6 *studied / been studying* a lot recently.
7 *done / been doing* all their homework this week.
8 *spent / been spending* a lot of money recently.
9 *been / been going* abroad this year.

b Write the questions you need to ask other students in the class. Find one person in the class who answers 'yes' to each one.

PRONUNCIATION

1 🎧 **6.4** Listen to this question from exercise 1a. Notice the weak forms of the auxiliary verbs. Which words are stressed?

/həv jə bin/
Have you been going out a lot recently?

2 🎧 **6.5** Listen to the other questions and practise saying them, paying attention to stress and weak forms.

2a Work in pairs. Read about Matt and Fiona. Think of reasons why Matt has been behaving in this way.

 Matt and Fiona have been going out for six months but recently, Fiona hasn't returned Matt's calls or responded to his texts.

b Write a conversation between Matt and Fiona when they meet on the street by chance. Use the prompts in the box in the correct tense.

I (try) to phone you	Why / you (avoid) me?
What / you (do)?	I (be) worried sick!
I (be) really busy.	You (have) doubts about us?

A: Hi, Fiona I've been trying to call you for days!
B: Oh, hi Matt. I'm really sorry. I …

▶ **> Unit 6, Study & Practice 2, page 147**

Wordspot
first

1 Use a word or phrase with *first* in the box to complete the sentences below.

first-class	first thing	in first place	first aid
at first sight	first-choice	first language	at first
first impression	first of all		

1 So you've never been to Russia before. Tell me, what is your _____ ?
2 _____ I felt a little bit nervous, but it was OK once I got started.
3 It's very difficult to attract really _____ teachers on the low salaries we offer.
4 At least one member of staff should be trained in _____ in case there's an accident at work.
5 As soon as I met Andrea, I knew we'd marry one day: it was a case of love _____ .
6 Good evening, everybody. Professor King will be answering your questions in a moment, but _____ let me introduce myself.
7 I'll email the details through before I leave work tonight, so we can discuss them _____ in the morning.
8 And as the runners come to the finishing line, it's still Kamouchi who is _____ .
9 It's a good idea to choose an alternative holiday, in case your _____ resort is not available.
10 Of the island's population, about 20 percent have Spanish as their _____ .

2 Complete the diagram with the phrases with *first* in exercise 1.

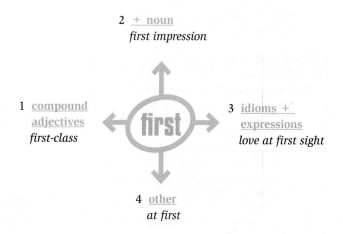

2 + noun
first impression

1 compound adjectives
first-class

3 idioms + expressions
love at first sight

4 other
at first

3a Study the words and phrases for a few minutes, and memorise as many as you can.

b Work in pairs. Turn to page 128 and take turns to ask and answer the questions using a phrase with *first*.

WORLD CULTURE

UNSUNG HEROES

Find out first

1a Work in pairs. Look at the list of British heroes below. Which have you heard of? Do you know what they are famous for?

- William Shakespeare
- John Lennon
- Diana, Princess of Wales
- Sir Winston Churchill
- Isambard Kingdom Brunel

b Try to match the people from exercise 1a with the sentences below.

He/She ...
1 was a songwriter and pop star.
2 led Britain during the Second World War.
3 designed and built bridges, ships, stations etc.
4 wrote plays and sonnets.
5 supported numerous charities

c Go online to check your answers or ask your teacher.

Search: William Shakespeare / John Lennon / Diana Princess of Wales / Winston Churchill / Isambard Kingdom Brunel

2 The people in 1a appeared in the top ten list of '100 Greatest Britons'. In what order do you think they came in the list?

View

3a You are going to watch a video about Isambard Kingdom Brunel, who is often thought of as an unsung hero. Look at the photos and read the statements below. Try to guess the correct answers.

1 His most famous work is **the Clifton Suspension Bridge / The Great Eastern ship / Paddington Station**.
2 His greatest mistake is considered to be **the Clifton Suspension Bridge / The Great Eastern ship / Paddington Station**.
3 He died at the age of **53 / 73 / 93**.
4 **The Clifton Suspension Bridge / The Great Eastern ship / Paddington Station** was completed five years after he died as a tribute to him.

b ▶ Watch the video and check your answers.

4 Watch the video again. Then work in pairs and explain the significance of the people and numbers below.

- 200 years ago
- photographers
- John Scott Russell
- the company directors
- six men
- 38 passengers
- 53 years old

5 Why was Brunel's 'greatest mistake' such a failure? Can you think of any other great mistakes famous people have made?

World view

6a ▶ Watch three people talking about an unsung hero that they admire. Complete the table.

	Name of person he/she admires	Biographical information	Achievements
Lizzie			
Sion			
Jeanette			

b Work in pairs. Compare your notes. Watch again if necessary.

7 Work in pairs. Can you think of any unsung heroes from your country or in your area of interest?

🔊 FIND OUT MORE

8a Choose one person from the list below (or choose your own unsung hero). Go online to find out more about him/her.

- **Mary Seacole** – the Jamaican woman who nursed soldiers in the Crimean War
- **Irena Sendler** – the Polish woman who saved thousands of children from death
- **Vasili Alexandrovich Arkhipov** – the Russian man who prevented nuclear war
- **Norman Borlaug** – the American man who 'saved a billion lives'

b Use the information you found out to prepare a short presentation about the person you chose.

....

Search: Mary Seacole / Irena Sendler / Vasili Alexandrovich Arkhipov / Norman Borlaug

....

c Give your presentation to the class. Decide together who the most impressive unsung hero is.

▶ Write up your research

9 Write one or two paragraphs about the person you researched. Use the prompts below to help you.

- … is credited with having saved/invented/prevented …
- … spent his/her early life in …
- At the age of … , he/she …
- Little is known about … because …
- His/Her achievements are important because …

AFTER UNIT 6 YOU CAN …

Describe a wide range of human achievements and their results.

....

Talk about different eras using appropriate tenses.

....

Give a presentation.

....

07

EVENTS

Speaking and vocabulary
Celebrations and protests

1 Look at the photo. What kind of event do you think it is? Think of five other events that draw large crowds like this.

2a Look at news extracts 1–8 below. Check the meaning of the words in bold. Do the the words in bold relate to:
- events   – people
- activities   – things?

b Can you think of any other words related to these categories?

1 The **demonstration** was largely peaceful with **protestors campaigning for an end to poverty**.

2 Hundreds of **supporters clapped**, **cheered** and **waved flags** as the team went past on their **victory parade**.

3 The **marchers** were carrying **placards** and **banners** calling for better pay.

4 When the minister **addressed the crowd**, a few people **booed**.

5 The **crowd** at the **festival went wild** when the final act came on.

6 A small group of **protestors** broke away and **clashed with** police.

7 The **carnival** was truly spectacular with so many **floats** and people wearing **costumes**.

8 The stadium is usually a venue for **outdoor concerts** and sporting events, but yesterday the crowd were there to **celebrate** the new year.

3 Work in pairs and discuss. What's the biggest protest or celebration that you have been to or seen on TV?

THE BIGGEST CONCERT IN HISTORY

A new record was set on 31st December 1994 [1]_____ a Rod Stewart concert in Rio de Janeiro, Brazil. The venue was Copacabana Beach, [2]_____ New Year's Eve every year. Some of the crowd [3]_____ were probably just celebrating as usual rather than attending the concert, but it is still recognised by the Guinness Book of Records as the largest ever.

THE BIGGEST PROTEST EVER

The largest coordinated anti-war rallies in history took place on 15th February 2003 all around the world. Protestors were campaigning against the war [4]_____ . The largest single protest, [5]_____ , attracted around three million people, many carrying placards and banners. The size of the protest surprised even the organisers, [6]_____ the march two hours early as a result. Most marchers didn't manage to hear the speakers address the crowd, as the public square wasn't big enough.

THE LARGEST CROWD AT A SPORTS EVENT

The 200,000 people [7]_____ in the Maracanã stadium in June 1950 remain to this day the largest stadium crowd at a sports event. The match itself was between Uruguay, [8]_____ , and Brazil. But the record for the largest crowd at a single sports event is probably held by the Tour de France. This race attracts 12–15 million spectators over the two weeks [9]_____ .

Language focus 1
Relative clauses

1 🎧 **7.1 Complete the news stories above with phrases from the box. Then listen and check.**

....

which was in Rome   who decided to start
where millions celebrate   that it is held
who watched the World Cup final   who were there
which was about to begin in Iraq   who won
when over 3.5 million people attended

....

GRAMMAR

Relative pronouns

1a The phrases in the box above are relative clauses. Underline the relative pronoun in each phrase.

b In which of the sentences below can the relative pronoun be omitted? Why?
This is the man who designed the stadium.
This is the stadium which he designed.

c Only one relative pronoun in the box above can be omitted from the news stories. Which one?

Defining and non-defining relative clauses

2 Read the sentences below and answer the questions.
*Those **who went home early** missed the party.*
*Pedro, **who went home early,** missed the party.*

1 Which clause in bold is necessary to understand the sentence? (This is a defining relative clause.)
2 Which clause in bold gives 'extra' information in the sentence? (This is a non-defining relative clause.)
3 Which type of relative clause needs commas?

▶ **Read Study 7.1, page 149**

PRACTICE

1a Complete the sentences below with a relative pronoun, if necessary.

Write the name of ...
1 a place _____ you'd really like to visit.
2 someone _____ you haven't seen for several years.
3 the month _____ you usually go on holiday.
4 something _____ you never leave home without.
5 someone _____ music you particularly enjoy.
6 someone _____ music you can't stand.
7 a place _____ you always feel relaxed.
8 something _____ you often forget.

b Write your answers in random order on a piece of paper.

c Work in pairs. Show your answers. Take turns to ask questions about the answers on the piece of paper, using relative clauses.

2 Combine the sentences below using a non-defining relative clause. Start with the words in bold.

1 **The UEFA Champions League final** takes place in May. It is the most-watched annual sporting event in the world.
The UEFA Champions League final, which takes place ...

2 **The Beatles** split up in 1970. They have sold more records than any other band in history.

3 **The Grand Bazaar** in Istanbul was built in the 15th century. It is the most popular tourist attraction in Europe.

4 Chongqing is a little-known city in south-west China. It is **one of the largest urban areas in the world.**

5 **Cuban singer Compay Segundo** made his first recording in the 1930s. He finally found international fame in the 1990s with Latin group The Buena Vista Social Club.

6 During the festival of Ramadan, **daytime eating and drinking are forbidden**. It takes place in the ninth month of the Muslim calendar..

> Unit 7, Study & Practice 1, page 149

WE SAW HISTORY IN THE MAKING

WE LOOK BACK AT SOME OF THE MOST FAMOUS CELEBRATIONS AND PROTESTS OF THE LAST CENTURY, AND HOW IT FELT TO BE THERE.

1929

1 THE WALL STREET CRASH AND THE JARROW MARCH

On Thursday 24th October 1929, at the New York Stock Exchange on Wall Street, the unthinkable happened. In one day, 13 million shares changed hands as prices collapsed and the dream of wealth was transformed into the nightmare of poverty. The Wall Street Crash led to a period of unemployment, homelessness and hunger all over the world. In the next few years, millions of ordinary people's lives were destroyed.

Over 5,000 km away, in the ship-building town of Jarrow in the north east of England, unemployment among skilled working men reached 65 percent as a result of the 'Great Depression' that followed the Wall Street Crash. In October 1936, 207 men from Jarrow set out on foot, to march the 480 km to London as a 'protest against starvation'. The Jarrow marchers were cheered and given food in every town they passed through, but when they reached parliament, nothing was done for them. The men were given £1 each for their train fare home.

1967

2 THE SUMMER OF LOVE

During the 1960s, rebellion against the establishment grew in many parts of the world, from the United States to Czechoslovakia. Young people began to adopt an alternative lifestyle characterised by long hair and colourful clothes, and to protest against the actions of their governments, such as the Vietnam War. In 1967, thousands of young people gathered in the Haight-Ashbury neighbourhood of San Francisco to promote peace, happiness and love in what became known as the 'Summer of love'. Music festivals, poetry readings, speeches and theatre events celebrated 'flower power'. However, by October 1967, events had taken an unpleasant turn as crime and drug abuse increasingly took over. The organisers held a 'funeral' and burnt a coffin labelled 'Summer of Love'.

Reading and speaking

1a Work in groups. Look at the photos and titles and make a list of anything you know about the events.

b Can you guess which event(s) the words below relate to?

the Stock Exchange	starvation
the campaign for Black rights	victory
an alternative lifestyle	reunify
the establishment	shares
a border crossing	homelessness
rebellion	to protest
reforms	

2a Read about events 1–4 above and check your ideas.

b Work in pairs and discuss the questions.

- When and where did these events happen?
- Were these events celebrations or protests?
- Why were the participants celebrating/protesting?
- Were other countries affected?

3 Work in pairs and discuss. What do you think it was like to experience these events at the time? Think of three words to describe each event.

4a Match comments A–E on page 69 to events 1–4. One event has two comments.

b What feelings or atmosphere does each person describe?

5 Read the texts and comments again. Are the statements below probably true (T) or probably false (F)? Underline the words that tell you.

Events

1 In 1929, people didn't believe that the stock market could collapse.
2 Ordinary people sympathised more with the Jarrow Marchers than the government did.
3 The organisers of the 'Summer of Love' thought it was a complete success.
4 The East German government was more or less forced to open its borders.
5 Obama only just won the 2008 presidential election.

Comments

6 The closure of the shipyards in Jarrow felt like a death sentence to the town.
7 Many older people in the1960s were shocked by the way hippies dressed.
8 People in the former East Germany did not trust the government.
9 Before Obama's election, black people did not believe that top jobs were open to them.

1989

2008

3 THE FALL OF THE BERLIN WALL

In autumn 1989, following reforms in the former Soviet Union, opposition to communist rule in the countries of Eastern Europe began to grow and their governments began to open their borders. Under overwhelming pressure, on 9th November, the East German government announced that the Berlin Wall, which divided the city, would be opened and that East Berliners would be free to visit the West. Within hours, thousands of people poured through the gates in the wall, where they were greeted with flowers and champagne by West Berliners. People from both sides began to knock down the wall with hammers and by 1990, East and West Germany were reunified.

4 OBAMA'S ELECTION NIGHT

On 5th November 2008, 47-year-old Senator Barack Obama shattered 200 years of US history and swept to victory to become the first black president of the United States. A crowd of a quarter of a million gathered in Grant Park, Chicago, to celebrate. Over a million people crammed the streets of the city and many millions more celebrated  around the US and across the world. Obama, who had started his presidential campaign as an outsider, had won millions of white votes as well as black ones with his famous slogan, 'Yes we can'. His election was seen by many as the culmination of a campaign for black rights that had begun with Martin Luther King in the early 1960s.

6   Work in groups. Discuss the questions.

- Whose account do you find most moving/interesting? Why?
- Which of these events do you think was most/least important? Why?
- Would you like to have experienced any of these events yourself? Which ones and why?
- Which other events in your lifetime do you think will be remembered by future generations? Why?

A We just couldn't believe it, then we saw pictures on television showing people at the border crossing … they were waving … it seemed impossible. The next day, we bundled our sleeping daughter into the car and drove to the border. We were worried it might be closed again before we could get there, but when we reached it we were waved through. People were getting out of their cars and giving flowers to the guards. It was a very peaceful sight. Someone greeted us with wine and chocolate for the child … I was shaking, I was so excited … the streets were full of people and everyone was embracing each other … there was a feeling of great joy.' *Carmen Blazejeweski*

B There was music and dancing and people being free and being wild … My parents came to visit and I remember my mother bursting into tears as someone wafted across the street in a cape with long plumed feathers.' **Martine Algier**

C It's one thing to hear someone say the sky is the limit, but now we can see that. We've had doctors and lawyers and we've known those were things we could achieve, but the presidency was always closed to us. If someone said the sky was the limit, we could say "not quite". That is no longer the case.' *God-Goldin Harrison*

D It was only natural for sons to follow their fathers, so that's what I did. My father was a riveter so when I was 14, I started with him as a rivet catcher … that was me with a job. Then one afternoon, the foreman came round and said "Con, you're finished tonight," just like that. So that was me finished, out … The town was murdered. A good town, just cut off like that, like a hangman dropping a noose. … It was really very depressing for the future and for our children' **Con Shiels**

E It seemed like anything was possible. Every kind of character appeared on the street because you could dress however you wanted … We put "free" in front of everything, we were exploring what freedom was, what a free society was. There were free stores, free meals, sometimes even a ceremony burning money.' *Ron Thelin*

Vocabulary and listening
Special events

1 Work in pairs and discuss the questions.

- What can you see in the photos?
- Which events do you associate these things/people with?
- Have you been to any events like these recently?

2 Cross out the word that does not match the event. Rewrite it in the correct place(s).

carnival:	floats, crowds, ~~a bridegroom~~, special costumes
wedding:	cake, speeches, a reception, mourners, *a bridegroom*
music festival:	presents, stewards, a stage, the headline act
anniversary/ engagement:	a party, guests, cards, merchandise, decorations
public holiday:	parades, fans, special meals, family gatherings
fair:	balloons, a bride, food stalls, queues
funeral:	a coffin, a ceremony, fireworks, flower arrangements

3 🎧 7.2 You are going to hear three people talking about an event from exercise 1, but the name of the event is bleeped out. Listen and decide which event each person is talking about.

4 Work in pairs. Make a list of positive or negative issues each speaker mentions. Listen again and check.

Language focus 2
Quantifiers

1a Choose the quantifier that best reflects what Harriet, Bethany and Dan said about the events they described.

Harriet
1 *Quite a few of / All of* my friends had huge weddings.
2 They had *one or two / hundreds of* guests.
3 My friend didn't know *some / any* of the guests at her own wedding.
4 She had *hardly any / enough* time to talk to her own friends.
5 We've invited *a few / loads of* old friends.
6 We'll have a party *a couple of / several* weeks later.

Bethany
7 Everyone eats *far too much / far too little* food.
8 *Very few / Most* people exchange presents.
9 You take *a little / a lot of* candy for the kids.

Dan
10 There are *too many / plenty of* food stalls.
11 There isn't *enough / any* water available.
12 I go to *no / any* festival I can.

b 🎧 7.3 Listen and check.

GRAMMAR

1 **Match the quantifiers in exercise 1 to the definitions below.**
  1 large quantities: *hundreds of*
  2 small quantities: *very few*
  3 neither: *enough*

2 **Are the quantifiers in exercise 1 followed by a countable noun (C), an uncountable noun (U) or both (B)?**

3 **What is the difference in meaning between the groups of sentences below?**
  1a We ate a lot of food.
   b We ate too much food.
  2a There are enough toilets.
   b There are plenty of toilets.
  3a Quite a few of my friends had big weddings.
   b A few of my friends had big weddings.
   c (Very) few of my friends had big weddings.
  4a My friend didn't know some of the guests at her own wedding.
   b My friend didn't know any of the guests at her own wedding.
  5a I go to any festival.
   b I don't go to any festivals.

▶ **Read Study 2, page 150**

PRACTICE

1a **Use the prompts below to make as many true sentences as you can about yourself, your country, town, etc.**

  1 In my country, there are very few / quite a few / too many carnivals / music festivals / public holidays.
  2 In my town, there are / plenty of / enough / not enough parks / supermarkets / facilities for children.
  3 At my house, there is a lot of / not enough / too much / not much space / noise.
  4 I like / I don't like some / any / most / rock music / classical music / opera.
  5 I like / I don't like some / any / most / fruit / fish / ice cream.

 b **Work in pairs and compare answers.**

2 **Work in pairs. Think of an event that you have been to. Describe it and say what was good or bad about it using quantifiers and the topics below.**

  • people   • speeches
  • noise   • excitement
  • space   • staff
  • toilets   • places to get food/drink

> **Unit 7, Study & Practice 2, page 150**

Wordspot
take

1 **Complete sentences 1–12 with a phrase from the word map below. Use the correct form of *take*.**

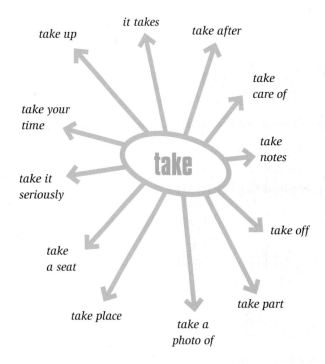

  1 Thousands of people _____ in yesterday's demonstration.
  2 Halloween _____ on 31st October.
  3 Excuse me, could you _____ us all with this camera?
  4 Don't worry, we're not in a hurry. You can _____ getting ready.
  5 _____ roughly an hour to get from the airport, depending on traffic.
  6 Fortunately, Carmen's father can _____ the baby while she's at work.
  7 Would you mind _____ for a moment? I'll tell Mr Evans you're here.
  8 Philip spends loads of money on tennis lessons. He really does _____ .
  9 I wish I'd _____ during the lecture, because I can't remember anything now.
  10 Everyone says Michael _____ his father, but I think he's more like his mother.
  11 It's getting hot in here – I think I'll _____ my jacket.
  12 Jo was getting unfit, so she decided _____ jogging.

2a 🎧 **7.4 Listen to 12 questions with *take* and write brief answers. How many of the questions can you remember from your answers? Look at audio script 7.4 on page 173.**

 b **Work in pairs. Ask and answer the questions with your partner.**

Task

Present ideas for an event

HOME | EVENTS | PREVIOUS WINNERS | GALLERY | CONTACT

Preparation Reading and vocabulary

1a Look at the photos. Which events in the box do they show?

art exhibition	classical concert	food festival
sports day	street party	summer fair
children's entertainment		traditional dancing
fancy dress competition		

b Work in pairs and discuss the questions.

- What are the people in each photo doing?
- Have you ever been to (or organised) any events like these?

2a Read the website and answer the questions.

1 What is the Mayor's Big Event?
2 How can you take part in the competition?
3 Which idea will win the competition?

b Read the advice for organisers below and check the meaning of the phrases in bold.

1 Consider **printing flyers** and **putting up posters**.
2 You can sell tickets for the event, **charge an entrance fee** or make it free.
3 Don't ignore easy **money spinners** such as selling bottled water.
4 If you're putting on a concert or festival then you need a **headline act** to **attract** people and encourage **word-of-mouth advertising**.
5 Think about **taking out an ad** in the local paper or sending out **a mailshot**.
6 Don't forget, if there are **stalls** at your event, you can **charge a fee** to the **stall holders** for taking part.

c Does each sentence describe a means of promotion or a way of raising money?

3 Work in pairs and discuss. What sort of event do you think would have the best chance of winning sponsorship from the mayor? Choose from the events in exercise 1a, or your own ideas.

the Mayor's Big Event competition

What event will you organise? The Mayor's Big Event has been running for six years. In that time, local residents have organised events such as concerts, fairs and art exhibitions. This year, the mayor will sponsor an exciting new event to raise money for local charities. Do you have an idea for such an event?

What is the Mayor's Big Event?

It's an annual event that is organised by local people, for local people. All the money that is raised goes to charity. The mayor pays for all the costs of organising and promoting the event.

Where does the event happen?

It can take place in the town hall, a local park, a shopping centre, or anywhere else you can think of.

Task Speaking

1a Work in groups of two or three. You are going to plan an event then present your ideas. Choose the type of event that you are going to plan.

b Discuss the questions below and make notes on your answers.

- What will be the main attraction at your event?
- What other activities and entertainment will be on offer?
- Where will you stage the event?
- What will you do about food and drink?
- How will you promote the event?
- What problems might you encounter and how will you solve those problems?

> Useful language a

Who can organise the event?

Anyone can present their ideas to the mayor on Saturday 11th April, between 2–5 p.m. in the town hall. The best idea wins.

What sort of event can I organise?

Anything that the local community will enjoy, and that will raise money for charity.

I have an idea for an event. What should I do now?

Plan your event in detail. For example, you should think about ...

- the activities that will be available.
- how to promote the event.
- how to raise the maximum amount of money for charity.

Then present your idea to the mayor on Saturday 11th April between 2–5 p.m. The most exciting and original idea that raises the most money for charity will win the sponsorship from the mayor.

Think big, act local!

2 Decide which pieces of information each member of the group will present. Then practise your presentation. Ask your teacher for any words/phrases you need. Try to make your ideas as attractive as possible.

> Useful language b

3a Take turns to give your presentation to the class and listen to the other presentations. Make notes on the topics below for each presentation you hear.

- event
- What's on offer?
- food and drink
- promotion and marketing

b At the end of each presentation, ask questions to see how well-planned the event is. Vote for the best idea (you can't vote for your own). Which idea got the most votes? Why?

> Useful language c

SHARE YOUR TASK

Practise giving your presentation until you feel confident.

Film/Record yourself giving your presentation.

Share your film/recording with other students.

Writing
A review of an event

1 Work in pairs and discuss. Have you been to see any well-known bands or singers in concert? If so, describe the experience. If not, which group/singer would you like to see?

2a Read the review and answer the questions.

1 What did the reviewer like about the concert?
2 What didn't he like?

b Tick the things below that the reviewer describes. What else do you think he should have described?

- the reason for going
- the reactions of the crowd
- how many people were there
- the quality of the performance
- the names of the band members
- the atmosphere
- the songs played
- the highlights
- the negatives

intune
on the edge of music

Coldplay aren't the youngest band on the music scene, or the coolest, but they're definitely one of the best live bands performing today. Consequently, as soon as I knew they were coming to Toronto, where I live, I booked my ticket!

Standing in the arena last night, the atmosphere was electric. The two women sitting next to me were cheering and singing (very badly) before the band had even come on stage. And when the concert finally started an hour later than planned, no one seemed to mind. The concert itself lasted for over two hours and included some of their biggest hits, such as 'Viva La Vida'. The crowd loved them all, though perhaps the highlight for me was 'Yellow', from their debut album *Parachutes*. Singing along to that with the thousands of other fans in the arena was an unforgettable experience.

The only problem for me was that their big hits weren't all that they played. Quite a lot of the songs were from their latest album, currently standing at the top of the charts. I haven't bought this album, although I think I was the only person in the arena who hadn't. As a result, when the concert finished, I felt like I'd been to my best friend's wedding but hadn't been given a piece of wedding cake. It was a great experience – but something was missing.

Next time Coldplay are in town, I'll definitely go again, but I'll make sure I know their latest album off by heart beforehand and I'll sit a bit further away from the two women with tuneless voices trying to sing louder than the lead singer!

3a Find sentences in the review which mean the same as the ones below. What are the differences?

1 They're definitely one of the best live bands who are performing today.
2 The two women who were sitting next to me were cheering ...
3 No one who was sitting in the arena seemed to mind.
4 Quite a lot of the songs were from their latest album, which is currently standing at the top of the charts.
5 I'll sit a bit further away from the two women with tuneless voices who were trying to sing louder than the lead singer.

b Cross out words from the relative clauses in the sentences below, if possible.

1 I felt sorry for the people ~~who were~~ queuing in the rain to get a ticket.
2 The band who I was watching on the main stage were awful.
3 The person who was sitting next to me fell asleep.
4 Who's that girl in the crowd who is waving at us?
5 The band that we are listening to are looking for a new drummer.
6 I haven't heard this song that is playing now.
7 I know that guy who is playing drums on stage.
8 Where did you download that music we're listening to?

4a Think of a festival, play, comedy show, etc. that you have been to or seen. Make notes on the topics in exercise 2b.

b Organise your notes into paragraphs, then write the first draft of your review.

5a Write a final draft of your review using the checklist below.

- Have you used interesting and rich language to describe the event?
- Have you used relative clauses correctly?
- Are the spelling, grammar and punctuation correct?
- Have you included information about some of the topics in exercise 2a?

b Work in pairs. Swap reviews with a partner and take turns to give each other feedback.

Speaking
Awkward social situations

1 Work in pairs and discuss. What would you say in each situation in pictures A–E?

2a 🎧 7.5 Listen to find out what Bella actually said. Was it similar to your answers above? How successfully did Bella deal with each situation?

b 🎧 7.6 Listen and complete the sentences. Then say the sentences, copying the polite intonation.
1 It was very nice but I'm really _____ .
2 No, really. I couldn't _____ any more.
3 Oh, don't _____ , Sally.
4 It doesn't _____ . These things _____ .
5 When was the last time we _____ ?
6 How's _____ going?
7 Oh sorry. I didn't _____ .
8 I hope I didn't _____ you.
9 I don't want to _____ you.
10 I'll call you if I get a _____ .

3a Work in pairs. Look at the awkward social situations below. Choose two and write conversations of five to six lines using sentences from exercise 2b.

- Someone keeps on offering you food but you aren't hungry.
- You are next to a very talkative person on a train. You want to do some work on your laptop.
- At a party, you comment that the food isn't very good. The other person says that he/she helped to cook it.
- Someone introduces you to Ivan at a party. Ivan says you've met before but you can't remember when or where.
- Someone spills a drink on your new sofa.

b Act out one of your conversations to the class. Listen to other students' conversations and decide which sound the most natural.

08

STRANGE BUT TRUE

IN THIS UNIT

- Grammar: Overview of modal verbs; Past modals

- Vocabulary: Mysteries and oddities; Extreme adjectives

- Task: Discuss two mysteries

- World culture: The Bermuda Triangle

Reading and vocabulary
Mysteries and oddities

1 Work in groups and discuss. Which of the mysteries below most interest you when you choose a film, book, etc.? Why?

- ghost stories and the supernatural
- detective stories
- mysteries of the natural world
- real-life mysteries

2 Work in pairs. Check you understand the phrases in the box. Think of examples of three of these things and tell the class.

a clever **hoax**	an **unexplained natural phenomenon**
a **supernatural event**	a **tragic incident**
a near **miracle**	a **popular myth**
an **unfortunate mishap**	an amazing **coincidence**
a **mysterious disappearance**	a stupid **publicity stunt**
a **practical joke** that went too far	

3 Read story beginnings A–E on page 77. Work in pairs and answer the questions below.
1 Which photos relate to each story?
2 Where and when did/does each story take place?
3 What strange events does it describe?
4 Match the topics in exercise 2 to each story.
5 How do you think each story ends?

4a Match the story endings 1–5 on page 77 with story beginnings A–E.

b Work in pairs and discuss the questions.

- Did you predict the endings correctly?
- Which strange events still appear to be unexplained?
- Have you changed your mind about the best topic from exercise 2 to describe each story? Explain why.

5 Work in pairs. Find the words/phrases below in the stories and explain in your own words what they mean, using the context to help you.

1 littered with (text A)
2 toiled (text B)
3 tormented (text B)
4 the baby's fall was broken (text C)
5 potentially deadly (text D)
6 faked (text 2)
7 lobe (text 4)
8 severed (text 4)

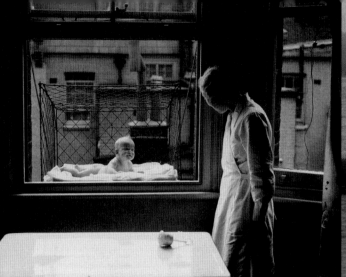

A

Science has provided the answer to many of nature's mysteries, but how about this?

In the Honduran province of Yoro, every May or June for the last hundred years there has been a 'Rain of Fish' or 'Lluvia de Pesces'. The rain, which is accompanied by thunder and lightning, lasts several hours. The city streets become littered with small fish, which local people collect and eat. Some scientists have suggested …

B

The 19th-century dutch artist Vincent van Gogh has gone down in history as a tragic genius.

He toiled all his life but died unrecognised and in poverty, while his paintings went on to fetch millions after his death. He was a man so tormented, the story goes, that he cut off his own ear and sent it to his mistress as proof of his love. However, recent studies indicate …

C

In the 1930s, a detroit street sweeper named Joseph Figlock played a remarkable part in the life of a young and apparently rather careless mother.

As Figlock was cleaning an alley, the woman's baby fell from a fourth-floor window onto Figlock. The baby's fall was broken and although Figlock and the baby were both injured, neither were killed. A year later …

D

After a terrible motorcycle accident at the age of 20 left him with no feeling in his legs, Californian David Blancarte spent over 20 years in a wheelchair.

Then in 2007, he was bitten by a rare brown recluse spider, whose venom is potentially deadly. Blancarte was immediately rushed to hospital.

E

In March 2002, when former teacher John Darwin disappeared while out canoeing near his home in the north of England, he was presumed dead by family, friends and the authorities.

Then in December 2007, Darwin walked into a London police station, saying that he had been suffering from amnesia and had no memory of what had happened to him in the last five years. His wife Anne issued a statement expressing her joy and amazement at his return and the case received huge publicity. Then, as the newspapers and police began to investigate …

1

… according to *Time* magazine, Mr Figlock was again cleaning an alley when another infant, two-year-old David Thomas fell on top of him from another fourth-floor window. Once again, both survived the event!

2

… the situation changed dramatically and both Darwin and his wife were arrested. It turned out that the couple had faked Darwin's 'death' in order to claim more than £600,000 in life insurance money. Anne Darwin had kept John hidden in the family home for over a year (lying even to their teenage sons about their father's disappearance) and then he travelled abroad on a false passport, until homesickness forced him to return in 2007. Eventually both the Darwins were convicted of fraud and sentenced to several years in prison.

3

However, as he was being checked over, the nurse discovered that the nerves in his legs had mysteriously 'come back to life' following the spider bite. Just five days later, Blancarte was walking again.

4

… that his friend, the artist Gauguin, cut off the ear in an argument and that van Gogh then lied to the authorities to protect his friend. What is almost certain is that only the ear lobe was severed, not the whole ear. And incidentally, the reason van Gogh received so little recognition in his lifetime was because he only worked as an artist for a few years: almost all of his famous paintings were produced in the last two years of his life.

5

… that strong winds collect the fish from the Atlantic and deposit them on Yoro, while others believe that they come from underground rivers. There have been cases all over the world of 'raining animals' but never in the same place at the same time every year. The truth is, no one has really been able to explain this occurrence. Locals believe it is a miracle.

Language focus 1
Overview of modal verbs

1a Work in pairs and discuss. Have you ever wondered about any of the questions below? Do you know the answers to any of them?

- Why can't we tickle ourselves?
- Why do we hiccup?
- Can we catch a cold from being cold?
- Why do we sleepwalk?

b Read the article below and check your ideas. Did you learn anything new?

2 Read the website again and choose the correct modal verbs.

GRAMMAR

Modals of ability

1 Look at the website. Why is *can* correct in 1 but not 2?

Modals of obligation

2 Find modals in the website that mean:
   1 it is necessary   _have to_   _____
   2 it is not allowed _____
   3 it is not necessary/it's optional _____
   4 it is a good idea, 'the right thing to do' _____ _____
   5 it is a bad idea or 'the wrong thing to do' _____

Modals of possibility or probability

3 Match the modals you chose to the meanings below.
   1 it seems certain that this is true _____
   2 this is possibly true _____ _____ _____
   3 it seems certain this isn't true _____
   4 this is a general possibility _____

4 Why is *can* correct in 8 but not possible in 7 in the website?

▶ Read Study1, page 152

Mysteries of the human body

Dr Jordan Wiley answers the questions you've always wondered about!

I find being tickled horrible, so this might seem like a strange question, but ... why can't I tickle myself?
Asked by Joshgrenton

Interesting question, Josh. If other people ¹**can / should** tickle us then logically we should ²**can / be able to** tickle ourselves – so why ³**mustn't / can't** we? The reason is simple: for something to tickle us, it ⁴**must / might** be unexpected. When we tickle ourselves, our brain is easily ⁵**can / able to** predict the feeling, so our body never feels tickled.

I sometimes get loud hiccups when I'm in a restaurant. What causes them? Asked by tbrcsmith

It ⁶**should / must** be embarrassing to get loud hiccups in public. What type of food are you eating when they start? You ⁷**might / can** be allergic to it. Hiccups come from a large muscle in your chest called the diaphragm. If it gets irritated, it ⁸**can / has to** start moving in a jerky way, causing hiccups. To make them go away you ⁹**mustn't / don't have to** do anything – they go away naturally and rarely last long (although one person did have an attack which lasted 68 years!).

My aunt often says to my daughter, 'You'll catch a cold if you go out in this weather.' Can you really catch a cold from being cold? Asked by eva_brooks44

The short answer, Eva, is no you can't, and your aunt ¹⁰**can't / shouldn't** try to keep your daughter indoors. Someone ¹¹**should / might** tell her that viruses cause colds, not the weather. In fact, cold viruses prefer warm, indoor conditions, so children (and adults) really ¹²**may / ought to** go outdoors as much as possible, even in winter.

Why do we sleepwalk? My flatmate does it and I sometimes find her asleep on the kitchen floor in the morning. Asked by younis_khan

It ¹³**can't / doesn't have to** be very nice for your flatmate to wake up in a strange room in the morning but she ¹⁴**couldn't / shouldn't** worry too much (although she ¹⁵**may / must** find it easier to lock her door at night). No one knows for sure what causes sleepwalking, though in adults it ¹⁶**could / must** be a sign of stress. Some people say that you ¹⁷**mustn't / don't have to** wake a sleepwalker, so if you see your friend sleepwalking, it's probably best to just lead her back to bed.

PRACTICE

1a Read the text below. What ability might some animals have that humans don't? Why?

Earthquakes

Rather than investing in expensive scientific equipment to predict earthquakes, perhaps scientists [1]*must / ought to / should* spend more time watching their pets.

Many scientists now believe that the behaviour of certain animals [2]*could / may / has to* help them to predict certain natural disasters. For example, Chinese scientists in the 1970s thought that reports of farm animals running round in circles [3]*can / could / might* indicate a coming disaster. They decided to evacuate the city of Haicheng, which shortly afterwards was hit by a huge earthquake. Thousands of lives were probably saved as a result.

Japanese scientists have also discovered that catfish become livelier several days before moderately strong earthquakes. Many scientists now accept that this [4]*can't / mustn't / may not* be pure coincidence – they believe that the explanation [5]*can / could / may* be linked to slight changes in the Earth's magnetic field. Although human beings [6]*aren't able to / can't / mustn't* perceive such changes, it is thought that the sensitive nervous systems of some animals [7]*could / have to / might* be affected by them. Now scientists [8]*have to / must / shouldn't* discover exactly which animals are affected in this way, so that more lives [9]*can / may / should* be saved in the future.

b Complete the text with the correct modals. There may be more than one possible answer.

2 Read the questions below about mysteries of the natural world. All of them were asked of experts in a science radio programme. What do you think the answers are?

1 Do fish sleep?
2 Why don't polar bears' feet freeze?
3 Can a loud sound kill you?
4 Can humans catch diseases from plants?
5 Why do chilli peppers taste hot?

3a Work in groups and discuss your answers to exercise 2. Use modal verbs of possibility to express your opinions.

> They must/can't (sleep) because …
>
> It might / may / could be possible that …

b 🎧 8.1 Listen to some experts on a science programme and compare your answers.

4 Do you have any questions that you've always wondered about? Write them down and then ask the class for possible answers.

> ▶ Unit 8, Study & Practice 1, page 152

Vocabulary
Extreme adjectives

1 Look at the sentence below. What is the meaning of the words in bold?

*Being tickled is both **hilarious** and **horrible** at the same time.*

2a Cross out the extreme adjective which does not belong in groups 1–5 below. Rewrite it in the correct group.

1 excellent, superb, ~~vast~~, wonderful
2 appalling, horrendous, terrible, terrific
3 amazing, gorgeous, extraordinary, remarkable
4 enormous, huge, incredible, massive, *vast*
5 awful, beautiful, exquisite, stunning

b Match the phrases in the box to groups 1–5.

very beautiful	very good	very bad
very big	very strange/impressive	

3 Match the extreme adjectives in box A with the meanings in box B.

A

deafening	exhausting	furious	tiny
starving	ridiculous	tragic	

B

very angry	very hungry	very loud
very sad	very silly	very small
very tiring		

4 Which intensifiers (*very, really, absolutely,* etc.) can you use before extreme adjectives?

The woman who vanished into thin air!

Listening and speaking
A mystery story

1a Look at the pictures about a woman who disappeared. Match the words/phrases in the box with the pictures.

the hotel register	red velvet curtains
the hotel doctor	a prescription for medicine
a carriage	to vanish completely
a mental asylum	the plague

b Work in pairs. Read the beginning of the story and guess what happened, using the pictures.

> The 'Great Exhibition', Paris 1889. The city was packed with visitors. Two wealthy English ladies, Eleanor Redwood and her mother Clara, arrived in the city looking for a hotel. They were on their way back to London from India.

2 🎧 8.2 Listen and compare your ideas. Were your predictions correct?

3a Work in pairs and answer the questions below.

1 Why had Eleanor and Clara Redwood left India?
2 What happened when they arrived at the hotel?
3 What happened when Eleanor called the doctor?
4 Where, why and how was Eleanor sent to get the medicine?
5 How long did the journey take?
6 Why was she surprised when she got back?
7 What did she find in room 342?
8 What happened when she went to the British Embassy with her story?
9 What about when she returned to Britain?
10 Did she ever trace her mother?

b Listen again and check.

4 Work in groups and discuss the questions below.

- What do you think happened to Mrs Redwood, and why?
- What do you think about the way the hotel and British Embassy treated Eleanor?
- Do you think Eleanor was insane?

5 🎧 8.3 Listen to a possible explanation for the disappearance. Do you find it convincing?

Language focus 2
Past modals

1 Read sentences 1–8 about the story on page 80 and choose the correct answers.

1 The ladies **could** / **managed to** speak very little French.
2 Eventually they **could** / **managed to** book two of the last rooms available in Paris.
3 Almost immediately, the mother fell ill and they **had to call** / **must have called** the hotel doctor.
4 The doctor said that he **can't have left** / **couldn't leave** Mrs Redwood because she was too ill.
5 Experts now believe that Mrs Redwood **must have** / **might have** brought the plague back from India.
6 The hotel manager **must have conspired** / **had to conspire** with the doctor in some way.
7 Surely the hotel staff **can't have disposed** / **mustn't have disposed** of the body and redecorated the room so soon?
8 The British Embassy **had to investigate** / **should have investigated** Eleanor's story more fully.

2 🎧 8.4 Listen and check.

GRAMMAR

Modals of ability

1 Look at sentences 1 and 2 in exercise 1. Match the modals to the descriptions below.
1 a general ability _____
2 something the person was actually able to do _____

Modals of obligation

2 Look at sentences 3 and 8 in exercise 1. Match the modals to the descriptions below.
1 something it was necessary to do _____
2 something that was a good idea but didn't happen _____

Modals of possibility

3 Look at sentences 5, 6 and 7 in exercise 1. Match the modals to the descriptions below.
1 something that seems logically certain _____
2 something that seems logically possible _____
3 something that seems logically impossible _____

▶ Read Study 2, page 153

PRACTICE

1 Rewrite the underlined words below using a past modal of possibility. Start with the words in brackets.

1 It is certain that the hotel manager and the doctor sent Eleanor away deliberately. (They)
They must have sent Eleanor away deliberately.
2 Surely the doctor sent a letter with Eleanor when she went to his surgery. (The doctor)
3 Surely it is impossible that they removed Mrs Redwood's signature from the hotel register. (They)
4 Perhaps they didn't take Eleanor back to room 342. Perhaps it was a different room. (They / It)
5 Surely someone else saw Mrs Redwood at the hotel. (Someone)
6 It is certain that the British Embassy didn't check Eleanor's story very carefully. (The British Embassy)
7 It is possible that Eleanor invented the whole story. (Eleanor)

2 Write sentences about what the people below should/shouldn't have done.

- Eleanor
- the doctor
- the hotel manager
- the British Embassy

Eleanor shouldn't have left her mother in the hotel. She should have … instead.

PRONUNCIATION

1 🎧 8.5 Listen and complete the sentences.

1 I'm so tired, I …
2 My parents are really late, they …
3 These shoes are killing me, I …
4 What's happened to Anna? She …
5 I can't find my phone anywhere, I …
6 It wasn't Isabel's fault, you …
7 I love your new bag – it …
8 I feel a bit ill, I …
9 I'm really sorry, I…

2 Listen again and check. Notice the weak form of *have*.

/əv/	/əv/
shouldn't have	might have

3 Practise the sentences, paying attention to the weak form of *have*.

3a 🎧 8.6 You will hear five people talking about the topics below. Match each speaker to a topic.

Something …
- you had to do recently but didn't enjoy.
- you should have done recently, but forgot about.
- people couldn't do 25 years ago.
- you didn't have to do ten years ago that you have to now.
- difficult that you've managed to keep doing.

b Work in pairs and discuss the topics in 3a.

> Unit 8, Study & Practice 2, page 153

Task

Discuss two mysteries

Preparation Reading and vocabulary

1 Look at the pictures and read the introductions to two classic mysteries. When and where did these mysteries take place and who was involved?

2 Work in pairs. Check the meaning of the words in the box below. Match the words with the two stories.

bolts	an abduction	aliens
a fortress	a UFO	a lie detector
a golden disc	to be nailed shut	a beam of light
gangsters	to hover	iron bars
screams	gunshot wounds	

3a Work in pairs or groups of four. Student/Pair A: Turn to page 128 and read the story of Isidor Fink. Student/Pair B: Turn to page 130 and read the story of Travis Walton.

b Make notes on the topics below.

- who the story is about and what happened to them
- who else was involved and what they did
- important details and clues

Task Speaking

1 You are going to tell your story to students who have not read it. Practise telling it, individually or with your partner. Ask your teacher for any words/phrases you need. Check any details you are still not sure of.

> Useful language a

2a Work in pairs or groups of four with students who have read the other story. Take turns to tell your stories. Answer any questions the other students have.

> Useful language a and b

b Discuss questions 1–6 under each story introduction.

> Useful language c

ISIDOR FINK:
A REAL LIFE 'LOCKED ROOM' MYSTERY

'Locked room' mysteries are commonplace in detective stories, but sometimes life is stranger than fiction. When immigrant Isidor Fink was found dead in his Fifth Avenue laundry on the night of March 9, 1929, New York City Police were presented with one of their most puzzling cases ever ...

What's your theory?

1 Did Isidor Fink commit suicide?
2 Did a burglar kill him?
3 Did the killer escape through a window?
4 Why did he have a bullet hole in his wrist?
5 Why was he so worried about security?
6 What is your theory about who killed Isidor Fink and how he came to die in a locked room?

3 Summarise your ideas to the class. Did you all reach similar conclusions?

> Useful language d

4 Work in pairs. Turn to page 129 and read what people have said about these cases since they happened. Discuss the questions below.

- Which case do experts now agree about? What solution have they come up with?
- What alternatives have been suggested in the other case?
- Did your class come up with any of the same ideas?
- Have you changed your mind about what happened?

Travis Walton:
abducted by aliens?

When forestry worker Travis Walton disappeared near his home in Arizona on November 5, 1975, it became one of the world's best-known cases of alleged alien abduction. Books have been written about the events of that night and what followed, and it was the subject of the 1993 film *Fire in the Sky*. According to UFO historian Jerome Clerk, 'few abduction reports have generated as much controversy as that of Travis Walton …'

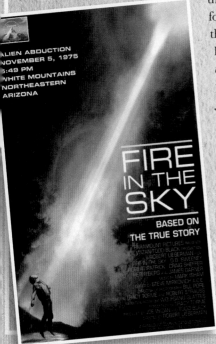

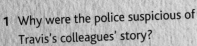

What's your theory?

1 Why were the police suspicious of Travis's colleagues' story?
2 Were his colleagues telling the truth?
3 In what ways was Travis's story convincing?
4 What reasons are there for doubting him?
5 What were his possible motives for lying?
6 What do you think happened to Travis during the five days that he was missing?

Follow up Writing

1a You are going to write about a mystery for the *Classic mysteries* website. Choose a mystery from another part of this unit or think of a real life mystery you know about.

b Make notes on the facts and different explanations for the mystery. If possible, research the details online.

c Write about the mystery, outlining the events and possible solutions.

USEFUL LANGUAGE

a Retelling the facts
Apparently,/It seems that …
One thing that is strange is that …
It's not really clear whether or not …

b Checking that you understand
There's one thing I don't really understand.
(Why … ?)
So remind me, (who … ?)
And do we know whether or not … ?

c Discussing explanations and opinions
He must have/can't have …
It seems likely/unlikely that …
He might/could have …
If … then … would have happened
Personally, I (can't) believe that …

d Presenting the group's opinions
We all felt/agreed that …
There were different opinions about …
Some people thought … , whereas other people thought …

SHARE YOUR TASK

Prepare to describe the possible explanations for one of the stories you discussed, and say what you think happened.

Practise describing the possible explanations until you feel confident.

Film/Record yourself giving your talk.

Share your film/recording with other students.

THE BERMUDA TRIANGLE

Find out first

1a Work in pairs. Read about the famous mysteries below. One detail in each description is incorrect. Which detail do you think it is?

The Mary Celeste

In 2002 the ship The Mary Celeste was found in calm waters in the Atlantic Ocean. It was in good condition and with plenty of food on board. The cargo and valuables were untouched but the seven crew were missing, along with one lifeboat. They were never found.

The Voynich Manuscript

The Voynich manuscript was written in the 15th century. It contains 1,240 pages of illustrations and information about plants and their medical uses. The plants, however, do not match any currently known and the text is written in a language that is unknown.

b Go online to check your answers or ask your teacher.

....

Search: Mary Celeste / Voynich manuscript

....

View

2a You are going to Watch a video about the Bermuda Triangle. Where is the Bermuda Triangle? Why is it famous?

b ▶ Watch the video and check your answers to exercise 2a. Then answer the questions below.

1 What did Columbus see when he first sailed into the Bermuda Triangle?
2 What is strange about the way the ships disappear?
3 Which three places mark the boundaries of theTriangle?
4 How many planes and people were involved in Flight 19?
5 According to the pilot, what problems were they having?
6 What event added to the mystery of Flight 19?

3a These numbers and dates from the video are incorrect. Watch the video again and correct them.

- thousands of lives
- 100 ships
- 1490
- 1,000,000 square miles
- 15th December, 1945
- 19 minutes later

b Work in pairs. Check your answers and explain the significance of each number.

4 Can you think of any possible explanations for the Bermuda Triangle mystery? Would you travel through it?

World view

5a ▶ Watch three people talking about a mysterious or paranormal experience. Complete the table.

	Where he/she was and who he/she was with	What happened	Possible explanations (if any)
Eben			
Heather			
Martin			

b Work in pairs and compare answers. Watch again, if necessary, to complete your notes.

6a ▶ Watch seven people answering the question 'Do you believe in the paranormal?'. Does each person say yes (Y), no (N) or they don't know/are open-minded (D)?

1 Elliot   5 Louisa
2 Wendy   6 Audrey
3 Jurgen   7 Luis
4 Guillem

b What reasons (if any) does each speaker give? Watch again to check

c Work in groups and discuss.

- Have you, or has anyone you know, had a mysterious or paranormal experience?
- Do you believe in the paranormal? Why/Why not?

FIND OUT MORE

7a Look at the names of mysterious things/places below. Which have you heard of before? What do you know about them?

- Stonehenge
- Area 51
- Easter Island statues

b Choose one of the mysteries from the list above. Go online to find out:

- more details about it
- how it became famous
- possible explanations.

Search: Stonehenge / Area 51 / Easter Island statues

Write up your research

8 Write one or two paragraphs on possible explanations for your chosen mystery. Use the prompts below to help you.

- The mystery began ... years ago in ...
- It is well-known that ...
- What is less well-known is that ...
- Some people believe that ...
- Other people have argued that ...
- To my mind, the most convincing explanation for the mystery is ...

AFTER UNIT 8 YOU CAN ...

Describe mysteries and strange events.

Speculate about unexplained events.

Retell and discuss mystery stories.

09

GETTING IT RIGHT

IN THIS UNIT

- **Grammar:** Use and non-use of articles; Different ways of giving emphasis

- **Vocabulary:** Phrasal verbs; *Right* and *wrong*

- **Task:** Collect and present tips

Reading and speaking

1 Work in groups. Do you think the quotation is true?

> If you want to be successful in life, it is necessary to get yourself noticed.

2a Which of the actions below are likely to get you noticed?

- wearing clothes that are different to other people's
- making eye contact with people when you first meet them
- referring to important people that you know (or claim to know)
- listening carefully to what other people say
- saying publicly what you believe in, even if it's unpopular
- keeping your opinions to yourself and avoiding making a fuss

b Read the article on page 87. Which ideas from exercise 2a are mentioned? What other ideas does the author mention?

3 Read the article again and answer the questions below.

1 Why should you look people in the eye when you make an entrance?
2 Why shouldn't you move your hands?
3 Why is it a good idea to hold your breath when entering a room?
4 Why can it be useful to mention the names of other experts?
5 How can language help you to sound like an expert?
6 When is it a bad idea to bluff?
7 In what ways was Rosa Parks a leader?
8 How are true leaders different from 'a lone voice in the wilderness'?
9 Why are narcissists bad leaders?

4 Work in pairs and discuss. How serious do you think this article is? Which piece of advice do you think is most/least useful?

HOW TO STAND OUT FROM THE CROWD

Do you want people to pay you more attention and show you more respect?
Read what the experts say and you'll never be overlooked again.

1 Make an entrance

You only get one chance to make a first impression, so here's how to stand out from the crowd when you walk into a room.

- **Make eye contact.** Look other people in the eye – it's the key to creating a connection with people.

- **Be a good actor.** If you don't feel confident, pretend you are. Before you walk in, think to yourself, 'I own the room.' Then, walk in holding your head high and smile. Soon, you will feel as confident as you look.

- **Raise your status.** In his book for actors, *Impro*, Keith Johnstone describes how we all play the status game, whether we know it or not. Our status is our social position compared to other people.

When you walk into a room, it's a good idea to 'raise your status' if you want to be noticed. That means holding yourself upright but relaxed, keeping your head and hands still, smiling and speaking slowly and clearly. People will pay more attention to you if you do these things (although they will find you aloof and unfriendly if you behave like this all the time).

- Hold your breath when you walk in. Steve Cohen, author of *Win the Crowd*, recommends this simple tip. Take a deep breath before you walk into a room and then hold it. It makes you 'more radiant and lively'. But remember not to hold it too long or you'll pass out!

2 Sound like an expert

Malcolm Gladwell, author of *Outliers*, says 10,000 hours of practice is necessary to really become an expert at anything. That's equivalent to about three hours a day for 10 years! If you haven't got that much time, here's how to fake it.

- Make a habit of name-dropping. Refer to famous experts as though they are your friends. For example, say 'Do you know Professor Russell Banks? He tends to agree with me on these matters.' It's hard to argue with experts and even harder to argue with people who aren't there.

- Use lots of abbreviations and acronyms. Someone who says 'I need to call HQ ASAP' sounds much more expert than someone who says 'I need to call headquarters as soon as possible.'

- Use words like *zeitgeist*, *paradigm* and *panacea*. Most people are familiar with words like this, but don't know exactly what they mean.

- Don't be afraid to make things up. If other people think you're an expert, they won't suspect you're making it up! However if you do meet a real expert, make your excuses and leave. They'll see through you immediately!

3 Act like a leader

Despite what you read in books and see in films, good leaders are not born that way, they learn to be that way. So if you don't feel like a leader, remember that you can become one. Here's how.

- Set goals. Present a vision and a path to achieve it. Let people know what you stand for.

- Stand up for what you believe in. In 1950s Alabama, black people were expected to give their seats on the bus to white people. One day in 1955, Rosa Parks, a black woman, refused to do this. 'I don't think I should have to stand up,' she said, and in doing so she sparked the American civil rights movement. All leaders at some point have to stand up for what they believe in.

- Listen and learn. Leadership is about communication and building relationships. It's about finding out which ideas really unite people and then expressing those ideas clearly.

- Treat the people who follow you as equals. The only difference between a leader and a lone voice in the wilderness is that the leader has followers, so treat them well.

- And finally, remember this. If you really, really want to be a leader and if you need other people to look up to you, then you're probably not a leader at all. You're a narcissist. Leadership is not about other people serving you, it's about you serving other people.

Vocabulary Phrasal verbs

1 Find phrases 1–6 in the article and choose the correct meaning of the phrasal verbs.

1 **stand out from the crowd** means *seem different from / the same as* everyone else
2 **pass out** means *stop breathing / become unconscious*
3 **make something up** means *invent / use other people's* information
4 **see through someone** means *know that someone is lying / ask someone questions*
5 **stand up for something** means *say publicly / try to decide* what you believe
6 **look up to someone** means *be jealous of / respect* someone

2a Think of a famous person or someone you know who:

- stands out from the crowd
- has passed out in public
- stands up for what they believe in
- makes up a lot of what he/she says
- you look up to
- looks up to you.

b Work in groups and compare your answers.

Weird interview questions

A

If you were a cartoon character, who would you be?

How would you get an elephant into a refrigerator?

Would the President of the United States make a good software engineer?

What is a normal person like?

How many people would you say there are at university in the UK/Mexico/your country?

How would you describe this company (Microsoft/Apple, etc.) to a visitor from Mars?

Why are manhole covers round?

If Hollywood made a movie about your life, which actor would you like to play the lead role?

B For many job seekers around ¹_____ world, getting
²_____ job with ³_____ top international company like
⁴_____ Google is ⁵_____ pinnacle of their ambition. But with so
many talented applicants how does ⁶_____ company find
⁷_____ brightest and best candidates?

In ⁸_____ last 15 years, there has been ⁹_____ trend amongst
top companies towards asking ¹⁰_____ weird and wacky
questions in ¹¹_____ job interviews, like the ones above.
¹²_____ idea of these questions is to test ¹³_____ creativity and
quickness of a candidate, and to find out more about
¹⁴_____ way that ¹⁵_____ candidate thinks.

Most candidates are unlikely to give ¹⁶_____ honest answer to ¹⁷_____
_____ stereotypical interview question like 'What is
¹⁸_____ biggest failure in your life?' But in answering a question
like 'What would I find in your refrigerator right now?' they may
reveal more about ¹⁹_____ kind of person that they are. So
what are ²⁰_____ correct answers to these sorts of questions?
According to ²¹_____ Professor Abdul Khalid, of
²²_____ London University, many of them do not have right or
wrong answers: ²³_____ most important thing is tackling
²⁴_____ question intelligently. When it comes to weird interview
questions, it seems ²⁵_____ only wrong answer is
'I don't know.'

Language focus 1
Use and non-use of articles

1 Work in pairs and discuss. Have you ever been to a job interview? What questions did they ask you? What would you expect to be asked in a job interview?

2a Read the examples of weird interview questions asked at job interviews in part A on the left. Which could/couldn't you answer?

b Work in pairs. Discuss the questions below, then check your answers in part B.
- What kind of companies tend to use job interview questions like these?
- What do you think is the point of them?
- What is the best way to respond if you are asked questions like this in an interview?

3 🎧 9.1 Complete the article with *a/an*, *the* or ø (no article). Then listen and check.

GRAMMAR

General rules for the use of articles

Look at the seven rules below. Find another example of each rule in the questions and article.

We use *a/an* when ...
1 the noun is 'one of many' and it hasn't been mentioned before.
   *For many job seekers, getting **a** job with **a** top company is their ambition ...*

We use *the* when ...
2 the noun has been mentioned before.
   *... to find out more about the way that **the** candidate thinks*

3 the noun is unique (or unique in that context).
   *For many job seekers around **the** world*
   *If Hollywood made a movie about your life who would play **the** lead role?*

4 the noun is defined by a phrase or clause that follows (an *of* phrase, a relative clause, etc.).
   ***the** idea of these questions*
   ***the** kind of person that they are*

5 the adjective before the noun defines it, for example, *right*, *wrong*, etc.
   ***the correct** answer*
   ***the first /second** time, etc.*

There is no article when ...
6 a plural or uncountable noun is used to make a generalisation.
   Why are ~~the~~ manhole covers round?

7 the noun is a singular proper name.
   ~~the~~ Google   ~~the~~ London University

▶ **Read Study 1, page 155**

PRACTICE

1a Complete the questions below with the correct article (*a/an*, *the* or *ø*).

More weird interview questions

1 You're in ¹___ rowing boat, which is in ²___ large tank filled with ³___ water. You have ⁴___ anchor on board which you throw overboard. ⁵___ chain is long enough that ⁶___ anchor rests completely on ⁷___ bottom of ⁸___ tank. Does ⁹___ water level in ¹⁰___ tank rise or fall?

2 How would you cure ¹¹___ world hunger?

3 If you were shrunk to ¹²___ size of ¹³___ pencil and put in ¹⁴___ blender, how would you get out?

4 If someone wrote ¹⁵___ biography of you, what do you think ¹⁶___ title should be?

5 (*At* ¹⁷___ *interview with a famous sandwich chain*) What's ¹⁸___ most important part of ¹⁹___ sandwich?

Answer: ²⁰___ smile that goes with it.

b Work in pairs and discuss. Which is the easiest/most difficult question to answer, in your opinion?

GRAMMAR

Specific rules for the use of articles

1 Complete rules 1–3 and find an example either from the article or the questions in exercise 1a above.
  1 With superlatives, we use *a/an*, *the*, *ø*.
    <u>the biggest failure in your life</u>
  2 With people's titles, we use *a/an*, *the*, *ø*.
  3 With institutions (universities, hospitals, etc.), we use *a/an*, *the*, *ø*.

2 Which places below use *the* before them? Check your answers in Study 9.1 on page 155.
  1 cities (Paris)
  2 continents (Asia)
  3 countries (Mexico)
  4 lakes (Victoria)
  5 mountain ranges (Andes)
  6 planets (Mars)
  7 rivers (Nile)
  8 seas and oceans (Atlantic)

3 Complete the time phrases below with *the*, *ø* or both.
  1 in _____ morning, afternoon, evening
  2 on _____ 5th March, 20th September, etc.
  3 on _____ Monday, Saturday, etc.
  4 in _____ summer, spring, etc.
  5 in _____ 1999, 2012, etc.
  6 in _____ 1970s, 1990s, etc.

2a Add articles, where necessary, to complete the quiz below.

FIVE-MINUTE QUIZ

A You are taking ^an 11-hour flight from Heathrow Airport in London to LAX airport in Los Angeles.
There is ^an eight-hour time difference between ^the two cities. If you leave at 2 o'clock in ^the afternoon, will you arrive …
  • ^the same day as you left, in afternoon?
  • same day as you left but in morning?
  • next day?
  • previous day?

B What is a ladybird?
  • female bird
  • exotic plant
  • red and black insect
  • very small woman?

C If you went for a boat trip on River Vltava, went climbing in Šumava Mountains, and went sight-seeing in Prague, which country would you be in?
  • Hungary
  • Poland
  • Czech Republic
  • Bulgaria

D If you are 'discharged', what do you do?
  • leave school
  • leave prison
  • leave hospital
  • leave university

E Which of the following seas does not exist?
  • Black Sea
  • Blue Sea
  • Red Sea
  • Yellow Sea

F 149.6 million kilometres is …
  • distance from sun to Earth.
  • distance from moon to Earth.
  • distance from sun to nearest star.
  • none of these.

b Work in pairs. Use your knowledge, logic or guesswork to answer the questions in the quiz.

c 🎧 9.2 Listen and check.

> Unit 9, Study, Practice & Remember 1, page 155

Language focus 2
Different ways of giving emphasis

1a Work in pairs and discuss. Have you ever given a presentation? If yes, how did you feel and how did it go? If not, would you like to?

b Read the conversation between Sophie and Paul. Why is Paul nervous? What advice does Sophie give?

2 🎧 9.3 Listen and write the missing words (marked ^) in the conversation. You may need to change some other words. What effect do these words have?

PAUL:	Thank you for coming. Before I start, I'd just like to say how wonderful you all look today … oh dear.
SOPHIE:	What are you doing?
PAUL:	Oh, I have to give a presentation in class tomorrow. I'm ^ nervous!
SOPHIE:	Why ^ are you nervous?
PAUL:	Why? Because public speaking is ^ terrifying, of course.
SOPHIE:	Don't be ^ a wimp. There are only nine students in your class.
PAUL:	You're calling me a wimp? ^ you ^ cried in the toilet before your last job interview!
SOPHIE:	That was an ^ important interview. It was different.
PAUL:	^ I need ^ sympathy right now, not criticism.
SOPHIE:	You're right. I'm ^ sorry. I ^ sympathise. When I'm stressed, ^ helps ^ to take deep breaths and listen to some relaxing music.
PAUL:	Oh, OK, thanks … and then you go and cry in the toilet?
SOPHIE:	Paul!

90

1 Look at the words you added to the conversation and answer the questions.
   1 Which of the four words you added go in front of an adjective to make it stronger? Can you think of any other words which make adjectives stronger?
   2 What is the difference between *so* and *such*?
   3 Find an example of an 'extra' auxiliary verb that adds emphasis.
   4 Find two more examples similar to the phrase in bold below.
   What I need is sympathy right now.
   5 Which words can be added to give emphasis to questions?

▶ Read Study 2, page 156

PRACTICE

1a Match sentences 1–10 with replies a–j.

   1 **I'm exhausted**. Let's stay in and watch a film.
   2 **I like living here** because **it's near** the centre.
   3 Thanks for everything, we've had **a nice evening**.
   4 I suppose you want to see Liz.
   5 **Why are we** inside on such a beautiful day?
   6 Ouch! This tooth is **painful**.
   7 What's all this broken glass! **What have you been doing?**
   8 Your friend **was lovely. I hope** you'll invite him again.
   9 Come on, let's go to that new club.
   10 **I think** you ought to apologise to her.

   a Yes, I will. I think **he enjoyed** the evening as well.
   b Well, **you wanted to** spend the day at a museum.
   c **Why** should I apologise? **I didn't start** the trouble.
   d You're welcome. Come again soon!
   e You know **you need** to go to the dentist's.
   f Look, **I think** it's time we went home. It's nearly three.
   g Oh, **you're boring** these days. I want to go out.
   h That's true, but it gets **noisy** at night.
   i No, actually **I wanted to see you**.
   j Don't blame me! **I didn't break** it!

b 🎧 9.4 How can you give the phrases in bold more emphasis? Listen and compare your answers.

PRONUNCIATION

1 Sentence stress is important for giving emphasis. Listen again and mark the words that are especially stressed on audio script 9.4 on page 175.

   I'm absolutely exhausted. Let's stay in …
   Oh, you're so boring these days. I want to go out.

2 Work in pairs and practise saying the conversations.

2 Work in pairs. Choose one of the conversations in exercise 1a and extend it to six or eight lines. Try to use different ways of giving emphasis.

▶ **> Unit 9, Study & Practice 2, page 156**

Listening and writing
Taking notes

1 Work in groups. Discuss the questions below.

- In what situations do you have to take notes?
- Do you write a lot of notes or just a few key points?
- What do you do with your notes afterwards?

2a You are going to listen to the first part of a talk on how to give presentations. First, predict which words connected to presentations you might hear.

slides, projector …

> *Rebecca Wade – How to Give Presentations*
>
> *presenting = no. 1 fear!*
>
> ## *important points*
> - *don't read it out*
> - *move around + talk fast*
>   *(esp at start)*
> - *start & finish @ right time – 'be nice to them and they'll be nice to you'*

b 🎧 9.5 Listen and make two corrections to the notes below.

3a Find examples in the notes of the techniques below.

bullet point	underlining
highlighting	abbreviation
main heading	sub-heading

b Do you know any other useful techniques for making notes?

4a 🎧 9.6 Listen to the second part of the talk and make notes on the topics below.

- planning
- delivery

b Work in pairs. Check that your notes are clear then show them to your partner. Can you understand each other's notes? Did either of you miss anything?

5 Work in pairs and discuss. Do you agree or disagree with any or all of the advice in the listening?

Wordspot
right and *wrong*

1 Look at expressions 1–10 with *right* and *wrong*. Then match the expressions with meanings a–j.

1 I'll be right back.
2 Everything's gone wrong.
3 Right here, right now.
4 That serves you right.
5 There's something/nothing wrong with it.
6 What's wrong?
7 It looks about right.
8 It's the wrong way round.
9 You were completely right/wrong about her!
10 That's all right by me!

a What's the problem?
b I'll return very soon.
c It seems to be correct.
d The front is at the back and the back is at the front.
e Everything's failed or turned out badly.
f Something is working/not working properly.
g That's a good plan.
h You judged someone fairly/unfairly.
i In this place, immediately.
j You deserved the bad thing that happened to you.

2 Study the expressions with *right* and *wrong* for a few minutes. Then rewrite the phrases in bold below using an expression with *right* or *wrong*.

1 My new laptop **stopped working** just a few hours after I bought it.
2 Move the picture a little bit this way … There, that **seems correct now**.
3 I know you hurt yourself but **it's your own fault** for playing with fire.
4 I didn't listen to your opinions at the time but **your ideas about her were correct**.
5 Pizza this evening? **That sounds like a good idea to me**.
6 He looked like such an idiot wearing his baseball cap **with the back at the front**.
7 The doctor said **I'm absolutely fine**. I'm so relieved!
8 When do I want to start? **Immediately, where we are**.
9 You seem very quiet. **Is there a problem**?
10 Wait here for me. **I'll return in a short time**.

Task

Collect and present tips

Do it right!   about us   contact us

>> **How to prepare for a job interview**

>> **How to choose the right career**

>> **How to dress for success in the workplace**

>> **How to learn a foreign language**

>> **How to be successful in exams**

>> **How to impress your colleagues and boss**

>> **How to manage your time**

>> **How to have a happy romantic relationship**

>> **How to be a good friend**

>> **How to improve your social life**

>> **How to get fit and stay fit**

>> **How to eat healthily and cheaply**

Preparation Reading

1 Work in groups. Look at the website above and discuss the questions below.

- What kind of website is it?
- Do you ever look on websites for tips about things you need to do? If so, what have you looked up recently?
- Which section(s) on this website would you find particularly useful? Why?
- Try to think of one tip for each topic on the website.

2a Match the tips from the website on page 93 to the correct sections in the website.

b Work in pairs and discuss. Do you think the tips give good advice?

3 Read the tips again and underline ten useful phrases for giving advice.

Task Speaking

1a Work in pairs. Choose a topic from the website that interests you or choose another topic that you both know about.

b Brainstorm as many tips as you can for the topic. Ask your teacher for any words/phrases you need.

c Mingle with the class. Take turns to talk about the topic and your tips. Make notes of any good ideas you hear.

d Prepare a short talk, giving advice about your chosen topic. Review your tips and select the best ones. Decide how you will present your tips.

> Useful language a–c

2 Work in groups. Listen to each other's tips and make notes on what each student says. Vote on the most useful set of tips.

OUR TOP TIPS

1. Always be honest. A dishonest person has no chance of making true friends, because it is hard to rely on a person who doesn't behave in a consistent or trustworthy way.

2. Most experts agree that only hard work, planning and starting early will maximise success. The first and most basic point is to make a clear solid revision plan. Research shows that those who break tasks down into small manageable parts achieve the best results.

3. One classic mistake is to try and progress too quickly. This often results in injuries, and puts you back at square one. So try to be realistic.

4. Take every opportunity to let your partner know what it is that you like most about them: what you admire, what makes you proud and what their strengths are in your eyes.

5. Never be afraid to ask for help. If you don't know what you are doing in a particular situation, then don't pretend that you do. It's far better to admit your ignorance and ask for help from someone who knows what they are doing. This has two benefits. Firstly, you appear willing to learn. Secondly, you make the other person feel important, which never does any harm.

6. Always remember that most organisations have a dress code about things like jewellery, nails, etc. Until you know differently, it's best to assume that your prospective employer or client is fairly conservative about these things.

7. Aim to find out as much as you can in advance about what is required, and then think about how you can best match your skills to the job.

USEFUL LANGUAGE

a What to do
Start by ...-ing
It's always advisable to ...
Take every opportunity to ...
It's very useful/best/better to ...
(You should) aim to ...
Never/Don't be afraid to ...

b What not to do
The last thing you want to do is ... so ...
Avoid ...-ing
One classic mistake is to ...
Whatever you do, don't ...

c Both
Most experts agree that ...
Be careful (not) to ...
It's absolutely essential that you (don't) ...
Always remember ...
It's far better to .... than ...
Don't panic if ...

Follow up Writing

1. **Choose a topic below.**

   - Imagine you are writing a blog, giving tips on one of the subjects you have discussed. Select the best tips, organise them into a logical order then write your blog post.
   - Write five tips to go on different sections of a website. Show them to other students. Can they guess which section they belong in?

SHARE YOUR TASK

Practise the talk you gave to the class or think of tips for a different topic and prepare a talk, explaining them.

Practise giving the talk until you feel confident.

Film/Record yourself giving your talk.

Share your film/recording with other students.

LANGUAGE LIVE

I'm so fed up

Speaking
Suggestions and advice

1 Work in pairs and discuss the questions.

- Do you know anyone who is fed up with their job? Why?
- What advice would you give them?

2a 🎧 9.7 Lisa is fed up with her job as a PA. Listen to her conversation with her friend Amy and choose the correct answers below.

1 Lisa wants a job that is **better-paid / more lively and interesting**.
2 **Lisa / Amy** comes up with the idea of becoming an estate agent.
3 Amy thinks Lisa has the **right personal qualities / the right qualifications** for the job.
4 Lisa is **unenthusiastic / interested** but a little unsure about the idea.
5 Amy suggests **applying for jobs online / contacting an acquaintance for advice**.

b 🎧 9.8 Now Listen to Lisa's conversation with Jenny, Alex's mum. Choose the correct answers below.

1 Jenny is **unwilling / happy** to advise Lisa.
2 She says that qualifications **are / are not** the most important thing.
3 She also mentions **interior design / computer skills**.
4 Her main suggestion is **doing a college course / getting some part-time experience**.

3a Try to complete the sentences below from the conversations. Then listen again and check.

Conversation 1
1 Any _____ ?
2 This might sound a bit strange, but have you _____ becoming an estate agent?
3 You ought to _____ , you know.
4 Yeah, _____ .
5 You _____ look online, I _____ .
6 Or why _____ into an estate agent's and just ask?
7 I know what you _____ .
8 Why _____ have a chat with her?

Conversation 2
1 I'd like _____ about careers.
2 I just wondered if you've got _____ about _____ do?
3 You should _____ look into that.
4 To be honest, _____ is personality.
5 Obviously, _____ to have good computer skills.
6 I would recommend _____ .
7 You know what I would advise? _____ that you try to get a weekend job with a local estate agent's.
8 That's a really good idea, _____ of that.
9 If I were you I _____ to all the estate agent's in the area.
10 That's great, thank you, _____ your advice.

b 🎧 9.9 Match the sentences in exercise 3a to the categories below. Then listen and check.

- asking for advice and suggestions
- giving advice and suggestions
- responding to advice and suggestions

c Practise saying the sentences. Do any phrases sound particularly formal or informal?

4 Work in A/B pairs. Turn to page 129 and act out one of the situations.

Writing
A speculative covering letter

1 Read Lisa's letter to a local estate agent's and answer the questions below.

  1 What does she say about herself?
  2 What does she say about the company?
  3 What else does she enclose?

2 Which phrases underlined in the letter can be replaced by the phrases below?

  1 this position or any similar vacancies   *g*
  2 I am a dynamic, creative person with lots of initiative
  3 I am currently in the final year of a degree in Business Studies and am hoping to pursue a career in Marketing.
  4 Please get in touch if you require any further information.
  5 With ten years of top-level experience, New Skills Training
  6 to enquire whether you have any internships or opportunities for work experience available
  7 Dear Sir/Madam, ... Yours faithfully,
  8 I have completed a two-month work placement with *Smart* publishers
  9 in reply to your advertisement for a trainee editor in *Publishing Weekly*
  10 I am fluent in both spoken and written English, and also speak French

3a Choose one of the options below and write a letter similar to Lisa's. You can either be yourself, or invent a persona.

  1 Write to *Quest,* a chain of fashionable clothes shops in London, to see if they have any vacancies for sales staff.
  2 Write to *Car* magazine, to see if they have any internships or opportunities for work experience in journalism.
  3 Write a reply to the advertisement on page 127.

b Think about the ideas below. Then write a first draft of your letter.

  • the qualities, skills, interests and experience to emphasise for this particular job
  • something positive to say about the company that you are writing to
  • phrases from Lisa's letter and exercise 2 to use in your letter

c Swap your letter with a partner and check each other's letters. Then write a final draft of your letter.

---

[1]8 Dean Court,
Hill Road,
Leeds,
LS2 1PD
01130 786543
[2]15th May 2013

[3]The Manager,
Dexters Ltd.,
6–8 Railton Rd,
Leeds,
[4]LS1 6DY

[a]Dear Mr Hunt,

My name is Lisa Allen, and I am writing [b]to enquire whether you have any positions available for a Saturday or part-time salesperson.

[c]I am currently working as a PA at Melton Sanjeev Solicitors, but I am hoping to make a new career as an estate agent. [d]With its excellent local reputation, Dexters is exactly the type of company that I would like to work for.

[e]I am an outgoing, enthusiastic person with good people skills and lots of drive. [f]I have good IT skills and can rapidly learn how to use new software.

My CV is enclosed and I would be grateful if you would consider me for [g]any current or future vacancies that might arise with your company. [h]I can attend an interview at any time that suits you.

I look forward to hearing from you soon,

[a]Yours sincerely,

Lisa Allen

10

MEDIA

IN THIS UNIT

- Grammar: Reporting people's exact words; Verbs that summarise what people say

- Vocabulary: The media; *Speak* and *talk*

- Task: Summarise an article and lead a discussion

- World culture: The Science of film

MEDIA: FACTS AND FIGURES

RESEARCH HAS SHOWN THAT HALF OUR WAKING HOURS ARE SPENT IN CONTACT WITH MASS MEDIA IN ONE FORM OR ANOTHER, SO CHECK OUT OUR MARVELLOUS MEDIA INFOGRAPHIC.

NEWSPAPERS AND MAGAZINES

UK newspaper **readership** is declining

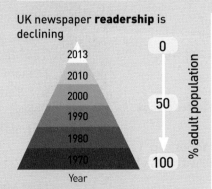

2013
2010
2000
1990
1980
1970

Year

0
50
100

% adult population

In the UK and the USA, **tabloids** have a higher circulation than **broadsheets**.

TABLOIDS
BROADSHEETS

The magazine with the highest **circulation** in the USA is for people over 50. In the UK, it's a TV listings magazine.
In Germany, it's a car magazine.
In Canada, it's a cooking magazine.

OVER 50
TV LISTINGS
CARS
COOKING

In most newspapers, **coverage** of foreign news has decreased and **foreign correspondents** have lost their jobs.
By contrast, there is more and more entertainment news.

Reading and vocabulary

The media

1 Work in pairs and have a race. Scan the media infographic and answer the questions below.

   1 What kind of people read the most popular magazine in the USA?
   2 How much time do teenagers spend in front of a screen?
   3 How much of our online time is spent on social media?
   4 What has happened to entertainment news in newspapers?
   5 Who is most likely to watch a horror film?
   6 How much video is uploaded or downloaded every minute (be careful!).
   7 What kind of newspaper is most popular in the UK?
   8 What sort of programmes are probably the most popular in India?
   9 What sort of website is Twitter?

2 Read the infographic more carefully and check the meaning of the words in bold. Work in pairs and discuss. Which information do you find most/least surprising? Why?

TV AND FILM

The most watched TV show ever in the UK is an episode of a **soap opera**. In the US, it is an episode of a **drama series**. In Canada, India and New Zealand, it is **coverage** of a sports event.

 Young teenagers in many countries get up to four hours of **screen time** a day. Most of that is still TV.

Product placement for a car in a James Bond film is reported to cost $50 million!

$50 MILLION

The **target audience** for horror films are males aged 15–24. They go to the cinema more than any other group.

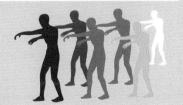

ONLINE

25% of all online time is spent on **social media**. It is the most **interactive** form of media.

 One million people set up a **microblogging** account every day (e.g. Twitter).

One million minutes of video is **uploaded** or downloaded every second.

 1 MILLION MINS

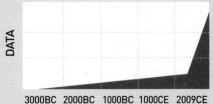 Humans generated more data in 2009 than in the previous 5,000 years combined.

DATA
3000BC 2000BC 1000BC 1000CE 2009CE
YEARS

3a Work in pairs and think of examples of the following from your country.

- a sports event that has received a lot of coverage recently
- a TV talent show
- the target audience of the most popular soap opera on TV
- a popular drama series
- a film with product placement
- the most popular social-media website
- a reality TV show
- a tabloid or magazine with a mostly male readership
- the broadsheet with the highest circulation

b Work with a new partner and compare your answers. Ask your partner for more information about some of his/her answers.
Why do you think a lot of people watch it?

4a Work in small groups. Can you think of more

media words to add to the three headings from the infographic?

1 newspapers and magazines: *headline, …*
2 TV and films: *director, …*
3 online: *video blog, …*

b Discuss the questions below.

- Why do you think newspaper circulation is falling? What impact will this have?
- What do you think is the most popular magazine in your country? Why?
- How much screen time do you get on an average day? How much of that is spent on social media?
- Do you like/dislike product placement? Why?
- Have you uploaded any videos to the internet? If yes, what were they?
- Do you think digital will ever completely replace print? Why/Why not?

Listening

Questions about the media

1 Work in pairs. Read questions 1–10 about the media. Which three questions would you most like to hear an answer to?

1 Who controls the media?
2 How can I protect my privacy online?
3 Will we still read newspapers in the future?
4 How has the internet affected the world of media?
5 What will happen to TV in the future?
6 Does the media reflect what we think or control what we think?
7 Does the media portray women in a negative way?
8 How does the media influence us?
9 What is the future of books?
10 Is TV bad for children?

2 🎧 10.1 Listen to an interview with a professor of media studies. Which questions do the callers ask?

3 Are the following statements true (T), false (F) or is there no information (NI)? Listen again and check.

1 The term 'mass media' includes the internet.
2 In the future, there will be fewer than six major media corporations.
3 Newspaper editors used to be more powerful.
4 We get all our news from big media corporations.
5 Media is more interactive now than in the past.
6 The top-rated TV show in the UK in 1986 was a soap opera.
7 Tabloid circulation has fallen in most countries.

4a Are the things Monica mentions evident in your country?

b Choose three or four questions in exercise 1 to discuss.

Language focus 1

Reporting people's exact words

1 Work in groups and discuss. Do you know any public figures who are famous for saying things that don't make sense, when speaking to the media?

2a The article above contains some unfortunate quotes that have been reported in the media. Read the first one. Why doesn't it make sense?

b Work in pairs. Read quotes 2–13. Which do you like best?

That might be what I said ...

but it wasn't what I meant!

When public figures talk to the media, sometimes the words don't quite come out right. Here are some of our favourite examples.

1 'I owe a lot to my parents, especially my mother and father.'
Australian golfer

2 'The lead car is absolutely unique, except for the one behind it, which is identical.'
Formula One Motorsport commentator

3 'If you exclude the killings, Washington now actually has a very low crime rate.'
ex-Mayor of Washington

4 'Were you present when your photograph was taken?'
Lawyer questioning witness in court

5 'Smoking kills people, and if you're killed, you've lost an important part of your life.'
American actress and anti-smoking campaigner

6 'I'd like to play for an Italian club like Barcelona.'
British footballer

7 'The word 'genius' is not applicable in football. A genius is a guy like Norman Einstein.'
American Footballer

3 Match reported speech sentences a–e below to five of the direct quotes in the article. Underline the parts which are different in the reported versions.

a The mayor told journalists that if you excluded the killings, Washington actually had a very low crime rate.
b The lawyer asked the witness whether she had been present when her photograph had been taken.
c The actress said that smoking kills people and added that if you are killed, then you have lost an important part of your life.
d The lawyer asked the witness how his first marriage had ended. The witness replied that it had ended with death. The lawyer then asked whose death had ended the marriage.
e The minister said that he didn't know what he had said, but that he knew what he thought and that he assumed that that was what he had said.

8 Lawyer: How did your first marriage end?
   Witness: With death.
   Lawyer: And whose death ended it?

9 '[This player] dribbles a lot and the opposition
   don't like it … you can see it on their faces.'
   British football commentator

10 Lawyer: Can you describe the person you
   saw?
   Witness: About medium height with a beard.
   Lawyer: Was this a male or a female?

11 'I just want you to know that when we talk
   about war, we are really talking about peace.'
   Former US President

12 Lawyer: What is your date of birth?
   Witness: July 15.
   Lawyer: What year?
   Witness: Every year.

13 'I don't know what I said, but I know what I
   think and … well … I assume that's what
   I said.'
   US politician

GRAMMAR

When we report what someone said, various changes are
made. Answer the questions below, referring to sentences
a–e in exercise 3.

Verb tenses
1 What generally happens to verb tenses in reported speech?
2 Look at sentence c. Why is this an exception to the rule?

Reported questions
3 Look at sentences b and d. Which conjunctions introduce
   reported questions?
4 What is the difference in word order between direct and
   reported questions?

Other changes
5 Look at sentence a. What happens to time phrases like *now*
   in reported speech?
6 Look at sentence e. What happens to interjections like *well*?
7 Look at sentences c and e. How do you report a series of
   statements?
8 Look at sentence d. How do you report an incomplete
   sentence like *With death*?

▶ **Read Study 1, page 158**

PRACTICE

1 Put the other quotes in the article into reported
   speech.

2a Look at the pictures. What do the speakers claim
   other people said?

Your mother
phoned about half an
hour ago. She said it was
nothing important and
that she'd ring back
later this evening.

She said I'd
taken some
money from her
purse!

It's my
turn.

Mum said I
can play as long as
I like and that you've
got to wait till I'm
finished.

b 🎧 10.2 Listen to the original conversations and
   report what was actually said.

Actually, she said …

PRONUNCIATION

1 🎧 10.3 Listen to two people reporting what another said.
   Who thinks Debbie is telling the truth: A or B?
   What is the difference in the stress pattern?

2 🎧 10.4 Listen to eight more statements. Which statements
   suggest the speaker doesn't believe what the other
   person said.

3 Look at audio script 10.4 on page 176. Practise saying the
   sentences, paying attention to stress patterns.

> Unit 10, Study & Practice 1, page 158

Language focus 2

Verbs that summarise what people say

1 Work in pairs and discuss. Do you watch celebrity interviews on TV? Do you know anything about the famous interviews in the photos?

2a Read the text on the right about two of the most famous TV interviews of all time. Complete the text with the phrases below.

confessed to making	admitted being
refused to accept	denied committing
accepted that	admitted that
invited Richard Nixon to be	explained that
accused her husband of having	

b 🎧 10.5 Listen and check. Why do you think each interview was so shocking at the time?

3a Read quotes 1–8. Can you guess which three are from the Diana interview and which are from the Nixon interview? There are two extra quotes.

1 My political life is over. (*accept / deny / invite*)
2 I had bulimia for a number of years. (*admit / deny / refuse*)
3 I let down my friends. I let down the country. (*invite / confess / accuse*)
4 I'm not going to talk about my private life. It's too personal. (*admit / refuse / confess*)
5 I don't see myself being queen of this country. (*explain / invite / deny*)
6 I did not commit, in my view, an ... offence. (*confess / deny / accuse*)
7 I can't tolerate it [the media] because it's become abusive ... (*deny / invite / accuse*)
8 Would you like to say a bit more about the crimes you committed? (*invite / explain / tell*)

b Choose the best verb in brackets in exercise 3a to report each quote.

GRAMMAR

1 The verbs in exercise 2a summarise what people say without repeating every word. Match them to patterns 2–7 below.

1 verb + object + *that*   *assure someone that*
2 verb + *that*
3 verb + gerund
4 verb + preposition + gerund
5 verb + object + preposition + gerund
6 verb + infinitive (with *to*)
7 verb + object + infinitive

2 Check the meaning of the verbs below. Match each verb to a pattern in exercise 1.

suggest	recommend	claim
agree	warn	apologise
blame	offer	point out

▶ Read Study 2, page 159

TV interviews that rocked the world

Diana, Princess of Wales

When Diana, Princess of Wales, was interviewed on television in November 1995, she was still married to Prince Charles. Diana [1]_____ in love with someone else during her marriage and [2]_____ the relationship had been more than a friendship.

At the same time, she [3]_____ a close relationship with another woman and [4]_____ the stress had led to an eating disorder. Coming from the future Queen of England, this was extraordinary. The hour-long interview caused a media storm. The following year, Diana and Charles divorced and two years later, she died in a car crash in Paris.

Richard Nixon

In 1977, young British reporter David Frost [5]_____ interviewed on television. Ex-US president Nixon was reported to have been paid $600,000 plus 20 percent of the profits for his involvement. It became perhaps the most famous TV interview of all time and was even made into a film. Nixon had resigned the presidency in 1974 after being accused of committing certain crimes.

In the interview, Nixon [6]_____ the crimes and [7]_____ he had done anything criminal. However, he [8]_____ he had let the American people down and he [9]_____ a lot of bad judgments.

The interviews were hugely successful and made Frost famous.

PRACTICE

1 Look again at exercise 3a and report each quote using the correct verb.

1 Nixon accepted that his political life was over.

2a Read quotes 1–10 below, which were reported by the media. Who said each one: a film star, the manager of a sports team, or a politician?

1 Why don't you write something positive about my team for once? (*suggest / deny / offer*)
2 The minister is lying now, he has lied in the past, and he will continue to lie in the future. (*confess / accuse / invite*)
3 I think you should all go and see my new film. It's great. (*offer / warn / recommend*)
4 I'm really sorry for all the mistakes we've made but I still think you should vote for us. (*deny / apologise / blame*)
5 It's true, I did hit the photographer at the Oscar ceremony. He was only doing his job, I guess. (*refuse / tell / confess*)
6 It was the director's fault that the film was so rubbish. (*blame / admit / offer*)
7 Despite what has been written about my future, I am very happy here and have no intention of leaving the club. (*confess / refuse / deny*)
8 Give me the details and I'll look into this problem. (*agree / offer / apologise*)
9 If you write a negative review, I'll sue you. (*accuse / warn / recommend*)
10 I think you're right. We should have won that game. (*recommend / apologise / agree*)

b Choose the best verb to report each quote. Then report the main message of each quote.

3 Work in pairs. Read an interview with a politician and report the information which is underlined.

A: So, Minister, I'm afraid I have to ask you this question. ¹Did you or did you not accept money from Mr Buckingham, the property developer?

B: ²I'm sorry but I'm not going to answer that question. I want to talk about important issues such as …

A: Minister! Our listeners want you to give a simple yes or no answer. ³Would you like to take this chance do that?

B: Well … ⁴yes, it's true that I did accept some money, but it wasn't a bribe. ⁵It was a business deal. ⁶I definitely didn't do anything illegal.

A: How much did you accept?

B: ⁷I'm sorry but I can't answer that. ⁸It's confidential. And I object to this line of questioning. ⁹You are being unprofessional.

A: It's an acceptable question, Minister. Why won't you answer?

> Unit 10, Study & Practice 2, page 159

Wordspot
speak and *talk*

1a Complete the sentences below with the correct form of *speak* or *talk*.

1 'Actions _____ louder than words' means that what you do is more important than what you say.
2 Someone who _____ their mind isn't afraid to say exactly what they mean.
3 It's rude for work colleagues to _____ shop when outsiders are present.
4 He knows what he's _____ about: he's an expert on gardening.
5 If you _____ highly of someone, you say good things about them.
6 A _____ point is a subject lots of people want to discuss.
7 _____ radio has phone-ins and interviews rather than music.
8 If your voice is very quiet, people may ask you to _____ up.
9 _____ to yourself is often considered to be a sign of eccentricity.
10 Small _____ is polite, friendly conversation about unimportant topics.
11 They had a huge argument. Since then, they haven't been on _____ terms.
12 Peace _____ are negotiations between the two sides in a war.
13 A _____-show features interviews with celebrity guests.

b 🎧 10.6 Listen and check.

2a Complete the diagrams with *speak* and *talk* phrases from exercise 1a.

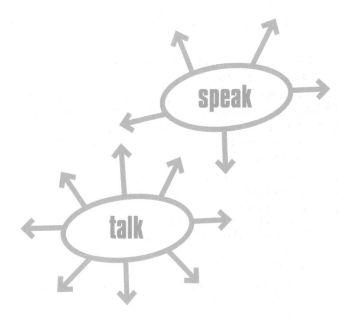

b Work in pairs. Spend a few minutes studying the phrases. Then turn to page 129 and ask and answer the questions.

Task

Discuss an article

Preparation Reading and vocabulary

1a Work in small groups. Look at the photos and headlines. Make three guesses about what each story is about.

b Look at the words and phrases in the box. Try to guess which article they are from.

forensic investigators	graphic violence
violate someone's privacy	ratings
uphold a complaint	in the public domain
undermine parental authority	untested in court
the Advertising Standards Authority	

2a Work in three groups. Group A: Read article 1. Group B: Read article 2. Group C: Read article 3. Which headline (A, B or C) does it relate to?

b Read the article again and memorise as much information as you can. Compare what you remember with another student from your group.

Task Speaking

1a You are going to summarise your article to other students, then lead a discussion about it. Practise summarising the article with your partner.

> Useful language a

b Think of at least four discussion questions to ask other students about your article.

> Useful language b

Do you think employers should try to find out about candidates' personal lives?

What do you think about violence on TV?

2 Work in groups of three with students who read other articles. Take turns to summarise your articles and ask and answer your discussion questions.

THE MOST POPULAR TV SHOW IN THE WORLD

YOUR PROSPECTIVE EMPLOYER IS CHECKING YOU OUT ON FACEBOOK

THE MOST OFFENSIVE TV ADVERT EVER!

CSI (Crime Scene Investigation) has been named as the world's most watched TV series – again. The show, which is set in Las Vegas, was presented with the International Television Audience Award for the highest ratings worldwide at the Monte Carlo Television Festival.

It is the fifth time it has won the award in the last seven years. CSI features a team of forensic investigators who solve crimes by examining evidence.

The series is frequently criticised by police experts for being inaccurate, and has also been criticised by parents' groups for its graphic images of sex and violence. However, it attracts an audience of almost 80 million in more than 50 countries worldwide. It was first aired in the US in 2000 and a 13th series has just been shown. In all, over 250 episodes have been made.

Other shows with top worldwide ratings include the medical drama *House*, starring Hugh Laurie, the long running series *Desperate Housewives*, as well as reruns of old favourites from the 80s and 90s such as *Baywatch* and *Friends*.

USEFUL LANGUAGE

a Describing the article
This article is about ...
According to the article ...
Apparently, ...
The main point that comes out if it is ...
I was surprised to find that ...

b Questions arising from the article
In your opinion, should ... ?
I'd be interested to know what you think.
What interests me is whether or not ...
It raises the question of whether ...

The UK Advertising Standards Authority (ASA) has published a list of the most offensive adverts of all time. Anyone guessing which adverts caused the most complaints would probably think that they contained sex, violence, swearing or blasphemy.

However they would be wrong. The most complained about advert of all time was actually a fast-food advert showing call-centre workers singing with their mouths full of food. The advert, which was broadcast in 2005, received a record 1,671 complaints because many parents were worried that it would encourage bad table manners among children. The ASA did not uphold the complaint; they ruled that the advert was unlikely to change children's behaviour or undermine parental authority. Other adverts that received large numbers of complaints included one in which a footballer kicked a cat across the pitch, and two with religious content. The number of complaints about adverts has been increasing, as in recent years it has become possible to complain via the web.

Depending what you read, anywhere between 40 and 90 percent of employers these days check out potential employees on Facebook, and increasingly, employers are asking job candidates to handover password details as a sign of "trust". So what are they looking for? Is this acceptable? Is it even legal?

In surveys, most employers deny that they are looking for reasons not to hire someone – although around 70 percent admit that they have at some point rejected a candidate based on what they found on a social-networking site. The most common reason given for rejection was not hard partying, however, it was discovering that candidates had lied about qualifications. Employers claim that they are mainly looking to see if the candidate is a well-rounded person who will fit in with their company culture.

In the USA, for example, it is legal to check material that is in the public domain (your Facebook page, for example) and this is something that we should probably bear in mind when job hunting. However, it is not legal to ask for password settings or to read private online conversations, as this also violates the privacy of others. But while this remains untested in court, many employers continue to demand this information.

Follow up Writing

1 Imagine you are commenting on a blog about one or more of the articles you have discussed. Write a short paragraph, giving your opinions.

SHARE YOUR TASK

Choose one of the topics you discussed. Prepare to give your opinion about it.

Practise giving your opinion until you feel confident.

Film or record yourself giving your opinion.

Share your film/recording with other students.

WORLD CULTURE

THE SCIENCE OF FILM

Find out first

1a Work in pairs. Do the film and photography quiz below.

THE HISTORY OF FILM AND PHOTOGRAPHY

1 **When was the first 3D film made?**
   a 1922   b 1970   c 2008

2 **When were the first moving colour images produced?**
   a 1849   b 1902   c 1938

3 **When was the first camera phone invented?**
   a 1997   b 2002   c 2007

4 **When was the the first photograph taken?**
   a 1726   b 1826   c 1926

5 **When was the first digital camera created?**
   a 1975   b 1985   c 1995

6 **When was the the first talking film made?**
   a 1887   b 1907   c 1927

7 **When was the first DVD sold?**
   a 1976   b 1986   c 1996

b Go online to check your answers or ask your teacher.

Search: first 3D film/colour film/ camera phone/photograph/digital camera/talking motion picture/DVD

View

2a You are going to watch a video about developments in film technology. Before you watch, read the definitions below and try to choose the correct answer.

slow-motion footage
a filmmaking technique in which the action happens *slower* / *faster* than in real life. This means that you can see events in detail which normally happen too *slowly* / *fast*.

time-lapse footage
a filmmaking technique in which the action happens *slower* / *faster* than in real life. This means that you can see in detail events which normally happen over a *short* / *long* period.

a time-slice photograph
a *2D*/*3D* record of a moment in time. You see a single moment in time from one *angle* / *many different angles*.

b ▶ Watch the video and check your answers.

3 Watch the video again and answer the questions.

   1 What did Eadweard Muybridge show for the first time?
   2 How many frames per second is a) normal film, b) slow-motion footage?
   3 How do you make a film that shows fruit rotting in 30 seconds?
   4 How do you take a time-slice image?
   5 What might we be able to do by the year 3,000?

World view

4a (▶) Watch five people talking about a film in which the special effects impressed them. Complete the table.

	Name of film	Special effects/ filming techniques	Effect on film
Sion			
Audrey			
Jeff			
Helen			
Elliot			

b Work in groups and compare answers. Watch again if necessary to complete your notes.

5 Work in groups and discuss the questions.

- Have you seen any of the films the speakers mention? If so, do you agree with what they say about the special effects?
- Which special effects in films have particularly impressed you? Why?

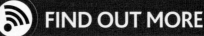

FIND OUT MORE

6a What do you know about the three film industries below?

BOLLYWOOD Nollywood **HOLLYWOOD**

b Go online and find out more about the film industries. Make notes about the following points:

- where they are located
- how many films they make
- what kind of films they make
- how much and how long the films take to make
- how many people work in each industry
- typical storylines
- how the films are sold and who watches them

....

Search: Bollywood / Nollywood / Hollywood

....

Write up your research

7 Write one or two paragraphs about your research. Summarise the similarities and differences. Use the prompts below to help you.

- All three industries ...
- There are further similarities in the way ...
- Whereas a Hollywood film costs ..., a Bollywood film costs ...
- Another big difference is ...
- Unlike Nollywood, Bollywood is ...
- Another way in which the film industries differ is ...

LIFE ISSUES

IN THIS UNIT

- **Grammar: Hypothetical situations in the present; Hypothetical situations in the past**

- **Vocabulary: Science and processes; *Life***

- **Task: Discuss a controversial issue**

- **Language live: Reporting opinions; A 'for and against' essay**

What if ... ?

In a world where science has made almost anything imaginable, think outside the box and imagine if the everyday things we all take for granted were different!

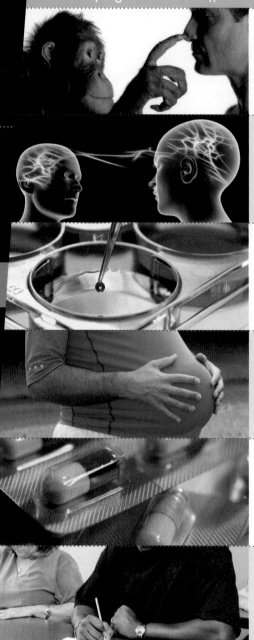

1 How would the world change if we learnt to communicate with other species, like dogs or cows?

Comment 💬

2 What if we had the power to read each other's thoughts – how would life be different?

Comment 💬

3 Imagine if everyone could choose their children's appearance – how would the human race change?

Comment 💬

4 Suppose that men could give birth just like women – how would the world change?

Comment 💬

5 Imagine that a harmless drug was invented so that we no longer needed to sleep. What would the effects be?

Comment 💬

6 What if people had to pass an exam before they could become parents – how would society change?

Comment 💬

Language focus 1
Hypothetical situations in the present

1 Work in groups. Read questions 1–6 on the website above and discuss the questions below.

- Have you thought about these questions before?
- Do you ever think about other questions like these?

2 Work in groups and discuss what you think would happen in the situations on the website. Which things would be beneficial to the world and which would be harmful?

3a Match the comments below to imaginary situations 1–6 on the website. Which situation has two comments? Which has none?

COMMENTS

Katy K
I think this would be horrible! I wouldn't be able to spend all those hours under my lovely duvet, I would have to spend more hours at work with my horrible boss! No, no, no!

Fabgirl 17
I really wish we could do this! I've got a dog and two cats and I wish I knew what they were thinking and what they really wanted. It would be so cool to have a chat with them.

PaulfromOz
It would be a bit difficult to carry on eating them, wouldn't it? It might feel a bit like cannibalism, I guess.

JeremyJ
Actually, I think it's time that people got some kind of qualification or training to become a parent. A lot of the world's problems are due to bad parenting if you look around.

JennyEP
LOL … if only this was true! I guess a painless way of giving birth would be invented pretty quickly, wouldn't it?

Amir K.
If we found out what our friends really thought of us, we'd get a few shocks, I imagine. I'm not sure this would be such a great idea!

b Work in pairs and discuss. Which comments do/don't you agree with? Why?

4 The people on the website are talking about imaginary situations. Underline all the language in situations 1–6 and comments that show this.

GRAMMAR

1 Answer the questions below.
1 Are the people on the website imagining situations in the past or present/future?
2 Look at the examples below. Which tense is used to describe the imaginary situations?
   I wish I knew what my pets really wanted – it would be so cool.

   If we found out what our friends really thought of us, we'd get a few shocks.
3 Which verb form is used to discuss the imaginary consequences of these situations?
4 Find at least three more phrases in the website used to introduce imaginary situations:
   I really wish …

   What if … ?

▶ Read Study 1, page 161

PRACTICE

1 Read imaginary situations 1–7 below. Complete the sentences with the correct form of the words in brackets.

1 What if the sun _____ (become) so strong that it _____ (burn) us immediately – how _____ (life change)?
2 Imagine that the government _____ (pass) a law banning people from eating meat. What _____ (happen)?
3 How _____ (life be) different if a drug _____ (be invented) that _____ (stop) people from ever feeling depressed?
4 Suppose couples _____ (not allow) to divorce – what _____ (the effects be)?
5 Imagine if we _____ (have) no sense of smell – what difference _____ (it make) to our lives?
6 How _____ (our lives be) different if a cure _____ (be discovered) for all colds and minor viruses?
7 Imagine if pollution _____ (get) so bad that the private ownership of cars _____ (be banned) – what _____ (happen)?

2a Choose five situations from the website on page 106 and write about what you think would happen.

b Work in pairs and compare your ideas.

3a 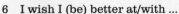 11.1 Listen to five people. Which sentences below are they completing? What ideas and wishes do they express?

Wishful thinking …

1 If I (could be) any animal I think I (be) …
2 I often imagine what it (be) like if …
3 If (I can change) one thing about my appearance I (change) …
4 I (not change) … for anything in the world.
5 If I (can change) places with a famous person for a day, I (choose) to be … because …
6 I wish I (be) better at/with …
7 If I (can) play one musical instrument well, I (choose) …
8 I (never) … under any circumstances.
9 I wish I (have/be) …
10 If I (can) wave a magic wand and speak another language fluently I (choose) … because …
11 I wish my friends/partner/parents/children …
12 I wish/If only …

b Complete at least eight sentences for yourself.

c Work in pairs and compare ideas, giving reasons.

> Unit 11, Study & Practise 1, page 161

Interfering with nature

Sixty-five million years ago, dinosaurs were roaming the earth when an asteroid struck, causing dramatic climate change and wiping them out. Seventy-four thousand years ago, early human beings almost suffered the same fate when Mount Toba in northern Sumatra, Indonesia erupted, triggering a ten-year volcanic winter across the planet. Global catastrophes are nothing new, but for the first time in history, humans may be making the technological advances to prevent some of them.

THE THREAT FROM CLIMATE CHANGE

Climate change is caused by the extremely high levels of dangerous chemicals in the atmosphere, particularly carbon dioxide (CO_2). It is estimated that average global temperatures will rise by between two and six degrees by the end of this century. We all know the effects could be catastrophic, but are we aware of the possible solutions?

Solution one: pump even more chemicals into the atmosphere

Crazy as it sounds, a group of academics from British universities is making a plan to build a 12-mile pipe, held up by a huge balloon, that would pump enormous quantities of toxic chemicals, such as sulphur dioxide, into the atmosphere. Surprisingly, there is good science behind the idea. The chemicals would form a protective layer around the earth that would reflect sunlight and so cool the earth, much like the effects of a volcanic eruption.

Cost: around $10 billion a year.

Benefits: this plan would produce almost instant results.

Risks: volcanoes have almost wiped out humanity in the past through the toxic chemicals released in the atmosphere, and the same thing could happen again with this plan.

Solution two: stir up the oceans

Intellectual Ventures, a company that invests in projects to combat global warming, has proposed building a million plastic tubes, each about 100 metres long, and using them to stir up the ocean. Why, you might be wondering, would we want to do this? Again, the answer is scientifically valid. The bottom of the ocean is almost freezing and by stirring it up, cold water would come to the surface and absorb heat and CO_2, and so cool the planet.

Cost: tens of millions of dollars.

Benefits: this plan is relatively cheap and technically possible now.

Risks: the tubes would disrupt and possibly destroy sea life, and the plan may not work.

Solution three: stop burning fossil fuels

This is undoubtedly the best solution but is it really likely to happen in the near future?

Cost: unknown, but in the short term it would probably involve global economic collapse.

Benefits: it's a simple and effective plan.

Risks: it may already be too late. Without radical action, this plan could just mean 'do nothing'.

THE THREAT FROM ASTEROIDS

In 1908, an asteroid measuring about 40 metres in diameter (quite small for an asteroid) struck Siberia and caused enormous damage. Had it landed on Beijing, New York, or any other large city, it would have destroyed it. So what preparations should we make to prevent future asteroid strikes?

Solution one: build a huge nuclear bomb

It's a simple solution: use a nuclear bomb to destroy an approaching asteroid. This solution would probably work for smaller asteroids but a huge nuclear bomb would be needed for larger ones, and that is a danger in itself. What if the rocket failed and the bomb fell to earth? The other danger is that the asteroid might not be destroyed but would split into two or three big pieces. Then we would have not one huge problem but three big, radioactive ones.

Cost: billions and billions of dollars.

Benefits: it may be our only option if there isn't much time before an asteroid strikes.

Risks: do we really want to build a bomb that could destroy the planet?

Solution two: build a giant umbrella in space

American geophysicist H Jay Melosh has proposed building a giant umbrella in space, one kilometre wide. The aim is not to stop asteroids raining down on our heads but rather to collect and focus solar energy, rather like a magnifying glass. This energy could be focused on an asteroid and over time, it would deflect it away from earth. It would take at least a year to work, however.

Cost: a few billion dollars.

Benefits: it wouldn't be a danger to humanity.

Risks: it might take too long to work.

Solution three: do nothing and hope

Any expensive solution has problems. If we decide to build a huge nuclear bomb or a giant umbrella, who pays? Who controls it? So the option to do nothing is always the simplest and most attractive. The question is, is it the right one?

Cost: nothing

Benefits: the cost

Risks: if an asteroid does threaten earth, we won't have the technology to deal with it.

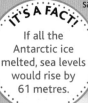

IT'S A FACT!
If all the Antarctic ice melted, sea levels would rise by 61 metres.

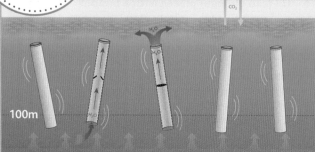

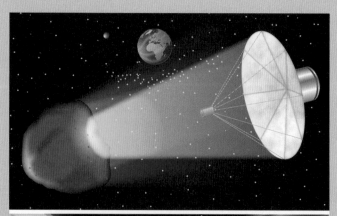

Reading

1a Look at the phrases in the box. Are they usually seen as problems that human beings face (P) or solutions to our problems (S)?

> an asteroid strike *P*   earthquakes   climate change
> wind power   nuclear bombs   rising sea levels
> volcanic eruptions   solar energy   burning fossil fuels
> toxic chemicals technological advances

b Work in pairs. Do you worry about any of the problems in exercise 1a? Which ones and why?

2a The text is about two of these problems: climate change and asteroid strikes. Read the introduction and look at the pictures. Match the pictures with the ideas below.

- pumping toxic chemicals into the atmosphere
- stirring up the oceans
- building a huge nuclear bomb
- building a giant umbrella in space

b Can you guess which problem each picture relates to and what the solution might be? Scan the text briefly to check.

3a Work in pairs. Student A: Read the section about climate change. Student B: Read the section about asteroids. Answer the appropriate questions below.
Student A
Which solution(s):
- copies what happens in nature?
- is unlikely to happen in the short term?
- might create a different catastrophe?
- would work quickly?
- would mean we have to change the way we live?
- would have side effects?

Student B
Which solution(s):
- would only work on some asteroids?
- is the easiest to choose?
- might create more problems than it solves?
- wouldn't destroy an approaching asteroid?
- seems to have the least risk?
- may be necessary if we don't have much warning?

b Ask your partner their questions from exercise 3a. Your partner should give reasons where possible.

4 Read the whole text and look at the pictures again. Explain in your own words exactly how each solution works and what the third solution is in each case.

5 Work in small groups and discuss the questions.
- Which threat do you think is the greatest?
- Which solution for each threat would you choose? Why?
- Which solution would you definitely avoid? Why?

PRONUNCIATION

1 How are the vowels in blue pronounced in the science/ nature words below? Which syllable is stressed?

asteroid	catastrophe	dioxide	dinosaur
eruption	fuel	nuclear	ocean
radioactive	scientific	solar	surface
temperature	volcanic	volcano	

2 🎧 11.2 Listen and check. Practise saying the words, paying attention to stress and vowel sounds.

Vocabulary
Science and processes

1 Read the true sentences below. What do you think the reason for each could be?

a In California, all flat roofs on new buildings have to be painted white.
b The residents of the island of Kiribati are making plans to move their entire nation to Fiji.
c There are 350,000 mirrors next to each other in the Mojave Desert in the USA.
d One gym in Hong Kong has incredibly low electricity bills.
e One nightclub in London lets people in for free if they walk or cycle to the club.
f Scientists put five tonnes of iron powder into the sea.

2 Check the words in bold below. Then match reasons 1–6 to sentences a–f in exercise 1.

1 They **reflect** sunlight onto water to generate 'clean electricity', which helps **prevent** climate change.
2 It is an eco-club which **combats** climate change by encouraging green behaviour.
3 They fear that climate change will **affect** sea levels and their island will **disappear** under water.
4 The exercise bikes and running machines **capture** energy when they are used and **turn it into** electricity, which the gym uses.
5 The iron **causes an increase in** tiny sea plants, which **have an impact on** the amount of toxic chemicals in the sea.
6 This is to **reflect** sunlight which heats the earth and **contributes to** global warming.

3 Choose the correct answer(s).

1 Recycling helps *to prevent / affect / contribute to* waste.
2 Black clothes don't *capture / combat / reflect* sunlight.
3 Travelling by aeroplane *contributes to / causes an increase in / combats* pollution.
4 Climate change is causing some glaciers to *prevent / disappear / capture*.
5 Greenhouse gases like CO2 can *affect / cause an increase in / reflect* global warming.

Task

Discuss a controversial issue

Preparation Listening

1 You are going to discuss three difficult cases of medical ethics. Look at the photos on page 111 and the key vocabulary below. Try to guess what each case is about.

Case 1
to be bullied
self-esteem
peer pressure
plastic surgery
to prescribe drugs

Case 2
attention deficit hyperactivity
  disorder (ADHD)
easily distracted
dependency
behavioural problems
long-term effects

Case 3
a lifelong smoker
a life-threatening illness
life expectancy
value for money
the taxpayer
the aging population

2a 🎧 11.3 Listen and check your ideas.

b Work in pairs. How much of each case summary can you complete?

c Listen again and complete the case summaries.

3 Read the fact file. Which case do you think each fact relates to?

Task Speaking

Option A

1 Work in pairs. Choose the case that most interests you. Think of three or four arguments for and against the surgery/drugs/treatment. Ask your teacher for any words/phrases you need.

> Useful language a and b

2 Work with another pair. Explain your arguments for and against, and discuss them with your group. Try to reach an agreement about what should be done. If you have time, discuss another case in a similar way.

> Useful language a–c

3 Present the arguments for and against the case, and your conclusions, to the class. What do the rest of the class think?

FACT FILE

A | In 2010, almost 77,000 teenagers in the USA had plastic surgery. The most common operations were rhinoplasty and ear pinning.

B | Between 3 and 4 million school-age children in the USA are thought to be taking Ritalin, the most common drug used to treat ADHD. Many of their parents and teachers say that the child cannot function effectively without the drug.

C | It has been estimated that the average course of treatment for cancer in the UK costs around $45,000.

D | Some child psychologists believe that regular outdoor activity can reduce the symptoms of ADHD by up to 30 percent.

E | One recent survey of National Health Service doctors in the UK showed that 52 percent believe that they should withhold non-urgent treatment from patients who smoke or are obese, and who refuse to take action about these issues.

F | According to a recent survey, two-thirds of British teenage girls say that they are considering plastic surgery, and say that this is because of the pressure they feel from seeing 'perfect' celebrities in magazines.

G | The average life expectancy for a woman in the UK is around 81, but according to a recent study, this is reduced by 14.5 years in lifelong smokers.

Option B

1a Work in two groups. Group A: Think about the arguments for the surgery/drugs/treatment in each case. Group B: Think about the arguments against surgery/drugs/treatment in each case.

b Work in pairs with a student in your group. Think of as many arguments as you can for each case. Ask your teacher for any words/phrases you need.

> Useful language a and b

c Work with other students in your group and compare ideas.

2 Work in pairs with a student from the other group. Discuss each case in turn, giving your arguments for or against. Try to persuade your partner of your side of the argument.

3 What is your real point of view? Compare your views with the class.

> Useful language b and c

CASE 1

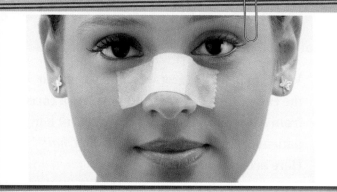

CASE SUMMARY

Miss K's background, age, etc.: _____

Miss K's wishes and reasons: _____

Her parents' position and reasons: _____

The key question: *Should _____?*

USEFUL LANGUAGE

a Arguments for and against

What if/Suppose (there were long-term effects on him)?

How would she/he feel if ... ?

What about the rights of (the child)?

It's a question of whether or not (the surgery is safe) ...

b Giving your opinion

He/She should(n't) be allowed to ...

I think people should have the right to ...

In my opinion, it's morally wrong to ...

I think you have to be practical ...

I feel really sorry for ... but I feel that ...

c Agreeing/disagreeing

I see what you mean, but ...

I totally agree (with ...)

I don't agree (at all).

CASE 2

CASE SUMMARY

Boy S's family background and personal details:

_____

His condition and the treatment prescribed:

_____

His mother's point of view and main arguments:

_____

His father's point of view and main arguments:

_____

The key question: *Should _____?*

CASE 3

CASE SUMMARY

Mrs X's personal background:

_____

Mrs X's health and treatment needs: _____

Dr Z's arguments: _____

What Dr Z's opponents say: _____

Why the case is causing public debate: _____

The key question: *Should _____?*

SHARE YOUR TASK

Choose one of these cases or a similar case that you have read about. Prepare to summarise the facts and give your opinion about what should happen.

Practise until you feel confident in expressing yourself.

Film/record yourself giving your summary.

Share your film/recording with other students.

Language focus 2
Hypothetical situations in the past

1 Read the quotes. Which do you most agree with? Why?

Never regret. If it's good, it's wonderful.
If it's bad, it's experience.
Victoria Holt, author

The stupid things you do, you regret ... and if you
don't regret them, maybe you're stupid.
Katharine Hepburn, actress

2a Read the text on the right. Whose regrets does
it describe?

b What words do you think are missing? Turn to page
126 and check.

3a The sentences below refer to hypothetical situations
in the past. Try to guess the missing words.

  1 She _____ _____ said 'yes' if I _____ asked
her out.

  2 I _____ be here now if I _____ followed my
parents' wishes.

  3 If I _____ kept in touch with her, we _____ be
friends now.

  4 If I _____ left work on time, I _____ _____ seen
my children before they went to bed.

b Match sentences 1–4 to regrets a–e in exercise 2a.

c 🎧 11.4 Listen and check. Which speakers
express regrets?

GRAMMAR

1a Look at the sentences with *if only* or *I wish* in exercise
2a. Do they refer to things which happened or didn't
happen?

b Which verb form follows *if only* and *I wish*?

2a Which sentences in exercise 3a refer to the past only?

b Which refer to the past and the present?

c Which verb forms are used in each case?

3 Complete the sentences below in two ways, one
referring to the past and the other to the present,
using the words in brackets.

  1 If I'd been a bit more ambitious, I
   (*be promoted / be manager*).

  2 If they hadn't suppressed their feelings
   for each other, they (*get together /
   be together*).

  3 If she'd made more of an effort to keep in contact, we
   (*not lose touch / still be friends*).

▶ Read Study 2, page 162

Regrets, I've had a few ...

What do people regret when they come to
the end of their lives? Bronnie Ware, a carer
from Australia, recorded the regrets of her
patients in her blog *Inspiration and Chai*.
Here are the top five.

a 'If only I'd had the courage to live a life true to
   ▨▨▨ , not the life others expected of me.'
  • It's very important to try to honour at least some
   of your dreams.

b 'I wish I hadn't worked so ▨▨▨ .'
  • This came from every male patient that I nursed.

c 'If only I'd had the courage to express my ▨▨▨ .'
  • Many people suppressed their ▨▨▨ in order to
   keep the peace with others.

d 'I wish I'd stayed in touch with my ▨▨▨ .'
  • It all comes down to love and relationships in the
   end.

e 'I wish that I had let myself be ▨▨▨ .'
  • Many people did not realise until too late that
   ▨▨▨ is a choice.

PRACTICE

1a Complete the sentences below with the correct form of the verbs in brackets.

1 If I *'d checked* (check) more carefully, it *would never have happened* (never happen)!
2 I wish I _____ (not do) it!
3 I wish I _____ (buy) it!
4 If I _____ (not meet) her, my life _____ (be) very different.
5 I wish I _____ (allow) more time.
6 If only I _____ (try) harder!
7 It _____ (be) much better if I _____ (not open) my mouth!
8 I wish I _____ (never go) to that party!
9 If only I _____ (can) turn the clock back five minutes I would do it all differently!
10 I wish I _____ (never set) eyes on him!

I wish ...

b Have you ever felt regrets like the ones in exercise 1a? Choose three situations and make notes about them. Think about what would have happened or what would be different now.

c Work in pairs and take turns to talk about the situations you chose.

2 Work in pairs and discuss. Do you think you will have the same regrets as Bronnie Ware's patients? Why/ Why not?

> Unit 11, Study & Practice 2, page 162

Wordspot
life

1a The word *life* has been omitted from the sentences below. Write it in the correct position.

life

1 Going on a safari has been a ^ long ambition of mine.
2 The actor Danny Mackay never answers questions about his private.
3 expectancy for both men and women is increasing in most parts of the world.
4 If the guard hadn't been on duty at the beach, the child might have drowned.
5 The accused was given a sentence for murder.
6 Don't worry, his illness is not threatening.
7 I've been offered a record contract! It's the chance of a time!
8 Although he can't actually throw us out, our landlord is making very difficult for us.
9 There is no danger of the ship sinking, but please put on your jacket.
10 Despite his tough screen image, in real Brad King is a quiet, gentle man.
11 The wax models are so like that you almost feel you could talk to them!
12 It's disappointing that you didn't win the prize, but that's! There's nothing you can do about it!

b Underline the word or phrase which goes with *life* in each sentence.

2 Complete the definitions below.

1 'In *real life*' means in reality, as opposed to what happens in stories.
2 A _____ is someone whose job is to save people from drowning on beaches.
3 A _____ is a long term in prison, possibly until the prisoner dies.
4 A _____ is something you wear to help you float.
5 A _____ statue looks exactly like the living person.
6 '_____ !' is what people say when they have to accept a situation they don't like.
7 If you make _____ for someone, you do your best to create problems for them.
8 A _____ disease is one that might kill you.
9 Your _____ is the part of your life concerned with your home, family, etc.
10 A _____ ambition/problem, etc. is one that has lasted through most of your life.
11 The _____ is the best opportunity you will ever have.
12 _____ is how long it is thought a person will live.

3 🎧 11.5 Listen and write down the five questions that you hear. Work in pairs. Ask and answer the questions.

1 *Do you have any lifelong ambitions?*

LANGUAGE LIVE

Speaking
Reporting opinions

1 Work in pairs and discuss. Why are animals used in medical research? What are the main arguments for and against, do you think?

2 🎧 **11.6** Listen to a reporter summarising public opinion polls on animal testing. Complete the four questions which the presenter asks.

   1 What do the ... ?
   2 What else do ... ?
   3 What do people feel about ... ?
   4 How would you ... ?

3 Listen again and choose the phrase you hear.

   1 Recent *research* / *opinion polls* have given new life to the debate on animal testing.
   2 Around *one in five* / *one in ten* people believe that it is never acceptable.
   3 *A quarter* / *Three-quarters* of people think that experiments on monkeys and other primates should not be allowed.
   4 More than *three out of five* / *four out of five* people think that experiments which cause severe suffering or pain should be banned.
   5 Just *over half* / *under half* the people polled also said that experiments on new medicines should be allowed.
   6 *The vast majority* / *A tiny minority* of people, over 90 percent, are against testing cosmetics on animals.
   7 *On the whole* / *Generally speaking*, it's a mixed picture. But the results show that more and more people are concerned about animal testing.

4 Read the research below about public opinion on smoking bans. Rephrase it using language from exercise 3.

85% of people are non-smokers.	35% of people think smoking should be made completely illegal.
65% of people support a ban on smoking in all public places. In 2001, only 35% of people supported the idea.	
	95% of people think that the minimum age to buy cigarettes should be 16 or higher.
48% of people support a ban on smoking in cars.	

5a Work in pairs. Student A: You are a presenter on a radio news show. Student B: You are a reporter who is summarising the research on a smoking ban. Act out an interview similar to the one in exercise 2.

b Swap roles and repeat.

Writing
A 'for and against' essay

1 Work in pairs and discuss the questions below.

   1 How many situations can you think of where animals are used for entertainment? *zoos, bullfights, ...*
   2 Can you think of any arguments for or against using animals for entertainment?

2 Read the for and against essay on page 115. Summarise the arguments on both sides. Were any the same as yours?

3 Choose the best answers below to complete the essay on page 115. Sometimes both answers are possible.

   1 *however* / *although*
   2 *At first* / *First of all*
   3 *It's important to remember* / *Don't forget*
   4 *Secondly* / *Second*
   5 *lastly* / *last*
   6 *on the other hand* / *however*
   7 *for example* / *such as*
   8 *Furthermore* / *What is more*
   9 *Another argument* / *Also*
   10 *In conclusion* / *To summarise*
   11 *In my opinion* / *To my mind*

Should animals be used for entertainment?

In zoos, aquariums, circuses and many other situations, animals are used to entertain people. Most of us take this for granted and see it as natural, ¹_____ , some people argue that animals deserve more respect. So what are the arguments for and against?

²_____ , those who believe it is OK to use animals for entertainment say that most animals have a safer and more enjoyable life in the entertainment business. ³_____ animals in the wild often have short and unpleasant lives and they are protected from that when they are used for entertainment. ⁴_____ , supporters argue, zoos, aquariums and other places which keep animals have an important educational function. It is the only way that most people will ever see a real wild animal. And ⁵_____ , they say, animals are adaptable and actually enjoy life in captivity.

Opponents of using animals for entertainment, ⁶_____ , disagree with the whole idea because it suggests that animals have no rights, ⁷_____ the right to freedom. ⁸_____ , they argue, most animals who are used in this way do not have safe and enjoyable lives. They are usually kept in cramped, unnatural conditions and their keepers often can't afford or can't be bothered to treat them well. ⁹_____ is that animals lose their true identity when they live around humans. Because of this, the educational aspect is lost.

¹⁰_____ , there are strong arguments on both sides of the debate. ¹¹_____ , however, the negatives of keeping animals for entertainment outweigh the positives and we should focus on protecting animals in their natural environment.

---

4 Cross out the phrase(s) below that are wrong or don't make sense.

1 In most countries, there are strict laws concerning which animals can be used for entertainment. *For example / Such as / Also* endangered species cannot be kept privately. *Furthermore / Another argument / What is more*, there are strict rules about which animals can be imported and exported.

2 In the USA, keeping wild animals as pets is illegal in some states, *another argument / however / although* it depends on the animal. *For example / Such as / At first*, in Florida, you can own a wolf as a pet if you get a licence.

3 Animal fights are illegal in most countries but *first of all / it's important to remember that / don't forget that* they often happen in secret. *For example / In conclusion / However*, dog fights still happen in the UK.

5a You are going to write a for and against essay. Work in pairs and choose one of the essay titles below. Make a list of arguments for and against.

- Should hunting be banned?
- Should the government encourage people to become vegetarian?
- Should experiments on animals be banned?

b Choose the two or three strongest arguments and think of an example or further point to support each one.

6a Read the checklist below, then write the first draft of your essay.

- Are there four paragraphs: introduction, 'for' paragraph, 'against' paragraph and conclusion?
- Have you made at least two arguments in each for/ against paragraph?
- Have you supported each argument with an example or a further point?
- Have you used several of the linking words/phrases in exercise 3a?
- Have you given your personal opinion in the conclusion?

b Work in pairs. Take turns to comment on each other's drafts. Use the checklist to guide your comments. Then, write a final draft.

12

FAME

Fifteen minutes of fame

In 1968, the artist Andy Warhol predicted that in the future, everyone would be world-famous for 15 minutes. In our modern, celebrity-obsessed world, Warhol's prediction seems to be coming true. But fame wasn't always so easy to get.

Reading and vocabulary
Fame

1 Work in pairs and discuss. Are you interested in celebrities? What about your friends and people in your country generally?

2a Work in pairs. Check the meaning of the phrases in bold below. Then choose five of the sentences. Write the name of a well-known person for each sentence.

He/She ...
- has been a **household name** for decades.
- **draws huge crowds** wherever he/she goes.
- is/was an **overnight sensation**.
- has been **splashed across the newspapers** recently.
- **has a reputation for** acting like **a diva**.
- tries hard to stay **in the media spotlight**.
- is **ill-equipped to deal with** the pressure of fame.
- is trying to **make a comeback**.

b Work with a new partner. Take turns to say the names on your list and guess why your partner chose that person.

In ancient times, some of the first celebrities were Roman gladiators. Rather like today's TV talent-show contestants, these men (and occasionally women) fought each other for the audience's entertainment. Gladiators, however, were fighting for their lives, not a record deal! Fast forward to the 18th century, and in the pre-photography age, it was politicians and preachers who were able to become celebrities through public speaking. George Whitefield, for example, a preacher from England, drew a crowd of 30,000 when he visited the US city of Boston. It's no wonder he was called 'Anglo-America's first modern celebrity'.

In the 19th century, the arrival of cheap newspapers created a sudden demand for exciting stories. All kinds of people began to get their 15 minutes (or more) of fame, including the legendary American outlaw and bank robber, Jesse James, and one of the world's first media celebrities, Sam Patch. Patch became famous for jumping into rivers from high places, and he became a household name by leaping into Niagara Falls. He survived every jump ... except the last one into the Genesee River in New York.

In the same way that the media is held responsible for celebrity problems today, people blamed the pressure of the media for Patch's sudden end.

By the end of the 20th century, TV show producers had begun to turn to the cheapest performers available – their audience. Finally, it seemed, anyone who wanted 15 minutes of fame could get it. And some people wanted it far too much.

Richard and Mayumi Heene, for example, launched a large helium balloon 2,000 metres into the air and then called a TV network to say that their six-year-old son, Falcon, was inside it. Planes were re-routed and Denver International Airport was briefly shut down. However Falcon was later found to have been hiding in the family's garage the whole time. The 'balloon boy' incident turned out to be a hoax and the Heenes were accused of doing it in the hope of landing their own reality TV show. Instead, they got a fine and a short prison sentence each – but they were certainly famous for a while.

So do we all want fame? Research suggests that a large number of us do. According to one recent survey, 30 percent of adults regularly daydream about being famous and 40 percent of us expect to experience some kind of fame in our lifetime. Statistics for teenagers are much higher! Perhaps a better question is: should we want to be famous? Do we really want every aspect of our private lives splashed across the newspapers and discussed on television? Some people, such as talent show contestant Susan Boyle, seem ill-equipped to deal with this kind of pressure, despite their talent. Boyle gained international fame for her extraordinary singing voice after appearing on TV talent show Britain's Got Talent and her debut album became the fastest-selling of all time in the UK. But the sudden fame didn't seem easy for her at first, and after the final of the show, Boyle was admitted to a private psychiatric clinic.

Furthermore, people who achieve fame often don't seem to like it once they have it. A survey of celebrities found that they worry about the press and paparazzi, critics, threatening letters, the lack of privacy, stalkers and the effect on their children (in that order). These are hardly worries that ordinary people have to deal with. They also, ironically, worry about what would happen if they were no longer famous. And there are plenty of people to ask about that. Take Donato Dalrymple, for example, a fisherman who rescued a boy from the sea and enjoyed the media spotlight for several months afterwards. When it ended, however, he resumed his job as a toilet cleaner. 'I know I'm a nobody,' he said when the attention had vanished.

'When the person has to go back to everyday life, there's a sense of disappointment, loss and being cheated out of something,' says Dr Robert Cancro of the New York University School of Medicine. And what's the name for this feeling? He calls it 'Andy Warhol Syndrome'.

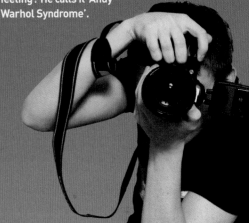

3a Read the introduction to the article and answer the questions.

1 In what ways do you think Warhol's prediction is coming true?
2 How do you think it was different in the past?

b Work in pairs. Read the whole article and discuss. How did the people in the box become famous? Had you heard of any of them before?

George Whitefield   Sam Patch   Falcon Heene
Susan Boyle   Donato Dalrymple

4 Complete the sentences according to the article.

1 _____ fight like gladiators for a record deal.
2 In the 18th century, there were fewer celebrities because there was no _____ .
3 In the 19th century, the rise of celebrities was caused by _____ .
4 Sam Patch died trying to _____ .
5 On TV, the cheapest entertainers are _____ .
6 Richard and Mayumi Heene were probably motivated by a desire for _____ .

7 _____ of teenagers expect to be famous.
8 Susan Boyle spent some time in a psychiatric clinic because _____ .
9 Celebrities' greatest single worry is _____ .
10 Donato Dalrymple possibly suffers from _____ .

5 Work in groups. Discuss the questions below.

• Would you take part in a reality TV show if you had the opportunity? Why/Why not? Which one?
• Do you ever daydream about being famous? If so, what kind of daydreams do you have?
• Why do you think celebrities have become so important in the modern world?
• Are celebrities mainly a good or a bad influence on modern life?

Have you got what it takes to become a celebrity?

Do our quiz and find out.

1 It's a friend's birthday and she wants to go to a club to celebrate, but she's not sure where. What do you do?
   a You suggest going somewhere fun where you're likely to bump into other friends.
   b You don't like making suggestions about where to go. You're happy to let other people decide.
   c You wait and see where your friend decides to go. If it's not 'the right place to be seen', you'll make an excuse and do something else instead.

2 You are at a party where you are introduced to various new people. How do you react?
   a You make a big effort to remember people's names and something about them.
   b You feel too nervous to remember people very well.
   c You expect other people to remember you better than you remember them – that's what usually happens.

3 A friend of yours is marrying someone wealthy, and they are having a big wedding with rich and famous guests. How do you go about choosing an outfit for the big day?
   a You ask other people what they are planning to wear and look for something similar.
   b You look for something special to wear, but it has to be something that you can wear again in the future.
   c You put a lot of effort into finding an outfit that outshines everyone else, including the bride! Impressing the right people at events like this is extremely important.

4 You meet someone who you're desperate to impress. Would you be prepared to tell lies about yourself to make the right impression?
   a No. If people don't respect you as you are, then that's tough.
   b You wouldn't dare tell lies – what if people found out?
   c Why not, if it helps to get you noticed?

5 A rather boring ex-classmate heads towards you at a social gathering. How do you react?
   a You pretend not to remember him and quickly find someone more interesting to talk to.
   b You have a friendly chat, then make an excuse to move on.
   c You are relieved to find someone who won't mind talking to you.

6 You are at a charity event and a reporter from the local newspaper asks you to be in a photograph. How do you react?
   a You aren't especially keen on being photographed, but you co-operate.
   b You pose happily. You've spent ages practising in front of the mirror, so you always look great in photos.
   c You manage to hide behind someone tall.

Scores
Q1: a= 2 b = 1 c = 3, **Q2:** a = 2 b=1 c= 3 **Q3:** a=1 b=2 c=3,
Q4: a=2 b= 1 c=3, **Q5:** a=3 b=2 c=1, **Q6:** a=2 b= 3 c =1

118

Language focus 1
Use of gerunds and infinitives

1 Work in pairs and discuss. If someone really wants to become a celebrity, what kind of personality are they likely to have? Have you ever met anyone like this?

2a Work in pairs and do the quiz.

b Add up your scores using the key below then turn to page 130 and check the quiz conclusions to find out if you have the kind of personality to become a celebrity. Do you agree with what it says?

GRAMMAR

1 Underline all the infinitives (*to* + verb) in the quiz and circle all the gerunds (verb + *-ing*).

2 Match verb patterns 1–10 below to other examples in the quiz.

  1 verb + gerund
    *You **suggest going** somewhere fun.*

  2 preposition + gerund
    *... put effort **into finding** an outfit*

  3 a gerund that is the subject of a sentence
    ***Being** famous is the last thing you would enjoy.*

  4 verb (+ object) + infinitive
    *A reporter **asks you to be** in a photo.*

  5 noun + infinitive
    *You make an **effort to remember** names.*

  6 adjective + infinitive
    *You're **likely to bump** into friends.*

  7 *too* + adjective + infinitive
    *You're too **sensible to worry** about it.*

  8 an infinitive that describes why someone does something (infinitive of purpose)
    *It's all done **to attract** attention.*

  9 (*some*)*where/one/thing* + (adjective +) infinitive
    *... suggestions about **where to go***

  10 verb + (object) + infinitive without *to*
    *You **let** other people **decide**.*

▶ **Read Study 1, page 164**

PRACTICE

1a Complete the quotes below with the correct form of the verbs in brackets.

'A celebrity is a person who works all his life [1]_____ (become) well-known, then wears dark glasses [2]_____ (prevent) people from [3]_____ (recognise) him.' *Fred Allen, comedian*

'[4]_____ (be) a star was never as much fun as [5]_____ (dream) about [6]_____ (be) a star.' *Marilyn Monroe, film star*

'If you don't want [7]_____ (be) forgotten as soon as you are dead, either write things that are worth [8]_____ (read), or do things that are worth [9]_____ (write) about.'
Benjamin Franklin, American statesman

'A writer's fame is the best kind [10]_____ (have): it is enough [11]_____ (get) you a good table in a restaurant, but not enough [12]_____ (mean) that you are interrupted while you are eating.' *Fran Lebowitz, writer*

'I don't want [13]_____ (achieve) immortality through my work. I want [14]_____ (achieve) it through not [15]_____ (die).'
Woody Allen, film director

'[16]_____ (be) a sex symbol was rather like [17]_____ (be) a convict.' *Raquel Welch, actress*

'There is only one thing worse than [18]_____ (be) talked about, and that is not [19]_____ (be) talked about.' *Oscar Wilde, playwright*

b 🎧 **12.1** Listen and check. Which quotes do you like best?

2a Complete the questions below with the correct form of the verbs in brackets.

1 How would you feel about _____ (go) to a big social gathering on your own?
2 On average, how much time do you spend _____ (get) ready before you go out?
3 At parties, etc., are you happy _____ (chat) to people you don't know, or do you tend _____ (stick) with people you know?
4 Are you better at _____ (remember) people's names or _____ (remember) their faces?
5 Do you mainly choose clothes _____ (get) noticed, _____ (fit) in with other people, _____ (feel) comfortable or some other reason?
6 Which do you prefer: _____ (take) photographs, _____ (be) photographed or neither?

b Work in pairs and discuss the questions.

> Unit 12, Study & Practice 1, page 164

Listening
Celebrities and the media

1 Work in pairs. You are going to hear two news stories about celebrities and the media. Check the meaning of the phrases in the boxes. What do you think each story is about?

Story 1

to have an extra-marital affair	to take legal action
to have a strong family image	to bully and tease someone
to be a hypocrite/hypocritical	to have a right to privacy

Story 2

a tabloid newspaper	to hack into someone's phone
to experience paranoia	to accuse someone wrongly
to appear in court	to receive compensation

2 🎧 **12.2** Listen to the two news stories and answer the questions.

1 Why has the 'unnamed entertainer' taken legal action?
2 What happened to Charlotte Morland and her mother?

3a 🎧 **12.3** Listen to a radio phone-in show. Are most listeners sympathetic to the unnamed entertainer and the Morland family?

b Match the listeners to opinions a–f.

Becky — a The public are to blame for buying the newspapers that print such stories.

Carl — b X is using his children as an excuse to protect himself.

Lesley — c Famous people have the right to privacy.

Carol — d It's X's fault if his children are hurt, not the newspaper's.

Gemma — e The treatment of the Morland family was wrong.

Robert — f If a celebrity creates a certain public image, and then behaves in a different way, people have the right to know.

c Listen again and answer the questions.

1 What reasons do they give for their opinions?
2 Does the presenter give any opinions?

4 Work in groups and discuss the questions below.

1 Who do you feel most/least sorry for in the news stories?
2 Which listeners in exercise 3a do/don't you agree with? Why/Why not?
3 Do things like this happen in your country? Can you give any examples?

Language focus 2
Different infinitive and gerund forms

1 Look at the photos. What do you know about each person? If you're not sure who each person is, check on page 130.

2 Read the article and match descriptions A–E with the celebrities in the photos.

3 Which celebrity currently earns the most?

4 Complete the article with the phrases below.

- he hated **being criticised**
- she desperately wanted **to be taken** seriously
- she often seemed **to be suffering**
- he became notorious for **not looking** after himself
- he decided **not to focus** on music any more
- most men would like **to have met**
- despite **having died** in 1977

RICHER
DEAD THAN ALIVE

A She died 50 years ago but achieved immortality through her roles in films such as *Some Like it Hot*. [1]_____ as an actor but she found it hard to deal with the pressure of fame and some directors found her unprofessional. Her death at the age of 36 was surrounded in mystery. Since then, she has become 'the most iconic person in the world' according to image experts, and she is still regularly voted the woman that [2]_____ . Her image currently earns around $27 million a year.

B Not many people know that he started out as an usher, guiding people to their seats in a cinema in Memphis. A recording of *That's Alright* got him noticed and he became an overnight sensation, adored for his good looks, and changing the face of popular music forever. Towards the end of his life, his career went into decline and [3]_____ – later photographs of him show that he had become bloated and unhealthy-looking. However, [4]_____ , he still makes over $55 million a year.

C Together with his band, he recorded his debut album in ten hours while suffering from a cold. The songs he wrote made him a living legend but in 1975 [5]_____ and instead devoted himself to looking after his young son. Five years later, just as he was making a comeback, he was shot dead in New York. He still sells millions of albums and earns around $12 million a year.

D He made his musical debut at the age of six, and had his first hit when he was just 11 years old, going on to become the most famous person on the planet. However, he found the media spotlight difficult, and [6]_____ in the press. Incredibly, in death, he may be making more money from touring than when he was alive, thanks to a stage show bearing his name. Along with sales of his music, he now earns about $170 million a year.

E Born in 1983, she got her first big break at the age of 16 when a record-company executive heard her demo tape by accident, and gave her a recording contract. She developed a reputation for being unreliable, and [7]_____ from drink or drug problems but her songs and performances were often brilliant. Tragically, she died of alcohol poisoning at the age of just 27. During her lifetime, albums such as *Back to Black* earned her $10 million, but after her death, she will probably earn much more.

GRAMMAR

Match the verbs in bold in exercise 4 to the descriptions below.
1 a negative infinitive _not to focus_
2 a negative gerund
   (*not + verb + -ing*) _____
3 a passive infinitive
   (*be + past participle*) _____
4 a passive gerund
   (*being + past participle*) _____
5 a continuous infinitive
   (*be + verb +-ing*) _____
6 a perfect infinitive
   (*have + past participle*) _____
7 a perfect gerund
   (*having + past participle*) _____

▶ Read Study 2, page 165

PRACTICE

1a Read 'Ten things to worry about if you're rich and famous' and choose the correct answers.

b Read 'Ten things to worry about if you're NOT rich and famous.' Complete the list with the correct form of the verbs in brackets.

2a Work in groups. Choose three of the situations below and make a list of five things to not worry about if:

- you're a teenager
- your partner is extremely good-looking and intelligent
- you haven't got a job
- you are a contestant on a reality TV show
- you move to a new city
- you can't speak more than one language
- you hate exercise
- you don't know how to use a computer.

b Work in pairs and compare lists.

PRONUNCIATION

1 🎧 12.4 Listen to six sentences and count the number of words in each (a contraction like *he's* is one word). Then write the sentences.

2a Listen again and mark the stressed words. How are these words pronounced?

b Practise saying the sentences. Listen again if necessary.

> Unit 12, Study & Practice 2, page 165

Ten things to worry about if you're rich and famous

1 Whether or not people really like you, or just like *seeing / being seen* with someone famous.

2 *Following / Being followed* by the paparazzi whenever you go to a fashionable party.

3 *Getting / Not getting* any peace because fans are always trying *taking / to take* photographs of you.

4 Whether or not your dress sense is going *to criticise / to be criticised* by fashion journalists.

5 Ex-boyfriends or girlfriends who threaten *selling / to sell* their story to the newspapers.

6 Whether it's possible for your children to *have / having* a normal childhood.

7 *To have / Having* trouble finding a reliable chauffeur, cleaner and cook.

8 Worrying about your family *kidnapping / being kidnapped*.

9 Wondering whether or not it's worth *selling / to sell* your third home.

10 *Not knowing / Not to know* if your accountant is cheating you.

Ten things to worry about if you're NOT rich and famous

1 Wondering why all your friends seem _____ (become) more successful than you.

2 Never _____ (invite) to fashionable parties.

3 _____ (not have) enough money _____ (be) able to go on holiday.

4 _____ (not have) any money _____ (spend) on new clothes.

5 Acquaintances who refuse _____ (see) with you because you're not successful enough.

6 Whether or not it was a mistake to _____ (have) children, in your financial position.

7 _____ (expect) to do the shopping, clean the house and cook dinner without any help.

8 _____ (not have) enough money _____ (buy) birthday presents for relatives.

9 The fact that your bicycle won't last much longer, and whether or not it's time _____ (sell) it.

10 _____ (give) the wrong change in the supermarket.

Task

Hold the floor!

The Fame Game

The things you would hate about being famous.

What's it like being the child of famous parents?

Why do celebrities' marriages seem to break up more than other people's?

Getting famous via the internet.

A person whose life has been ruined by fame.

Is it easier or more difficult to make friends if you are famous?

A celebrity you can't stand.

Would you ever appear on a reality TV programme?

Hollywood stars.

The things you would enjoy about being famous.

Someone who is famous without having any talent.

If you had to be famous, what would you like to be famous for?

Should there be privacy laws to protect famous people?

Is it possible to be normal if you are a superstar?

Gossip columns and magazines.

RULES

1 Work in groups. Take turns to choose and speak about a topic from one of the cards. Each topic can be chosen only once.

2 The speaker must attempt to speak on the topic without hesitation or repetition.

3 The speaker wins three points if they speak for 30 seconds and 10 points if they speak for a minute. Another member of the group should keep time.

4 If the speaker hesitates for too long or repeats the same idea/point, another group member can say 'challenge'. If the group members agree, the speaker loses a point. The speaker should then try to continue speaking for the remaining time.

Preparation Listening and speaking

1a Work in groups. Make a list of situations when you have to speak at length in front of other people.

in meetings at work, ...

b How do you feel about 'holding the floor' like this?

2a You are going to play a game in which you speak at length about different topics. Read the rules of the game and check that you understand what to do.

b 🎧 12.5 Read the topics on the cards. Then listen to three people playing the game and answer the questions.

- Which topics from the game are they talking about?
- Who did best and why?
- What did the unsuccessful players do wrong?

Task Speaking

1a Work in groups of between three and five. Make a list of ideas for each topic before you play the game. Ask your teacher for any words/phrases you need.

b Look at the Useful language box and think about how you can use the phrases to express some of your ideas.

> Useful language a and b

2 Play the game, following the rules. Who had the highest score in each group?

> Useful language c

Follow up Writing

1 Choose one of the options below.

- Write a comment for a website about one of the topics in the game, giving your opinion.
- Write an imaginary interview with a celebrity of your choice in which you ask them about one or more of the topics in the game. Imagine the answers he/she would give.

USEFUL LANGUAGE

a Putting yourself in someone else's position
I (don't) think I would enjoy (being the centre of attention).
I imagine it's very stressful when ...
It must/can't be very easy (to make friends).
It's probably (very strange) when ...
... would be really amazing

b Making points
The way I see it is ...
To my mind ...
I don't like the way ...
It seems right/wrong to me that ...
It must be difficult ...

c Playing the game
Challenge – repetition!
Challenge – you hesitated!
Well done – that's 30 seconds.

SHARE YOUR TASK

Choose one of the topics from the game that interests you and prepare to speak about it for a minute.

Practise speaking until you feel confident.

Film/Record yourself speaking.

Share your film/recording with other students.

WORLD CULTURE

CHANGING LIVES IN MALAWI

Find out first

1a Work in pairs. Try to complete the factfile about Malawi by choosing the correct answers.

FACTFILE MALAWI

Population:	Around *15 / 55 / 125* million
Life expectancy:	*55 / 65 / 75* years
Average amount to live on per day:	*60 pence / £6 / £16*
Percentage of adults who can read:	*34 / 54 / 74*
Extraordinary fact:	20% of land is covered by *a desert / water / a forest*

b Go online to check your answers or ask your teacher.

Search: Malawi statistics / Malawi factfile

View

2a You are going to watch a video about Martha, a girl from Scotland who changed the lives of children in Malawi. Look at the pictures. How do you think she did this?

b ▶ Watch the video and put the events in the order they happened.

a Martha and her family flew to Malawi.
b Martha's local council banned her from taking photos.
c Martha raised over £100,000 through donations on her site.
d She started a blog about her school dinners.
e Martha became fed up with her school dinners.
f The money was used to build a kitchen in Malawi.
g The site became even more popular.
h The blog went viral.

3 Match the start of a phrase from the video to an ending. Then watch the video again and check your answers.

1 Martha raised	a the headlines at the age of nine.
2 Her simple blog won	b from taking photos.
3 Martha posted photos	c head to Malawi.
4 She didn't expect to hit	d longer go hungry.
5 Her local council banned her	e money to buy meals in Malawi.
6 The donations rolled	f on 60p a day.
7 Martha and family decided to	g worldwide attention.
8 Many Malawians live	h to her blog.
9 Two thousand children will no	I in.

4 Work in pairs. Use your answers to exercise 2b and 3 to retell the story of Martha and her blog.

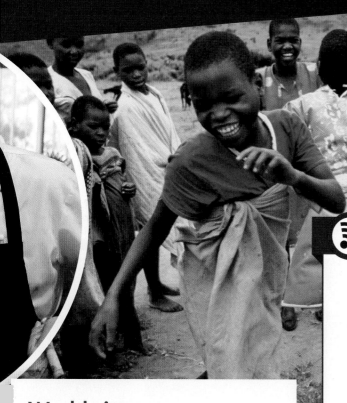

World view

5a ▶ Watch five people answering the question 'Have you ever felt moved to donate money to or help a charitable cause?'. Complete the table (some speakers may not answer every question).

	What was the charity/ cause?	Why were they moved to help?	What did they do?
Jurgen			
Fauzia			
Helen			
Jeanette			
Martin			

b Work in pairs and compare your answers. If necessary, watch again to complete your notes.

c Work in groups. Choose one of the questions below and discuss it.

- Which of the causes mentioned do you feel most moved by?
- Are there any other charitable causes that you feel strongly about?
- Have you ever donated money or done anything to help a charity? If so what and why?
- Which are the most important or popular charities in your country?

🔊 FIND OUT MORE

6a Have you heard of any of the charity events below? Go online to find out where each event takes place.

- Thrill the World
- Red Nose Day
- The Mongol Rally
- Twestival

b Choose one of the global fundraising events and go online to find out more about it. Make notes about the following points:

- how long it has been going
- what the event involves
- how much money it has raised
- what the money is used for

....

Search: Thrill the World / Red Nose Day / Mongol Rally / Twestival

....

Write up your research

7 Write one or two paragraphs about the fundraising event that you researched. Use the prompts below to help you.

- This event has been taking place since ...
- Participants have to ...
- They raise money through sponsorship/donations.
- Each year, the event raises about ...
- Since it began, it has raised around ...
- They money goes towards ... / to help ...

Communication activities

Unit 1: Wordspot
Exercise 3, page 11
Student A

1 Ask Student B the questions below. Student B should give the answers in brackets.

   1 What phrase with *get* means 'to improve'? (get better)

   2 What phrasal verb with *get* means 'to continue with'? (get on with)

   3 What do people hope to get on their birthday? (presents)

   4 What can you get if you don't have a map? (get lost)

   5 Why do people sometimes not laugh at a joke? (they don't get it)

   6 What's the opposite of 'leave the house'? (get home)

2 Answer Student B's questions.

Unit 4: Vocabulary and listening
Exercise 2, page 37

Things to buy/do in town

new toothbrush

post letters

bread

light bulbs

shampoo

birthday card for Granny

envelopes

milk

phone top-up card

have passport photos taken

collect dry-cleaning

cheese

Unit 4: Language focus 1
Practice, exercise 2, page 37

1 Rewrite these passive sentences in a more conversational style, using the active form and the words in brackets.

Brain facts

1 It is said that there are about 100 billion cells in the human brain. (They) They say that there are about 100 billion cells in the human brain.

2 Brain cells can only be seen with a microscope. (You)

3 It is still not known exactly how many aspects of the human brain work. (We)

4 It is often thought that the right side of the brain is the 'artistic' side. (People)

5 In fact, both sides of the brain are used when we listen to music. (We)

6 It has been calculated that messages in the brain travel at over 250 kilometres per hour! (Someone)

7 In ancient times, it was believed that the purpose of the brain was to cool the blood. (People)

8 Research is being done into how the brain is formed. (They)

Unit 11: Language focus 2
Exercise 2b, page 112

What do people regret when they come to the end of their lives? Bronnie Ware, a carer from Australia, recorded the regrets of her patients in her blog, *Inspiration and Chai*. Here are the top five.

a 'If only I'd had the courage to live a life true to myself, not the life others expected of me.'
   - It's very important to try to honour at least some of your dreams.

b 'I wish I hadn't worked so hard.'
   - This came from every male patient that I nursed.

c 'If only I'd had the courage to express my feelings.'
   - Many people suppressed their feelings in order to keep the peace with others.

d 'I wish I'd stayed in touch with my friends.'
   - It all comes down to love and relationships in the end.

e 'I wish that I had let myself be happier.'
   - Many people did not realise until too late that happiness is a choice.

Unit 2: Reading and speaking
Exercise 3, page 18
Student B

Happiness facts and myths

Talk to strangers

Most of the time, we avoid strangers. It's one of the first lessons we learn as children. But according to Dr Richard Wiseman, it's a habit we should change. Talking to strangers opens up new possibilities in life. It increases the chances of finding luck and friendship. Choosing which strangers to talk to obviously requires a bit of common sense and judgement, but Liz Barry and Bill Wetzel from New York were so inspired by the idea that they started the Talk to Me project. For three years, they sat at bus stops, on street corners and any other place they could find in New York, holding a sign saying 'Talk to me'. They encountered hostility and suspicion sometimes, but in general they were surprised by the kindness they encountered. 'In an ideal world,' Bill said, 'we would never need the sign.'

A wandering mind is not a happy mind

Many philosophical and religious traditions tell us that happiness can be found by living in the present. Now there is some scientific support for this belief. Recent research by Harvard University psychologists found that we spend 46.9 percent of our waking time daydreaming. And when we daydream, we are less happy, the research found. Activities which make us focus on the present, such as exercising or talking to friends, tend to make us happier than ones which allow us to daydream, like resting or using a computer. There is an 'emotional cost', as one of the researchers put it, to thinking about what is not happening.

Clean your way to happiness

How many people actually enjoy doing housework? Not many, you might think, but a recent study by Dr Caroline Gatrell of the University of Lancaster found that men are happier if they do regular housework. Dr Gatrell interviewed over 1,000 fathers and found that those who do more housework are less stressed than those who do a smaller amount. They're also more likely to stay married. However, that doesn't mean that all men in the UK are following the path to happiness. If current rates of change continue, it will be 2050 before men and women are sharing the household chores equally.

The sunnier the country the happier the people?

Most people would expect this to be true. After all, who doesn't feel happier when the sun is shining? But global surveys continually show that some of the happiest countries in the world are colder than average. The northern European countries of Norway, Denmark and Sweden are all in the top five of the Legatum Prosperity Index, which measures how happy a country is. To be fair, weather probably isn't very important in these surveys; they measure other factors like education, health and safety. But it does go to show that it takes more than sunny weather to make us feel good.

Unit 5: Language focus 1
Practice, exercise 2a, page 47

plans for a party or celebration in the near future

journeys you are likely to make in the next few months

your career plans

sporting fixtures in the next couple of months and your predictions for them

what the weather will be like over the next seven days

your plans for the rest of this week

your plans for when you finish this English course

how the world will be different in 80 years' time

your plans for this weekend

your hopes for the future

your plans for this evening

your next birthday

how your life will be different in ten years' time

what you're planning to do with your money over the next few months

Unit 9: Writing
Exercise 3a, page 95

PART-TIME CHILDMINDER

Responsible, friendly and enthusiastic person (male or female) required 15 hours a week to care for two boys (aged 8 and 10) before and after school, to supervise homework, cook meals, etc. Driving licence essential.
Would suit student.
Please apply in writing to Sylvia Markoni, 99 Apple Tree Drive, Bath, BA23 7TD.

Communication activities

Unit 1: Wordspot
Exercise 3, page 11
Student B

1 Answer Student A's questions.

2 Ask Student A the questions below. Student A should give the answers in brackets.

1 If it's too far to walk, and you can't afford a taxi, what can you get? (get the bus)
2 What phrasal verb with *get* means 'have a good relationship'? (get on well with someone)
3 What phrase is the opposite of 'get better'? (get worse)
4 What will probably happen if you walk for ten kilometres? (you'll get tired)
5 If you are travelling in a lift and it stops between floors then it ...? (gets stuck)
6 What's the opposite of 'leave work'? (get to work)

Unit 6: Language focus 2
Exercise 1b, page 62

Answers
1 In 2009, Agris Kazelniks ran 20 metres in 11.40 seconds. He was carrying 300 kg at the time.
2 Tom Sietas set a new world record when he swam 200 metres. He did it underwater.
3 Paddy Doyle completed 1,868 press ups in one hour in 1993. He only used one arm.
4 In 2004, Sonya Thomas ate 5 kg of cheesecake. She did it in nine minutes.
5 In 2010, Andrew Dahl inflated 23 balloons in three minutes. He used his nose.

Unit 6: Wordspot
Exercise 3b, page 63

Which expression with *first* ...
1 has the same meaning as 'mother tongue'?
2 means 'initially'?
3 is the opposite of 'last thing at night'?
4 means the thing or place that you or want most?
5 means 'of the very best quality'?
6 means you fall in love with someone as soon as you meet them?
7 means that you are in the leading position?
8 is the idea of people or things that you get when you first see them?
9 is a type of simple medical care?
10 means 'before everything else'?

Unit 8: Task
Preparation, exercise 3a, page 82
Student A

Isidor Fink: a real life 'locked room' mystery

On 9th March 1929, the body of 31-year-old Isidor Fink was found in the back room of the laundry he owned on Fifth Avenue, New York. Fink was an immigrant from modern day Lithuania and it seems that he had very few friends and no family. On that evening, he had made several laundry deliveries before returning to his living quarters at 10:15 p.m. At 10:30 his neighbour heard screams (but no gunshots) and decided to call the police.

A police officer happened to be nearby and managed to reach the scene only a few minutes after the first screams had been heard. After interviewing the neighbour, the officer tried the front door but found that it had been locked from the inside. Testing the windows, he found them all nailed shut on the inside, too. Because the windows were too small for an adult to get through, the police officer asked a small boy to climb in and unlock the front door.

The officer was finally able to get into the apartment and survey the scene. Fink's body lay on the floor, ten metres from the doorway. There were three gunshot wounds to the body: two in the chest and one in his left wrist. However, there was no gun in the apartment, and no valuables had been stolen: there was money both in Fink's pocket and in his cash register.

The police searched the premises for hidden doors, but none were discovered. They investigated Fink's background, but found no connections with the gangsters who terrorised much of New York at that time. However, Fink was certainly frightened of something: he had made the laundry into a kind of fortress. All the windows had heavy iron bars, and it was equipped with the best locks that money could buy.

No one was ever arrested for the murder of Isidor Fink and no motive was ever found. Two years later in a radio interview, the officer in charge of the investigation, Commissioner Mulrooney, declared the case 'an unsolvable mystery' and to this day it remains in the 'unsolved cases' files of New York City Police.

Unit 5: Speaking
Exercise 4, page 54

1 Who is speaking?
  a boyfriend/girlfriend
  b customer/telephonist
  c two colleagues
  d two friends
  e other
2 Why/What about?
  a for a friendly chat
  b to make a complaint
  c to arrange a business meeting
  d to arrange a night out
  e other
3 What problem occurs?
  a it's a bad time to call
  b keep getting the wrong person
  c problems on the line
  d other
4 How is the problem resolved?
  a you arrange to phone back another time
  b you get cut off
  c you hang up
  d other

Unit 8: Task
Speaking, exercise 4, page 82

Crime experts now believe they know what happened to Fink. No gun was found, so he can't have committed suicide. And his murderer can't have got into the room and escaped, because of the barred windows and locked doors. The only other possibility, therefore, is that he was shot at the door and then somehow managed to lock the doors himself, before staggering across the room and collapsing dead on the floor. This might also explain why he had a bullet hole in his wrist: the murderer may have shot at his hands as he was struggling with all those bolts and keys.

The Walton case was unusual in many ways: there are few cases where there have been so many eye witnesses to corroborate someone's account of an abduction, and few cases where the police have been so closely involved throughout. On the other hand, there have been many who are sceptical about the story. It has been suggested that the whole story was cooked up to get money out of the forestry company that the men worked for; experts point out that a TV programme about UFO abductions had been broadcast shortly before and may have given the men the idea. It has even been claimed that Walton was friendly with a local LSD addict and may have spent the missing days with him, and hallucinated about aliens. However, none of this has ever been proven. To this day, no one knows for sure whether Travis Walton's story is the truth or a clever hoax.

Unit 9: Speaking
Exercise 4, page 94

a Choose one of the situations below.

Situation 1
- Like Lisa, A hates his/her job and wants a change. B, a friend, makes suggestions.
- A is fed up and wants to take up a new interest or do an evening course. B, a friend, makes suggestions.
- A has met an attractive member of the opposite sex, but fears that he/she has not noticed him/her. B, a friend, makes suggestions.

Situation 2
- B has to give a presentation to work colleagues next month and doesn't know how to go about it, so he/she approaches A, a senior colleague with a lot of experience of presentations for advice. (A, turn to audio script 9.5 on page 175 for ideas.)
- B is a student who needs to improve their spoken English rapidly for a new job. He/She approaches A, an experienced English teacher, for advice.
- B wants to get a job in A's field of work. A gives advice.

b Think about how formal the situation is. Spend a couple of minutes planning what you will say.

c Act the situations out using appropriate phrases from exercise 3a on page 94.

Unit 10: Wordspot
Exercise 2b, page 101

1 What are the main talking points in the news today?
2 If you're not on speaking terms with someone, how do you feel towards them?
3 According to the saying, what speaks louder than words?
4 Do you ever listen to talk radio? Why/Why not?
5 Do you tend to speak your mind about things, or do you keep your opinions to yourself?
6 If someone spoke highly of you, would you be angry or pleased?
7 What reasons might there be for someone to talk to himself/herself?
8 Do you think you know what you're talking about when it comes to cooking?
9 If people 'talk shop', what are they talking about?
10 Can you name a popular talk-show host in your country? Do you like him/her?
11 What kind of people would probably take part in peace talks?
12 On what occasions do you hear a lot of small talk?
13 Do people sometimes ask you to speak up?

Communication activities

Unit 8: Task
Preparation, exercise 3a, page 82
Student B

Travis Walton: abducted by aliens?

On 5th November, 1975, a forestry worker called Travis Walton was driving home through the woods near Snowflake, Arizona with six of his colleagues, when apparently, a golden disc about six metres wide suddenly appeared, hovering above the ground ahead of them. The seven men stared in amazement. Then Travis did something extraordinary. He got out of the truck and walked towards the disc. 'I was afraid it would fly away and I would miss the chance of a lifetime,' he wrote later.

As Travis got closer, the disc made a loud noise. Then, according to all seven men, a beam of blue-green light shot out from the disc and held Travis above the ground before throwing him backwards. He landed several metres away and didn't move. 'Let's get out of here!' screamed one of the men in the truck and they drove away.

After a short distance, the men stopped and decided to go back and find their friend. When they got to where the disc had been, it was gone, and so was Travis. The police were soon involved and searches began. But no trace of him could be found.

As the days passed, police became suspicious of the men's story. All of the men were given a lie detector test, which they all passed. Then, five days after the disappearance, Travis's brother-in-law received a phone call: 'This is Travis and I need help. Come and get me.' Travis was found on the floor of the phone booth wearing the same clothing as when he had disappeared. He seemed afraid and upset and kept talking about aliens with terrifying eyes. He thought he'd only been gone for a few hours.

After he recovered, Travis told an extraordinary story of being inside the UFO. He described strange aliens with enormous brown eyes and humans who smiled but said nothing. Soon after the event, Travis was given a lie-detector test. He failed. A few months later, he took two more tests, both of which he passed.

Unit 12: Language focus 1
Exercise 2b, page 118

9 points or less

You lack confidence, and tend to hide behind other people (sometimes literally!). You worry too much about what other people think and are frightened to stand out from the crowd. Being famous is the last thing in the world you would enjoy. There's nothing wrong with that, but try to believe in yourself a bit more. If you don't, no one else will!

Celebrity potential: 0/10

9 to 13 points

You are self-confident and comfortable in your own skin and you always try to treat other people with consideration. You are far too sensible to worry about being famous. If you attract attention in life that's great, but you aren't going to lose any sleep over it!

Celebrity potential: 5/10

14 to 18 points

You are supremely confident that other people find you fascinating, and almost everything you do is done to attract attention. Getting noticed is more important to you than other people's feelings. (Other people's feelings don't really matter to you.) Perhaps you'll get lucky and make it big, but you may find it lonely at the top!

Celebrity potential: 10/10

Unit 12: Language focus 2
Exercise 1, page 120

- From left to right: Michael Jackson, Elvis Presley, Marilyn Monroe, John Lennon, Amy Winehouse.

STUDY 1

Past and present verb forms

1 Present simple and Present continuous

While the Present simple is used for things that happen **regularly** or that we see as **permanent**, the Present continuous is used for things that we see as **temporary**, **incomplete** or happening over a **limited period of time**.

*Normally, I **take** the train to work ...* (= this is what I usually do)
*... but this week I**'m coming** by bicycle.* (= for a limited period)

2 Past simple and Past continuous

- The Past simple is used to describe actions or states in the past that we see as **complete**. The time when the action happened is often stated or understood.
  *Jane **went** to visit her aunt in hospital **yesterday**. She **got** home at about eight.*
- The Past continuous is used to describe actions or states that were **in progress** at a point of time in the past, or that we see as in some way **incomplete**.
  *I **was driving** along when suddenly, a dog ran into the road.*

3 State and action verbs

- A number of verbs (state verbs) describe states rather than actions. They are rarely found in continuous forms. These include:
  a verbs that describe thought processes and opinions
    agree, believe, disagree, forget, know, remember, think
  b verbs that describe emotions
    adore, detest, like, love, hate, want
  c verbs that describe the five senses
    feel, hear, see, smell, taste
  d others
    be, belong, have, seem, own
- Some verbs can describe both states and actions, but there is a change of meaning.
  state: *He's very friendly.* (= this is his character)
  action: *He's **being** very friendly.* (= he is behaving this way, he is not usually like this)
  state: *They **have** an apartment near the town centre.* (= possess)
  action: *They**'re having** a coffee.* (= taking)
  state: *I **think** you're absolutely right.* (= this is my opinion)
  action: *I**'m thinking** about what you said.* (= considering, it is in my mind)

4 *Used to*

We use *used to* for describing habits and states in the past. We can always use the Past simple instead of *used to*, but we cannot use *used to* for actions that happen only once. With *used to*, we don't say how many times or how long.
*I **used to** go to my grandmother's every Sunday.*

5 Present perfect and Past simple

- The Present perfect is used when an action happened in the past, but is linked to the present. It is still relevant or important **now**.
  *She's **broken** her leg.* (= her leg is broken now)
  *I **haven't read** 'War and Peace'.* (= I am unfamiliar with it now)
- The Past simple is used for actions or states which we see as being **completely in the past**. These time phrases are often used with the Past simple.
  Last (week/summer, etc.), ago, after, before, then, in 2009, etc.
- If an action continues over a period of time up to the present, we use the Present perfect. To describe a finished period of time in the past, we use the Past simple.
  *I've **worked** in Singapore for two years.* (= I still work there now)
  *I **worked** in Singapore for two years.* (= completely in the past, I don't work there now)

6 Past perfect

- The Past perfect is used for things which happened **before a point of time in the past**.
  *Claire **had left** by the time he arrived.*

- Compare this to the Present perfect, which is used for things which happened **before the present** but are linked to the present.
  *Oh no! Claire's already **left**.* (= she's not here now)

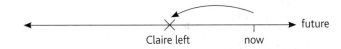

PRACTICE 1

1 Look at sentences 1–4. Are statements a–c below true (T) or false (F)?

1 We used to go to Spain for our holidays.
  a We went to Spain once. ☐
  b We went to Spain more than once. ☐
  c We go to Spain now. ☐
2 They'd started dinner when we arrived.
  a When we arrived, they began eating. ☐
  b When we arrived, they were eating. ☐
  c When we arrived, the meal was finished. ☐
3 I worked as a travel courier for several years.
  a I'm a travel courier now. ☐
  b I used to be a travel courier. ☐
  c I was a travel courier but I'm not now. ☐
4 Jamie's lost his wallet.
  a His wallet was lost but he's got it back now. ☐
  b His wallet is lost now. ☐
  c We don't know if his wallet is still lost. ☐

2 Choose the correct verb form.

1 When I was younger, I *have played* / *play* / *used to play* football on the beach with my friends.

2 In his 20s, Michael *has lived* / *lived* / *used to live* in the US for a year.

3 This week, Kate *is looking after* / *looks after* / *used to look after* the shop for the owner.

4 Unfortunately, the concert *had started* / *started* / *used to start* when we got there, so we missed the first song.

5 I *read* / *was reading* / *used to read* the newspaper the other day, when I saw an interesting job advertisement.

6 I *have seen* / *saw* / *used to see* Neil yesterday.

7 Can I call you back later? We*'re having* / *have* / *have had* lunch right now.

8 *Did it rain* / *Was it raining* / *Has it rained* when you last looked outside?

9 *Does* / *Is* / *Has* this umbrella *belong* / *belonging* / *belonged* to you?

STUDY 2

Uses of auxiliary verbs

Auxiliary verbs are often used to emphasise things, show interest, ask questions or avoid repetition.

- **To emphasise**
  *I **do** hate it when my neighbour plays his music so loud.*
  *I'm sure I **did** lock the door.*

- **In questions**
  You can show interest in what someone said by responding with a short question using an auxiliary verb. The auxiliary verb must agree with the tense and person of the main sentence.
  A: *I've got six grandchildren.*
  B: ***Have you**? How lovely!*
  A: *We didn't like the film at all.*
  B: *Really, **didn't you**, why not?*
  Notice here that positive questions are used with positive sentences, and negative questions are used with negative sentences.

  Question tags at the end of a statement encourage the listener to respond. Here, negative questions are used with positive sentences, and positive questions with negative sentences.
  *You've remembered (+) your keys, **haven't** (−) you?*
  *It isn't (−) a very nice day, **is** (+) it?*
  If there is no doubt about the statement, the voice goes down.

  *It isn't a very nice day, **is** it?*
  If there is an element of doubt, the voice goes up.

  *You've remembered your keys, **haven't** you?*

- **To avoid repetition**
  We also use auxiliary verbs to avoid repeating whole phrases.
  *I enjoyed the film very much, but most of my friends **didn't**.*
  (= enjoy the film very much)
  *The other students in the class don't understand Italian, but Alexandra **does**.* (= understand Italian)
  This is common in answers to *yes/no* questions.
  A: *Have you done your homework yet?*
  B: *Yes, actually, I **have**.* (= done my homework)

PRACTICE 2

1 Write an auxiliary verb in the correct position in each sentence.

was

1 The test wasn't as difficult as we expected, ^ it?

2 You don't like Marta very much, you?

3 Kate wasn't keen on sport before, but she now.

4 **A:** Steve's decided to look for a new job.
   B: he? What made him want to leave?

5 **A:** Did you see anything unusual in the park, Mr Ball?
   B: Yes, I. There was a group of young men acting suspiciously.

6 Marina looks well, she?

7 **A:** We haven't been here before.
   B: you? That's surprising.

2 Rewrite the underlined verbs with an auxiliary, to give the sentence greater emphasis.

I <u>enjoyed</u> the concert last night, it was really good.
I did enjoy the concert last night, it was really good.

1 I <u>love</u> your new hairstyle.

2 Alex <u>makes</u> me laugh.

3 I <u>heard</u> you the first time.

4 I <u>think</u> you're right.

5 I <u>waited</u> for you for ages.

6 You <u>speak</u> good English!

3 Match sentences 1–10 to responses a–j.

1 Does Amy like cats?

2 We went to Paris at the weekend.

3 Do you take sugar?

4 Are you sure you want to come?

5 I was 21 yesterday.

6 Have you seen *Star Trek II*?

7 Are you Japanese?

8 We've got four cats.

9 I'm going shopping. Can I get you anything?

10 Did you speak to Sarah yesterday?

a I haven't but the children have.

b No, she doesn't.

c I do need some sugar.

d Yes, I do want to, honestly.

e I do, but John doesn't.

f I am but Kim isn't.

g Oh! Did you?

h Really? Were you?

i Have you?

j Yes, I did.

REMEMBER THESE WORDS

RELATIONSHIPS

to be close to someone
to be fun to be with
to be loyal/disloyal to someone
to be jealous of someone
to be supportive
to be violent towards someone
to compete with someone
to confide in someone
a destructive relationship
to fall out with someone
to feel inferior/superior to
  someone
to feel threatened by someone

to (not) get on with someone
to gossip about someone behind
  their back
to (not) have a lot in common
(a relationship) isn't going
  anywhere
to keep a promise
to lie to someone
to loathe someone
to put someone down
to respect someone
a rivalry
a sibling
to tell the truth
to trust someone

PHRASES WITH *GET*

to get $50,000 a year
to get a better job
to get a cold
to get a flight
to get a joke
to get a present
to get a shock
to get angry
to get better/worse
to get home

to get lost
to get on (well) with someone
to get on with your work
to get over an illness
to get stuck
to get the bus
to get tired
to get to work
to get what someone is saying

OTHER

to boast
a civil war
a coincidence
to cost a fortune

to do something against
  someone's advice
to end up doing something

PRACTICE

1 How many missing adjectives/verbs can you complete
  without using a dictionary? Use a dictionary to complete
  the rest of the table.

verb	adjective
1 to compete	
2	destructive
3 to respect	
4	supportive
5 to trust	

2 Find at least eight verbs in the 'relationships' word
  list that can be used with *each other*. Write example
  sentences. Remember any necessary prepositions.

  Katie and her brother are very jealous of each other.

3 Cover the word list and complete the sentences below
  with the correct word in the box (there is one extra
  word).

| on | down | out | on | up | over |

1 I hate my boss, he's always putting me _____ .
2 Can you stop talking and get _____ with your work.
3 Pat's very easy going. She gets _____ with everyone.
4 You children be good – no falling _____ please!
5 I've had a really bad cold, but hopefully I'm getting
  _____ it now.

4 Choose the best phrase.

1 If you don't take the SatNav you'll *get lost / get a cold*.
2 That's a funny one! I *get the joke / get on well with it*.
3 I had quite a frightening experience today – I *got stuck /
  got angry* in a lift.
4 If you want to *get better / get a better job* you need to
  get some qualifications.
5 I *got a shock / got tired* when I saw him lying there.
  Thankfully, he was fine.
6 Take this pill. It'll help you *get over it / get a present*.

STUDY TIPS

Five steps to better writing

1 What are your most common problems with written
  English? Choose from the list or your own ideas.

  - spelling
  - grammar
  - coming up with ideas
  - using natural phrases
  - organising your ideas
  - finding the right words

2 The five steps below will help you to write more
  effectively in English. Which steps do you already follow?

  1 Preparing and gathering information
  List the topics and examples you might include.

  2 Structuring
  Put your ideas into a logical order. Remove any ideas
  which don't fit your structure.

  3 First draft
  Write a first draft within a time limit.

  4 Checking and feedback
  Show your draft to another student or check it
  yourself. Ask questions such as: *Is there a better
  word/phrase that I could use? Have I used enough
  punctuation? Have I used the correct verb forms?*

  5 Final draft
  Use the feedback to write your final draft. Check it
  for spelling, grammar and punctuation.

3 Write a paragraph about the qualities that a best friend
  should have. Follow the five steps above. Is there a big
  difference between your first and second draft?

STUDY 1

Forming adjectives

1 Prefixes used to form opposites

prefix	examples
dis-*	disloyal, displeased
il-	illegal, illiterate
im-	immature, impossible
in-	inexperienced, insecure
un-*	unhappy, unpopular

* Note that these prefixes can also be used with some verbs, e.g. *disagree*, *unlock*.

prefix	examples	meaning
anti-	anti-social, anti-war	against
mis-	misunderstood, mismanaged	badly, in the wrong way
non-	non-stop, non-smoking	without, not
over-	over-cooked	too much
post-	post-war	after
pre-	pre-war	before
pro-	pro-European	in favour of
re-	reunited, recharged	again
self-	self-confident	relating to itself
under-	under-cooked	not enough
good/well/better	good-tempered	good
bad/badly	bad-tempered	bad

2 Common suffixes for adjectives

suffix	examples
-able*, -ible	miserable, responsible
-al	physical, psychological
-ant, -ent, -ient	pleasant, violent, efficient
-ed	depressed, talented
-ful	powerful, successful
-ic	enthusiastic, scientific
-ure	insecure, unsure
-ing	exciting, frustrating
-ive	aggressive, intensive
-less	restless, hopeless (= without)
-ious, -ous	anxious, nervous
-y	grumpy, wealthy

* This suffix sometimes means 'can be' (*washable* = can be washed)

REMEMBER!

Many adjectives to describe feelings have both an *-ing* and an *-ed* form. The *-ed* form describes how you feel.
*I'm very **tired** this morning*
The *-ing* form describes what makes you feel that way.
*Looking after babies can be very **tiring**.*
However, not all *-ed / -ing* adjectives have both forms.
*Ben is a very **talented** musician.*
*Fortunately, her illness isn't **catching**.*

PRACTICE 1

1 Add prefixes to form the opposite of the adjectives below.

1 ___experienced
2 ___popular
3 ___loyal
4 ___attractive
5 ___possible

6 ___friendly
7 ___polite
8 ___respectful
9 ___enthusiastic
10 ___correct

2 Choose the correct definition.

1 anti-war = *against / in favour of* war
2 non-violent = *against / without* violence
3 over-confident = *too confident / not confident enough*
4 pre-paid = paid for *in advance / afterwards*
5 post-natal = *before / after* birth
6 misinformed = *given the wrong information / informed again*

3 Which word in each group does not belong with the suffix?

1 *success- / power- / talent-*   ful
2 *confid- / persist- / pleas-*   ent
3 *disappoint- / enthusiast- / pessimist-*   ic
4 *health- / import- / wealth-*   y
5 *hope- / imagine- / penni-*   less

Forming nouns and gerunds

1 Common suffixes for nouns

- **-ance** and **-ence** are often used to form abstract nouns from adjectives ending in -ant or -ent.
  patient → patience
  tolerant → tolerance
- **-ee** is used to describe a person on whom an action is performed.
  employee (= person who is employed)
  trainee (= person who is being trained)
- **-er, -ian** and **-or** are often used for people or things that do a particular job.
  act → actor
  music → musician
  football → footballer
  open → can opener
- **-hood** is used to form abstract nouns, especially those concerned with periods of life or relationships between people.
  child → childhood
  mother → motherhood
- **-ism** is often used to describe particular religions or ideologies, and with some abstract nouns.
  Buddhism, liberalism, criticism, cynicism
- **-ist** is used to describe people's beliefs and sometimes their occupation.
  communist, journalist, pianist
- **-ity, -iety** and **-y** are used to form nouns from adjectives.
  anxious → anxiety
  immune → immunity
- **-tion, -(s)sion, -ion** and **ation** are ften used to form nouns from verbs.
  imagine → imagination
  admit → admission
- **-ment** is often used to form abstract nouns from verbs.
  enjoy → enjoyment
  move → movement
- **-ness** is very commonly used to form abstract nouns from adjectives.
  happy → happiness
  nervous → nervousness
- **-our, -iour** and **-ure** are often used to form abstract nouns.
  behaviour
  pleasure
- **-ship** is used to form abstract nouns, usually about relationships.
  friend → friendship
  member → membership

REMEMBER!

Many other nouns are exactly the same as the verb form.

to comment → a comment
to drive → a drive
to decrease → a decrease
to study → a study

2 Gerunds

The gerund (-ing form) is used in the same way as a noun, either as the subject or object of the sentence, or alone. It is commonly used:

- to describe general activities or abstract ideas. (We cannot use the infinitive here.)
  Trusting your children is very important.
  Walking and swimming are my favourite forms of exercise.
- when there is no single noun to describe that idea.
  Going to the dentist's makes me really nervous.
- when ideas or activities are not put into complete sentences. These can be in written lists:
  Our priorities for next year are:
  – cutting costs;
  – expanding into new markets.
  or in conversation:
  A: So, what's your idea of relaxation?
  B: Having a nice long bath and reading my book.

▌PRACTICE 2

1 Complete the nouns below with the suffixes in the box.

-ee   -ence   -iety   -ion   -our   -ism
-ment   -ness   -ship   -ance

1 hon_____	6 move_____
2 depress_____	7 interview_____
3 evid_____	8 anx_____
4 pessim_____	9 annoy_____
5 member_____	10 tired_____

2 Complete the second sentence with a noun so it means the same as the first.

1 Were you happy as a **child**?
   Did you have a happy _____ ?
2 To do this job, you need to be very **creative**.
   To do this job, you need to have a lot of _____ .
3 Roy and I have always been very close **friends**.
   Roy and I have a very close _____ .
4 I can understand why you are so **anxious**.
   I can understand your _____ .
5 He is **employed** by the post office.
   He is an _____ of the post office.
6 The staff were very **hostile** to their new manager.
   The staff felt a lot of _____ towards their new manager.

3 Underline the words in bold which should be in the -ing form.

1 Many people who wish to **improve** their fitness **find** that **go** to the gym is easier and more sociable than **do** exercise at home.
2 **Join** an internet chat room has become a popular way of **meet** new people.
3 Don't you **think** that **go** out and **take** exercise in the fresh air is better for you than **spend** half your life **sit** in front of a computer screen?
4 **Change** your lifestyle is a better way of **lose** weight than **go** on a crash diet.

REMEMBER THESE WORDS

ADJECTIVES TO DESCRIBE FEELINGS

amused	impatient
awkward	insecure
cheerful	panicky
curious	unsociable
dissatisfied	upset
enthusiastic	optimistic
frustrated	pessimistic
grumpy	

WORDS WITH PREFIXES THAT CHANGE THE MEANING

antisocial	postgraduate
bad-tempered	pro-/anti-government
being a (non)conformist	self-aware
financial (in)security	self-centred
good and bad things in life	self-confident
over/underpaid	self-critical
non-/anti-smoking	underfed
non-stop	well-being
non-violent	

OTHER

an active social life	to inherit a fortune
to commute	intellectual stimulation
companionship	a lack of confidence
contentment	a lack of money
criticism	loneliness
to daydream	random
determined	rational
an employee	to pay taxes
exhaustion	a purpose
fascinating	support
to get into debt	to take a nap
to giggle	talented
to give you the creeps	to track something
hostility	violence

PRACTICE

1 Complete the gaps.

	adjective	noun
1	exhausting	*exhaustion*
2	_____	security
3	financial	_____
4	intellectual	_____
5	panicky	_____
6	_____	impatience
7	_____	hostility
8	enthusiastic	_____
9	curious	_____
10	aware	_____
11	creative	_____
12	_____	contentment
13	optimistic	_____
14	fit	_____

2 Complete the sentences.

behaviour   creeps   fortune   giggle
nap   security   social life

1 The silly picture on Jake's T-shirt made everyone _____ .
2 My grandparents are 80, but still have an active _____ .
3 Lola decided to join the civil service because of the financial _____ .
4 That mask you are wearing really gives me the _____ .
5 When his father died, Alistair inherited a _____ .
6 I think the children should take a _____ before we go out, or they'll be tired.
7 Our neighbours have been reported to the police for anti-social _____ .

STUDY TIPS

Using a dictionary for wordbuilding

1 Use the extracts below to find ...

• the past tense, -ing form and third person (*he, she, it*) form of *satisfy*.
• the noun from *satisfy*, and its opposite.
• three adjectives from *satisfy*. Find the difference in meaning, and the opposite of each one.

satisfaction \ˌsætɪəsˈfækʃən\ *n* a feeling of happiness because you have achieved something [opposite = *dissatisfaction*]

satisfactory \ˌsætɪəsˈfæktəri\ *adj* something that is satisfactory seems good enough for a particular situation [opposite = *unsatisfactory*]

satisfied \ˌsætɪəsfaɪd\ *adj* pleased because something has happened as you want, or because you have got what you want [opposite = *dissatisfied*]

satisfy \ˌsætɪəsfaɪ\ *v* satisfied, satisfying, satisfies to make someone pleased by doing what they want

satisfying \ˌsætɪəsfaɪ-ɪŋ\ *adj* making you feel pleased and happy, because you have got what you wanted [opposite = *unsatisfying*]

2 Complete the sentences below with a word related to *satisfy*. For each missing word, think about ...

• whether you need a verb, noun, adjective, etc.
• if there is more than one adjective, noun form, etc. Make sure you choose the word which makes sense in the gap.
• if you need to add any prefixes, suffixes, etc. (there may be more than one).

1 It was very _____ to beat our rivals United in the final.
2 Although we could still do better, our overall progress has been _____ .
3 There is much _____ with the government over recent failures.
4 This work is _____ . You will need to do it again.
5 He's _____ with the investigation, and wants a new one.

STUDY 1

Narrative tenses

Past simple	I work**ed**	Verb + -ed (regular verbs)
Past continuous	you **were** work**ing**	was/were + verb + -ing
Past perfect simple	she **had** work**ed**	had + past participle
Past perfect continuous	she **had been** work**ing**	had + been + verb + -ing

1 Past simple and Past continuous

- The Past simple describes the **main events** in a past narrative.
  *I **called** the police and they **arrived** more or less straightaway.*

- The Past continuous describes **actions in progress** at the time of the main events.
  *When they **got** home, everyone **was waiting** to greet them.*

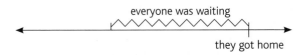

2 Past perfect simple and Past perfect continuous

- Both these tenses describe events **before** the events in the main narrative. They are 'the past of the past'.
  *The suspects **had disappeared** when the police arrived.*

The Past perfect continuous emphasises the duration of an event, and often describes actions which continue up until the main past events.
*He **had been waiting** for hours when we **got** there.*

PRACTICE 1

1 One of the Past simple verbs in each sentence below should be in the Past perfect simple or Past perfect continuous. Correct the verbs. You may need to change the word order.

had been crying
1 It was obvious that she ~~cried~~ because her eyes were red.
2 As soon I saw his new girlfriend, I realised that we met before.
3 The passengers were very frustrated by the time someone finally made an announcement. They waited for several hours.
4 Everyone was amazed at his appearance – they never saw anyone with dyed blue hair before.
5 When I looked out of the window in the morning everywhere was white – it snowed all night.
6 Two hours before his best man's speech, John still didn't decide what to say.
7 When they got married, they only knew each other for a few months.

2 Put the verbs in the story in the correct tense: Past simple, Past continuous, Past perfect or Past perfect continuous. There may be more than one correct form.

My friend ¹_____ (travel) on a domestic flight in South America a few years ago when something quite funny ²_____ (happen). They ³_____ (fly) for about 40 minutes, when the pilot ⁴_____ (suddenly start) speaking excitedly in Spanish. Most of the passengers ⁵_____ (run) forward, shouting, and in panic my friend ⁶_____ (get) into the crash position, leaning forward with his head between his knees. He ⁷_____ (sit) like that for some minutes when one of the cabin crew kindly ⁸_____ (explain) to him that they ⁹_____ (fly) over the Angel Falls, and ¹⁰_____ (ask) if he would like to look out of the window like the other passengers!

3 Choose the correct verbs.

Knock, Knock!

Last Monday I ¹*worked / 'd worked / was working* at home when someone ²*knocked / 'd knocked / was knocking* on the door. It was the postman.

'I have a packet for you, which needs a signature,' he said. ³*I'm living / I lived / I'd been living* in my house for three years and I ⁴*hadn't seen / didn't see / hadn't been seeing* this postman before, so ⁵*I asked / I was asking / I'd asked* him, 'Could I see some identification, please?'

⁶*He'd looked / He looked / He'd been looking* at me strangely.

'Madam, if I'd wanted to break into your house, I would have used these,' he said and ⁷*pulled / was pulling / had been pulling* the keys out of the front door.

STUDY 2

Continuous aspect in other tenses

Present continuous	He **is** work**ing**	subject + *be* + *-ing*
Present perfect continuous	She **has been** work**ing**	subject + *have/has been* + *-ing*
Future continuous	We **will be** work**ing**	subject + *will be* + *-ing*

Continuous verb forms can:

* emphasise that an action lasts for some time.
  I've cut my finger! (= action lasts for only a moment)
  I've been cutting firewood. (= action lasts for some time)
* describe an action that is in progress but not complete.
  I think I'll watch a film tomorrow. (= a complete action)
  Don't call me. I'll be watching a film. (= in progress at that time)
* emphasise that an action is repeated.
  I rang you this morning. (= once)
  I've been ringing you all morning! (= several times)
* describe a situation which is temporary.
  She'll stay with her sister after university. (= perhaps long term)
  She'll be staying at her sister's house for a few days. (= temporary)

REMEMBER!

* If you give the number of times that something happened you always use the simple form, not the continuous.
  He has won three Oscars.
  NOT *He has been winning three Oscars.*
  I called you five times yesterday.
  NOT *I was calling you five times yesterday.*

* Verbs that describe states are not usually used in the continuous form (see Unit 1, Study 1)

PRACTICE 2

1 Choose the best alternative in the context.

1 **A:** What's wrong?
  B: I've *been hurting / hurt* my arm.
2 You seem out of breath. Have you *been running / run*?
3 She didn't hear the doorbell because she *dried / was drying* her hair.
4 I've *bought / been buying* this new scooter. Do you like it?
5 We've *finished / been finishing* our work. Can we go out now?
6 This time next week, I'll *travel / be travelling* to Australia!
7 The Australian swimmer has *been winning / won* the gold medal twice before.
8 It had *rained / been raining* all night, so everywhere was soaking wet.

2 Each pair of sentences below is correct. What is the difference between each pair?

1 a Kristina's gone to the gym.
  b Kristina's been going to the gym.
2 a He changed his mind.
  b He was changing his mind.
3 a She had phoned my parents secretly.
  b She had been phoning my parents secretly.
4 a I'll write the report at the weekend.
  b I'll be writing the report at the weekend.
5 a I left when he arrived.
  b I was leaving when he arrived.

3 Tick the best response, a, b or c.

1 A: Where were you at seven o'clock last night?
  B: a I had dinner. Why?
     b I was having dinner. Why?
     c I've been having dinner. Why?
2 A: What's the problem with your thumb?
  B: a I've been breaking it.
     b I'd broken it.
     c I've broken it.
3 A: When's the best time to phone?
  B: a Oh any time. We won't do anything special.
     b Oh any time. We don't do anything special.
     c Oh any time. We won't be doing anything special.
4 A: Have you spoken to Mrs O'Brien yet?
  B: a No, I've been trying to get her since nine o'clock.
     b No, I'm trying to get her since nine o'clock.
     c No, I tried to get her since nine o'clock.
5 A: Oh no, I've lost my wallet.
  B: a When have you last been using it?
     b When were you last using it?
     c When did you last use it?
6 A: You look tired.
  B: a Yes, I've been running.
     b Yes, I ran.
     c Yes, I've run.
7 A: What's your address?
  B: a I'm staying with my parents at the moment.
     b I stay with my parents at the moment.
     c I've been staying with my parents at the moment.
8 A: Did they offer you a place at university?
  B: a Yes, and I've been accepting it.
     b Yes, and I've accepted it.
     c Yes, and I accept it.
9 A: I need this letter posting.
  B: a I do it.
     b I'll be doing it.
     c I'll do it.
10 A: Would you like a doughnut?
  B: a No thanks, I've been eating biscuits all morning.
     b No thanks, I've eaten biscuits all morning.
     c No thanks, I ate biscuits all morning.

REMEMBER THESE WORDS

MISHAPS

to bang your head	to lock yourself out
to break (something)	to lose your keys
to break down	to miss your train
to damage something	to oversleep
to drop something (valuable)	to run out of petrol
to get confused	to slip on some ice
to get lost	to spill your drink
to get on the wrong train	to trip and fall over
to get stuck in traffic	

CRIMES

antisocial behaviour	(to commit) plagiarism
begging	to play truant
drink-driving	possession of illegal drugs
(to commit) fraud	to write graffiti on ...

PUNISHMENT

to be charged (with ...)	to be sentenced to
to be evicted	(six months in) jail
to be expelled	to be taken into care
to be fined	to get/receive a warning
to be given community service	to get/receive a suspended
to be let off (with a warning)	sentence
to be prosecuted	to lose your licence
to be suspended	

HEADLINES

to back something	a toll
to be set to do something	to vow

ADVERBS FOR TELLING STORIES

after a while	eventually
all of a sudden	for some reason
amazingly	ironically
by this stage	(un)fortunately

OTHER

to access someone's email account	to pay off a debt
to claim a prize	to reimburse a person
to go through a divorce	to violate someone's privacy

PRACTICE

1 COLLOCATIONS. Cross out the word that does not fit with each verb.

1 I banged my *hair / elbow / head*.
2 We missed *the train / our ID / the plane*.
3 She slipped on *a glass of wine / some ice / a banana skin*.
4 I spilt *some shampoo / a drink / the pavement*.
5 He got on the wrong *train / bus / taxi*.
6 He dropped *his wallet / his train / a precious vase*.
7 They got stuck in *the lift / bad traffic / a drink*.

2 Correct the words in bold. Use a dictionary if necessary.

1 The **lose** of his licence was very hard because he was a taxi driver.
2 Did you **plagiarism** this essay?
3 She was charged with **possess** of illegal drugs.
4 You can't read my emails! It's a **violate** of my privacy.
5 I will **warning** him about playing truant.
6 She got on the wrong train. It was a silly **confused**.
7 The insurance claim was revealed to be **fraud**.

3 Complete the sentences with the words in the box.

down   out   out   over   off   off

1 My granny has fallen _____ and broken her arm.
2 He's working two jobs so he can pay _____ his debts.
3 He's had a row with his wife and she has locked him _____ , so he's sleeping on our sofa tonight.
4 It was the first time he had been in trouble with the police, so they let him _____ with a warning.
5 They were late back from the school trip because the bus had broken _____ .
6 We got stuck on the motorway because we had run _____ of petrol.

STUDY TIPS

Noticing and remembering collocations

1 A collocation is a combination of two or more words that frequently occur together. Using collocations in your speech and writing will help you to sound natural in English. Collocations are often ...

- adjective + noun
  antisocial behaviour; a steep hill
- verb + noun
  miss a bus/train/flight; spill your drink; call the police

2 Look at the articles on page 33 and find ...
- a verb often used with *the police*.
- a verb often used with *immediate action*.
- an adjective used with *ticket*.
- an adjective used with *survey*.

3 Look at the dictionary entry for fraud. Find four collocations.

fraud /frɔːd/ [C,U] the crime of deceiving people in order to gain something such as money or goods: **tax/insurance/credit card, etc.** fraud *He's been charged with tax fraud.* | electoral fraud | *She was found guilty of fraud.*

4 Make a note of useful collocations from *Happiness Facts and Myths* on page 18.

earn money, average income ...

STUDY 1

Use and non-use of the passive

1 The active and the passive

- In active sentences, the subject is the agent (or 'doer') of the verb.
  *The two firefighters **rescued** the child.*
       (subject)   (verb)   (object)
- In passive sentences, the subject is **not** the agent of the verb.
  *The child **was rescued** by the two firefighters.*
  (subject)   (verb)   (agent)
- The passive is formed with *be* + past participle.

	active	passive
Present simple	it makes	it **is made**
Present continuous	it is making	it **is being made**
Present perfect	it has made	it **has been made**
Past simple	it made	it **was made**
Past continuous	it was making	it **was being made**
Past perfect	it had made	it **had been made**
Future simple	it will make	it **will be made**
infinitive forms	make/to make	**be made/to be made**
-ing form	making	**being made**

2 Reasons for using the passive

- The main topic of the sentence is not the agent. In English, the main topic of the sentence normally comes at the beginning, and new information about the topic comes at the end.
  *James Cameron **directed** 'Avatar'.* (From a profile of Cameron, who is the main topic of the sentence.)
  If the agent is not the main topic of the sentence, we use the passive.
  *'Avatar' **was directed by** James Cameron.* (From an article about *Avatar*, which is the main topic of the sentence.)
- The agent is unknown, unimportant or obvious.
  *My bicycle **has been stolen**!* (= we don't know who did this)
  *The mice **are kept** in cages.* (= it's not important who does this)
  *A man **was arrested**.* (= it's obvious the police did this)

REMEMBER!
If we include the agent in the sentence, we use *by*.

- In more formal texts, the passive is preferred because it is less personal. This is especially true in newspapers and in scientific, technical or academic writing. The following passive constructions are particularly common in this kind of formal writing.
  It is said that ...
  It is thought that ...
  It is believed that ...
  It has been proved that ...

3 Alternatives to the passive/avoiding the passive

In informal speech, we can avoid using the passive by using a subject like *we, you, they, people, someone,* etc. This sounds more personal and friendly. Compare the following pairs of sentences.
*Gregor **is said to be** interested in living abroad.*
***They say** Gregor is interested in living abroad.*

*The Gold Label credit card can **be used** all over the world.*
***You can use** the Gold Label credit card all over the world.*

*More computers **are being** bought than ever before.*
***People are buying** more computers than ever before.*

PRACTICE

1 Choose the correct verb forms.

It must be true – I read it in the tabloids

Magistrate Isabelle Le Tessier [1]***sentenced** / **was sentenced*** her old school teacher in Rouen, France last week. He [2]***forced** / **was forced*** to write 'I must not break the speed limit' 25,000 times.

Lars Homberg and Anka Edlund of Karlstadt, Sweden [3]***have decided** / **have been decided*** to get married after spending 19 hours stuck in a lift together earlier this month. Before their ordeal they [4]***had not introduced** / **had not been introduced***.

The State of Andhra Pradesh in India [5]***has passed** / **has been passed*** a law saying that anyone who [6]***catches** / **is caught*** cheating in school exams [7]***will send** / **will be sent*** to prison for ten years.

Failed pilot Larry Walters [8]***attached** / **was attached*** 42 helium balloons to a kitchen chair and spent 14 hours flying above Los Angeles earlier this week. Mr Walters who [9]***had turned down** / **had been turned down*** by the US air force because of bad eye sight [10]***almost hit** / **was almost hit*** by two planes after he [11]***blew** / **was blown*** unexpectedly in the direction of the city's airport.

2 Complete the gaps with the correct form of the verb (active or passive) in brackets.

Fortune-teller offers to remove curse on money

A fortune-teller in Colorado, USA, [1]_____ (arrest) a few years ago after she [2]_____ (trick) a pensioner into giving her $30,000. While [3]_____ (tell) a 64-year-old widow her fortune, Sonya Adamson, 24, persuaded the woman that a curse [4]_____ (place) on all her money by evil spirits, and that she needed to take the money to the fortune teller and leave it with her for the curse [5]_____ (remove). The woman did this, but when she [6]_____ (return) in order to pick up her money, she [7]_____ (find) that Adamson [8]_____ (disappear) and all the furniture [9]_____ (take) from her apartment. Police [10]_____ (arrest) Adamson as she [11]_____ (board) a plane to Miami – her tickets [12]_____ (paid for) in cash a few minutes earlier with the old woman's money. 'I [13]_____ (not usually deceive) so easily,' [14]_____ (say) the old lady. Her money [15]_____ (return) to her a few months later.

STUDY 2

Passive forms with *have* and *get*

- The passive form *have* + object + past participle is used to talk about something we pay other people to do for us.
  *She **had her nose pierced** when she was a teenager.*
- We use *have/get* + object + past participle when it was difficult to have something done.
  *After many years of trying, he finally **had/got his book published**.*
- We can also use *get* + object + past participle. It is more informal but the meaning is the same.
  *She **got her hair cut** yesterday.*
  *She **had her hair cut** yesterday.*
- We use *get* + past participle for things that happen by accident, or things which happen to us that are unpleasant.
  *It's common for things **to get broken** when you move house.*
  *My luggage **got stolen** somewhere at the airport.*

PRACTICE

1 Use the prompts in brackets to complete the sentences with *have/get* + past participle.

1 Last year I _____ (my eyes / treat) by laser, because I had got very short-sighted.
2 Joe is going to _____ (his tattoo / remove) as soon as he can afford it, because he really regrets _____ (it / do).
3 My sister _____ (her hair / dye) orange recently.
4 Why don't you _____ (your photo / take) with your brother and give it as a present to your parents?
5 Poor Rachel _____ (her credit card / steal) yesterday.
6 Could I _____ (two copies of this / make), please?
7 _____ (our house / burgle) when we were on holiday.

2 Write at least one thing that you have or get done at these places. Use the verbs in the box.

do   (re)shape   straighten   dye   cut   wax
lift   remove   mend   check   treat

- a garage
  You get your car repaired.
  You have your tyres checked.
- a shoe-repair shop
- a dry-cleaner's
- a hairdresser's
- a beautician's
- a cosmetic surgery clinic
- a doctor's
- a dentist's
- an optician's

3 Choose the best response, a, b or c.

1 **A:** Can you give me a booking form please?
  B: a I'll have printed one for you.
    b I'll have one printed for you.
    c I'll get printed one for you
2 **A:** Can I help you, sir?
  B: a Yes. Can I get my car washed here?
    b Yes. I can get washed my car here?
    c Yes. Can I get washed my car here?
3 **A:** Your hair looks nice.
  B: a Thanks, I'd just cut it.
    b Thanks, I've just had it cut.
    c Thanks, I just have had it cut.
4 **A:** I like this room.
  B: a Thanks. We had it redecorated last month.
    b Thanks. We had redecorated it last month.
    c Thanks. We have redecorated it last month.
5 **A:** Do you need any help?
  B: a Yes. Where I can get some photocopying done?
    b Yes. Where can I get done some photocopying?
    c Yes. Where can I get some photocopying done?
6 **A:** Your car engine's making a strange noise.
  B: a I know. I need to have it looked at.
    b I know. It needs looking at it.
    c I know. I need to have looked at it.
7 **A:** My watch is slow.
  B: a When did you last repair it?
    b When did you last have it repaired?
    c When did you last have repaired it?
8 **A:** What does that sign say? I can't read it.
  B: a You should get your eyes tested!
    b You should test your eyes!
    c You should get tested your eyes!

REMEMBER THESE WORDS

TYPES OF INTELLIGENCE

emotional intelligence	organisational skills
logic	problem-solving skills
mathematical skills	visual/spatial intelligence

PHRASES WITH *MIND*

absent-minded	Mind your own business!
to change your mind	My mind went blank.
to have something on your mind	Never mind.
I don't mind.	open-minded
to make up your mind	to speak your mind
Mind your head!	Would you mind + –ing?

PERSONAL CHARACTERISTICS

argumentative	individualistic
arrogant	introvert
attention-seeking	jealous
calm	needy
extrovert	rebellious
good in a team	resilient
hot-tempered	self-sufficient
humourless	talkative
humorous	uncommunicative

OTHER

to analyse	to implant
to assess	infamous
an astronaut	to monitor
blank	to paint your nails
a cross-section	to shape
to dye	simulated
to erase	to take your blood pressure
to execute	to trace
to fund	a volunteer

PRACTICE

1 Complete the table with the noun/adjective forms.

adjective	noun
arrogant	
calm	
humorous	
jealous	
	logic
rebellious	
resilient	
	volunteer

2 Which characteristics/mental skills are not desirable/ necessary for each person?

1 A carpenter should have *emotional intelligence / mathematical skills / spatial intelligence*.
2 A mountaineer is *resilient / self-sufficient / extrovert*.
3 A boss should be *arrogant / calm / good in a team*.
4 A mathematician needs *logic / organisational skills / problem-solving skills*.
5 The perfect girlfriend/boyfriend is *attention-seeking / humorous / needy*.

3 Tick the best sentence for each situation.

1 You are shopping with your sister, and she has been trying to decide which dress to buy for half an hour.
  a 'Please make up your mind!' ☐
  b 'Please change your mind!' ☐
2 You need to talk to your partner about a problem.
  a 'My mind's gone blank.' ☐
  b 'I've got something on my mind.' ☐
3 Your younger brother is trying to find out about your new girlfriend/boyfriend, but you don't want to tell him.
  a 'Mind your own business!' ☐
  b 'I don't mind!' ☐
4 Your flatmate has lost her glasses – again!
  a 'You're so absent-minded!' ☐
  b 'You're open-minded!' ☐
5 A small child has his hand near a door that is closing.
  a 'Mind your fingers!' ☐
  b 'Never mind!' ☐

STUDY TIPS

Guessing meaning from context

1 Decide if each word below in bold is a noun, verb, adjective or adverb. Here is some information to help.

- typical endings for different types of words
  verbs: *-ed, -ing, -s*   adjectives: *-ive, -ful, -ible*
  nouns: *-ion, -ness, -ance*   adverbs: *-ly*
- words which come before ...
  nouns: *a, the, adjectives*
  verbs: auxiliary or modal verbs (*be, have, may, should*, etc.)

Do polygraphs work?

Polygraphs, also called 'lie **detectors**', are far from **infallible**. They measure certain **physiological** changes such as heart rate and blood pressure, which are **correlated** with lying. The belief is that **deceptive** answers produce physiological responses that can be **differentiated** from truthful ones. Certain rules and procedures should be **rigorously** applied when taking polygraph tests. For a start, the person who **administers** the test should not be the one who judges the results, and ideally more than one person should offer an **interpretation**.

2 Think of a word that could replace each word in bold.

STUDY 1

Review of future forms

Plans and decisions in the future

1 *Will*

We use *will/won't* for a decision made at the moment of speaking.
I'll phone you later.
Will is also used for promises and offers.
I'll call you this evening.   Here, I'll carry that for you.

REMEMBER!

Don't use *will* after *if, when, before, after, in case, as long as,
as soon as, once, unless, until,* etc. Use the Present simple instead.

2 *Going to*

We use *going to* to express present intentions for the future. The
action may be distant or in the near future.
I'm never going to get married.

3 Present continuous

We use the Present continuous to talk about something we have
arranged for the future.
I'm meeting Henry for lunch on Friday.

REMEMBER!

- The use of *going to* and the Present continuous is very similar. You
can always use *going to* instead of the Present continuous to talk
about the future.

  I'm going to meet Henry for lunch on Friday.

- The use of the Present continuous is more limited. You only use it
to talk about definite arrangements.

  I'm going to get married before I'm 30. (= general intention)

  I'm getting married in June. (= this has been arranged)

- When the main verb is *go*, the Present continuous is often
preferred to the *going to* form.

  We're going (to go) to Greece for our holiday.

4 Present simple

When an action in the future is part of a regular timetable or has
been officially fixed, the Present simple is used.
The show begins at eight o'clock.

5 Future continuous

We use the Future continuous for something that will happen
without any particular plan or intention, but as part of the normal
course of events.
I expect you'll be going to the swimming pool tomorrow.
This form is also used when we make requests, to suggest that
something will not cause trouble to other people.
I'll be turning off the electricity for a while later. Is that OK?
Will you be going to the supermarket? We need some milk.

6 Other phrases

Many other phrases can express future intentions and plans.
I've decided to … , I'm hoping to … , I'm planning to … , I'm thinking of …

Predictions

We use *going to* and *will* to make predictions about the future.

- When the prediction is based on some evidence in the present,
we usually use *going to*.
  Watch out! You're going to drop those plates if you're not careful!
  (= I can see you're not carrying them properly)

- When the prediction is based on our own beliefs and
expectations rather than present evidence, we use *will*.
  A: *I wonder where Anna is?*
  B: *Don't worry. I'm sure she'll get here soon.*

- In many cases, there is no important difference in meaning.
  Who do you think is going to/will win the Champion's League?

- To express a simple fact about the future, we use *will*.
  My birthday will be on Tuesday this year.

- There are many other phrases to make predictions about the
future, such as: *to be certain to …; to be (un)likely to …; to be
bound to …; there's a good chance that …; I bet …; certain to,* etc.
  My mother is bound to buy me a pair of socks for Christmas.
  In this heat, it's likely to be an uncomfortable journey.
  There's a good chance that I'll be accepted.

PRACTICE 1

1 Choose the correct verbs.

JAMES: Richard, how're you doing? Listen, the reason I'm
calling is [1]*I'll take / I'm going to take* my nephew
Sam to his first football match on Saturday. United
[2]*are playing / will play* City, as I'm sure you know.
I just wondered if you fancy coming, too?

RICHARD: I'd love to … ah, but I've just remembered …
[3]*we're having / we'll have* lunch over at my mum's
on Saturday, so it depends on the time …

JAMES: Well, [4]*it's going to start / it starts* at five … I've just
checked online.

RICHARD: Five o'clock? Hmm … that means I'd have to
leave about half three … yeah, I'm sure Mum
[5]*doesn't mind / won't mind* if [6]*I leave / I will leave*,
then … [7]*I'll tell / I'm going to tell* her it's something
really important. I'm sure [8]*she'll understand /
she's going to understand*.

JAMES: Well, what could be more important than going to
your first football match?

RICHARD: Exactly. By the way, have you thought about how
to get there? [9]*Are you going to take / Do you take*
the train like we did last time?

JAMES: No, I've decided [10]*I'm going to drive / I drive*. It's
easier with my nephew. My sister [11]*drops /
's dropping* him at my place around three, so that
we've got plenty of time. [12]*I'm going to pick you up /
I'll pick you up* from your mum's if you like.

RICHARD: That would be great. About what time?

JAMES: We'd better leave about four, in case the traffic
[13]*is / will be* bad.

RICHARD: Yeah, it's [14]*likely / unlikely* to be pretty busy, I
guess. I tell you what, give me a call just before you
[15]*leave / will leave* for Mum's.

JAMES: Yeah, that's a good idea. Speak to you then.

More complex question forms

1 Compound questions

- After *what* or *which*, you can use a noun to form questions.
  Which restaurant did you go to?
  What information do you need?
- After *how*, you can use an adjective or adverb to form questions.
  How trustworthy do you think he is?
  How quickly can you get here?

2 Questions with prepositions

Some verbs and adjectives take prepositions, for example, *rely on*, *talk about*, *frightened of*, etc. The preposition comes after the verb or adjective. Don't omit the preposition.
*Who do you **rely on**?*
*What were you **talking about**?*
*What are you **frightened of**?*

3 Statements and negative questions

- Statements with a rising intonation often function as questions. They are often used to express surprise at what someone has just said or to check information.
  A: *I bought three pairs of shoes.*
  B: *You bought three pairs of shoes?*

  A: *Sophie arrived yesterday.*
  B: *She arrived yesterday? I thought she was arriving today.*
- Negative questions also express surprise, an opinion or check that information is correct.
  Didn't you like the book?
  Don't you think it would be better if you talked to her?
  Doesn't it start at two?
- Notice the way we answer negative questions.
  Didn't you hear what I said?
  No, I didn't. (What did you say?)
  Yes, I did. (You said we were late.)

4 Indirect questions

- Indirect questions are often more polite or more formal than normal questions. Use phrases like *Could you tell me* at the start of the question. We use affirmative word order in indirect questions.
  Could you tell me where the bank is?
  Do you know if that restaurant is open?
  I wanted to know what you thought of her.
- Other phrases can be used for indirect questions: *I wonder ...*; *Tell me ...*; *Can you remind me ...?*; *I'd like/love to know ...*
  Tell me when you are ready to leave.
  Can you remind me what time our flight is?
- Don't use *do* or *did* in the Present simple and Past simple.
  I wanted to know what you think of her.
  NOT *I wanted to know what did you think of her.*
- Use *if* or *whether* for *yes/no* questions.
  Could you tell me if there's a bank near here?
  Do you know whether the meeting's going ahead?

5 Other ways of asking questions

The words *on earth*, *exactly*, *precisely* can be used to make a question stronger.
*What **on earth** are you doing?*
*Where **exactly/precisely** do you think it is?*

PRACTICE 2

1 Complete the questions.

1. *Which* café do you want to go to?
2. How _____ do you know her?
3. _____ food are you going to take to the picnic?
4. _____ surprised was he when he saw you at the station?
5. _____ airport are you flying in to?
6. What are you thinking _____ ?
7. Who is she married _____ ?
8. What are they famous _____ ?
9. Who are you shouting _____ ?
10. How _____ have you known her?

2 Write a negative question to express surprise at what the speaker says. Use the verbs in brackets.

1. A: That was an awful film.
   B: *Didn't you like it?* (like)
2. A: I didn't know she was getting married.
   B: _____ ? (tell)
3. A: I'm still doing my homework.
   B: _____ ? (finish)
4. A: Can I borrow your mobile phone?
   B: _____ ? (have got)
5. A: Can you explain it again?
   B: _____ ? (understand)
6. A: Hello. What's your name?
   B: _____ ? We met last year. (remember)

3 Rewrite the questions to make them indirect.

1. What does she do for a living?
   Do you know what she does for a living?
2. How old is your sister?
   I _____ .
3. Have you been learning English for long?
   Could _____ ?
4. How good are your listening skills in English?
   I _____ .
5. When will you be finished in the bathroom?
   Do _____ ?
6. Are you going to go out this evening?
   Do _____ ?
7. How do you say 'Of course' in your language?
   Could _____ ?
8. Will it be expensive?
   Do _____ ?

REMEMBER THESE WORDS

WAYS OF MEETING

an appointment	a dinner party
a blind date	a family get-together
a business meeting	a house-warming party
a celebration meal	an online forum
a conference	a school reunion
a conference call	a social networking site
a dating website	a summit

PEOPLE

an acquaintance	an ex-classmate
a business associate	a political leader
a client	a speaker
a delegate	

COLLOQUIAL LANGUAGE

Alright?	to grab (a chair/coffee)
to be like (+ what someone said)	How come?
to be (totally) stressed out	Just kidding.
booze	a mate
to chill out (v) / chilled out (adj)	a rip off
he's/she's doing my head in	wanna
a fiver/tenner	way beyond …
to go cold turkey	What's up?
gonna	

IDIOMS

to be economical with the truth	to take something with a
to fall hopelessly in love (with …)	pinch of salt
to keep an eye out for	to tell (little) white lies
to stretch the truth	

OTHER

to be considerate	long-standing
to charge (something up)	long-suffering
to download	to register/registration
to exaggerate	to scroll through
to have followers/follow someone	to tweet
on Twitter	to update/an update

PRACTICE

1 Replace the underlined phrases with a different phrase.

1 It's a <u>party for members of my extended family</u>.
   family get-together
2 I'm going on a <u>date with someone I've never met before</u> this evening.
3 He's <u>not a friend, but I know him</u>.
4 She is <u>someone who used to be in my class</u>.
5 We're having a <u>party for people who used to be in my year at school</u>.
6 We're having a <u>party to celebrate moving to a new house</u>.
7 Can we have a <u>telephone call with more than two people on the line at the same time</u>?

2 Rewrite this conversation to make it less colloquial. Replace one phrase/word in each line.

A: ~~Alright~~, Jon. *Hello*
B: Hey Tonya. What's up?
A: I'm really upset with one of my best mates, actually.
B: How come?
A: He's totally doing my head in. He always borrows money.
B: That's terrible. By the way, can I borrow a tenner?
A: Don't! I'm totally stressed out.
B: Just kidding!

3 One word in each sentence is wrong. Replace it with the correct word.

1 I've fallen helplessly in love with my best friend.
2 I don't believe her. She's stretching her truth a bit.
3 I told him what he wanted to hear. It was a little blue lie.
4 Don't believe what she says. Take it with a pinch of pepper.
5 I've known him a long time. He's a long-sitting friend.
6 I'm going to stop give up coffee. I'm going to go cold chicken.
7 Is that true or are you being economic with the truth?
8 Be careful. Keep an eye in for dangerous drivers.

STUDY TIPS

Improving your listening skills

1 What is your most common complaint when trying to understand spoken English?

· People speak too fast.
· The words all merge together.
· I can't understand different accents.
· There are too many words I don't know.
· Other? What?

2a You can improve your listening skills by practising a little bit every day. Which of the tips below seem most useful to you?

· Go online every day and listen to or watch one video clip in English. Choose a topic you are interested in. Websites such as YouTube and bbc.co.uk can be very useful.
· Focus on the important words, usually the stressed words. Try to guess the meaning of words that you don't understand.
· The vast majority of English speakers in the world are not native English speakers. Try to listen to English spoken by people with other first languages. Again, the internet is a good resource.
· Consider buying an audio book and listening to it in your car, on your MP3 player or smart phone. Choose a book that you would like to listen to in your language. Many classic works, for example by Orwell or Tolstoy, can be downloaded legally for free.
· Avoid trying to understand every word. If a listening seems too difficult, try asking easier questions. What is the speaker talking about? What is his/her attitude towards the subject?

b Discuss what you are going to do to try to improve your listening skills.

STUDY 1

Perfect tenses

Present perfect	I have/He has arrived	I haven't/He hasn't arrived	Have you/Has he arrived?
Past perfect	I/she had arrived	I hadn't arrived	Had you arrived?
Future perfect	I/he will have arrived	I won't have arrived	Will you have arrived?

All perfect tenses link two points in time. They show actions <u>before</u> a particular time in the present, past or future.

1 Present perfect

The Present perfect links actions in the past to the present.

This can happen in a number of ways.

- The action is not finished, but continues into the present.
  We have lived here all our lives. (= and we still live here now)
- The action took place in a period of time which is not finished.
  We've all been ill this year. (= this year is not finished)
  I've been to Italy several times. (= in my life)
- The action happened very recently and is still 'news'.
  They've just had a baby.
- The results of a past action are still important now.
  I've lost my mobile phone!
- The Present perfect is often found with these time phrases.
  already   ever   for   just   never   since   so far
  this month/morning/week   today   yet

REMEMBER!

If you relate the action to a specific past time, use the Past simple.

I first met John when I was 21 / in 2004.

---

2 Past perfect

- The Past perfect links a point in the past with a time further in the past. It describes actions that happened 'before the past'.

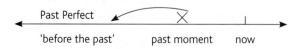

She had been ill for some time before she died.
When I got home the cat had escaped.
- Many of the time phrases often used with the Present perfect are also used with the Past perfect.
  Had you ever seen the man before that night?
  Mary hadn't been abroad for many years.
- We can use *by* + past time phrases with the Past perfect.
  By eight o'clock last night, they had managed to clear all the roads.

- We can also use clauses with *by the time*, *when*, etc.
  The party had finished by the time I arrived.
  We went on holiday when we'd finished our exams.
- Notice that when we use *before* and *after*, the order of events is obvious, so the Past perfect is not always necessary.
  I remembered to lock up before I went to bed.

3 Future perfect

The Future perfect links two actions or times in the future.

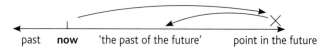

We use the Future perfect when we look forward to a time in the future and then think about something that will be completed before that time. It is often introduced with *by* + future time phrase:
Come over about ten. We'll have eaten by then.
By the time I'm 50, I hope I'll have earned enough money to retire.
Notice the word order of Future perfect questions.
1   2   3
Will you have finished by tomorrow?

PRACTICE 1

1 Look at sentences 1–3. Are statements a–c true (T), false (F) or it isn't sure (NS)?

1 They've lived in France for nearly two years.
   a They live in France now. ☐
   b They used to live in France. ☐
   c They moved to France around two years ago. ☐

2 Dave had had his dinner when Sally arrived home.
   a Dave finished eating before she arrived home. ☐
   b Dave was eating when she arrived home. ☐
   c She arrived before Dave's dinner. ☐

3 We'll have raised more than €100,000 by the end of January.
   a We haven't raised €100,000 yet. ☐
   b We'll have €100,000 before February. ☐
   c We've already raised €100,000. ☐

2 Complete the sentences with the correct form of the verbs in brackets.

1 The grass is extremely dry, it _____ (not rain) for weeks.

2 We _____ (sit) at the table for about 25 minutes before anyone came to take our order.

3 By the time he was five, Joe _____ (learn) to play the guitar.

4 At the end of next month, we _____ (live) in this flat for exactly one year.

5 It was no good trying to persuade him – he _____ (make) up his mind a long time ago.

6 Come and call for me about seven, I _____ (finish) my homework by then.

7 I don't think I would recognise Anita any more – I _____ (not see) her for years.

STUDY 2

More about the Present perfect simple and continuous

Both the Present perfect simple and the Present perfect continuous link the past and the present as described above. Sometimes there is no important difference in meaning between the two.

He's been living here for a long time.
He's lived here for a long time.

However, in most cases, there are differences in emphasis which mean we choose a particular form.

1 'Long' / 'repeated' vs 'momentary'

If an action lasts only for a moment or a very short time, the simple form is used. The continuous form emphasises that the action continues for a period of time, or was repeated.

Oh no! I've broken my glasses! (= lasts only for a moment)
Be careful. It's been snowing. (= lasts some time)
I've been phoning all my friends to tell them the news. (= I've made several calls)

2 'Complete' actions vs 'incomplete' actions

If we see the action as completed, we tend to use the simple form. The continuous form emphasises that the action is incomplete, or we could continue it later.

I've done my homework. Can I go out now? (= completed)
He's been working on his assignment. (= it's not necessarily finished)

3 Activities vs results

The continuous form often describes an activity. It answers the question 'How have you spent your time?' We use the simple form when we emphasise the result of an activity. It answers the question 'What have you achieved?'

A: *What have you been doing today?* (= interested in activity)
B: *I've been mending my bike*
A: *What have you done today?* (= interested in result)
B: *I've fixed my bike!*

If you give a number, the Present perfect simple is always used, because we are emphasising completion or results.

I've been to the gym three times this week.
I've sent 15 emails so far today.

REMEMBER!

Some verbs describe states, and are therefore not usually used in the continuous form.

PRACTICE 2

1 Match sentences 1–8 to descriptions a–h.

1 Kate has been doing her homework.
2 I've seen this movie hundreds of times.
3 They've been waiting outside for several hours.
4 You've spilt my drink!
5 I've been trying to contact you all morning.
6 What have you been doing up there?
7 Have you fixed the printer?
8 I've always liked water polo.

a an action which lasts only for a moment
b a state
c a longer action
d the number of times something has happened
e an action which is repeated
f an action which is not necessarily finished
g a question about the results of an activity
h a question about an activity

2 Complete the sentences with the Present perfect simple or the Present perfect continuous form of the verbs in brackets.

1 Oh no! I think I _____ (leave) my bag at the restaurant.
2 _____ (you finish) with that DVD I lent you?
3 He's _____ (try) to fix his motorbike all morning.
4 I _____ (send) five texts but she _____ . (not reply)
5 I _____ (never see) such an untidy room!
6 Gwen _____ (work) on her presentation all day – she must be nearly finished now.

3 Choose the best verb forms in the article below.

RECORD BREAKERS

The world's biggest breakfast
Cooks in Croatia [1]*have used / have been using* 1,111 eggs to create the world's largest portion of scrambled eggs. Before their successful record attempt, no one [2]*has ever tried / had ever tried* to set a world record for scrambled eggs.

The world's longest marriage
When Liu Yang Wan [3]*has died / died* peacefully in her sleep at the age of 103, it [4]*brought / has brought* an end to the world's longest marriage. She and her husband [5]*have been married / had been married* for no fewer than 85 years. But they [6]*have lived / had lived* in the same house for even longer. In accordance with the traditions of the time, she [7]*went / has gone* to live in her husband's parents' house at the age of just five.

The biggest Pepsi Cola fan
Dr Christian Cavaletti from Corropoli, Italy, [8]*has been collecting / has collected* Pepsi Cola cans since 1989. In this time, he [9]*has collected / has been collecting* more than 3,000 cans from over 70 countries.

Exploding population!
The world's population [10]*has increased / has been increasing* by about 1.5 percent each year for the last 30 years. It is estimated that it [11]*has reached / will have reached* nine billion by the year 2050.

REMEMBER THESE WORDS

ACHIEVEMENTS

to affect (dramatically)	to found an organisation, etc.
to cause	to inspire others/future
to cure a disease, etc.	generations
to defeat an army, etc.	to lead to
to develop a theory/machine, etc.	to lead a political group, etc.
to discover	to make something possible
to donate money to charity	to mean that
to enable	to raise money for charity
to explore space, etc.	to result in
to have an impact on	to set/break a (new) world record
to have an influence on	a step forward
to give a (great) speech	to transform
a (great) advance	

TIME PHRASES

a decade (or so)	the 7th century BC/AD
in the early/mid/late 16th century	within 30 years

PHRASES WITH *FIRST*

at first	first-choice
at first sight	first impression
in first place	first language
first aid	first of all
first-class	first thing

OTHER

a bar code	to load
a container	shipping
a crane	to standardise
to flush (a toilet)	to take something for granted
international time zones	to unload

PRACTICE

1 Decide if each pair of sentences mean the same thing. If not, what is the difference?

1 a Brad Pitt has raised a lot of money for charity.
  b Brad Pitt has donated a lot of money to charity.
2 a We will probably find a cure within the next ten years.
  b We will probably find a cure within the next decade.
3 a The detective discovered a strange story.
  b The detective invented a strange story.
4 a Penicillin has enabled us to cure many illnesses.
  b Penicillin has made it possible for us to cure many illnesses.
5 a The conquerors explored the Western Islands.
  b The conquerors defeated the Western Islands.
6 a Mobile phones have transformed our lives.
  b Mobile phones have influenced our lives.

2 Complete the article with words in the box.

had   influence   means   led   in   on
enable   make   cause   take   had

No one doubts that modern technology has ¹_____ a huge impact ²_____ working life, but has it ³_____ a positive or negative ⁴_____? Email and the internet ⁵_____ us to communicate with colleagues all over the world in an instant, but they have also ⁶_____ to a culture where we expect instant responses. Because of global time differences, this can result ⁷_____ a situation where people end up working late and unsociable hours. Similarly, mobile phones ⁸_____ it possible for us to be away from our desks without colleagues or clients knowing that we are actually on the beach, but those we work with also ⁹_____ it for granted that they can get hold of us whenever they need to. This ¹⁰_____ that it is harder to switch off from work completely, and can ¹¹_____ a lot of disruption to family life.

3 Write the noun forms of the verbs. Which nouns and verbs are the same?

1	to affect	6 to donate
2	to cause	7 to explore
3	to cure	8 to influence
4	to defeat	9 to transform
5	to discover	

STUDY TIPS

Improving your speaking in the classroom

1 As your English becomes more advanced, it is important to improve your accuracy and fluency when speaking. Which tips will help make you more accurate, fluent or both?

1 Always use English during pair and group work.
2 Always use English to ask questions in class.
3 Try to speak as much as you can during class discussions.
4 In class (and at home) listen to the pronunciation of new words and phrases and practise saying them.
5 Try to think in English whenever you can, and try to avoid translating word for word from your own language.
6 Give full answers rather than answering with a word or two.
7 Ask your teacher to write down important corrections and tell you about them afterwards
8 Where possible, take a few moments to plan what you are going to say and think of the best words, grammar structures, etc. to express what you want to say.
9 Listen when your teacher corrects other students.

2 Which three suggestions could you work more on?

STUDY 1

Relative clauses

1 General

Relative clauses give us information about things, people, possessions, places and times using a relative pronoun (*which*, *that*, *who*, *whose*, *where*, *when*).

- **Things** (*which*, *that*)

  *It's a shop **which/that** sells electronic goods.*

REMEMBER!

It is incorrect to use *what* after a noun.

It's a festival which raises money for charity.

NOT *It's a festival ~~what~~ raises money for charity.*

- **People** (*who*, *that*)

  *A spectator is a person **who/that** watches a public event.*
- **Possessions** (*whose*)

  *A widow is a woman **whose** husband has died.*
- **Places** (*where*, *which/that* + preposition)

  *This is the room **where** Leo sleeps.*

  *This is the room **which/that** Leo sleeps in.*

  Notice that we drop prepositions with *where*.

  That's the room where Leo sleeps ~~in~~.
- **Times** (*when*)

  *A public holiday is a day **when** all the shops close.*

REMEMBER!

- In the examples above, the relative pronoun is the subject of the clause. If a person or thing is the object of the relative clause, you can omit *which*, *who* or *that*.

  *A ring is a metal thing **(which)** you wear on your finger.*

  *Look! There's the man **(who)** I met at that party the other night.*
- When we combine sentences with a relative clause, words which refer to the subject like *here* and *then* are omitted. Pronouns are also omitted.

  This is the city. The president was born here.

  → *This is the city **where** the president was born ~~here~~.*

  He's a man. Everyone admires him.

  → *He's a man **(who)** everyone admires ~~him~~.*
- Prepositions normally go at the end of the clause.

  *That's the woman **(who)** I was talking **about**.*

  But in very formal English, they can go before the relative pronoun. Notice that in this case we use *whom* instead of *who*.

  *That's the woman **about whom** I was talking.*

---

2 Defining vs non-defining relative clauses

Defining relative clauses (without commas)

Sometimes the relative clause is necessary to tell us which thing or person we are talking about. In this case, there are no commas.

*That's the man **who offered me a lift home**.*

(we need the relative clause to know which man)

*I've just finished the book **you gave me for Christmas**.*

(we need the relative clause to know which book)

Non-defining relative clauses (with commas)

Sometimes the relative clause is not necessary to tell us which thing/person we are talking about – it gives extra information. In this case, there are commas before (and if necessary after) the clause.

*Christmas Day, **which is on a Thursday this year**, is always a public holiday.*

*He gave me a photograph, **which I keep in my wallet**.*

REMEMBER!

You cannot use *that* in non-defining clauses.

*Christmas Day, **which is on a Thursday this year**, is always a public holiday.*

NOT *Christmas Day, ~~that~~ is on a Thursday this year, is always a public holiday.*

You cannot leave out the relative pronoun in non-defining clauses.

*He gave me a photograph, **which I keep in my wallet**.*

NOT *He gave me a photograph, ~~I keep in my wallet~~.*

PRACTICE 1

1 Complete the sentences with a relative pronoun only where necessary.

1 That's the man _____ photo was in the paper the other day.

2 Chiang Mai, _____ is one of the biggest cities in Thailand, is in the north of the country.

3 This is the place_____ a new library is going to be built.

4 For dinner we had *bouillabaisse*, _____ is a kind of fish stew.

5 Sunday's the day _____ we all go and visit my grandmother.

6 Cate Blanchett's first film *Paradise Road*, in _____ she played a young nurse, was released in 1997.

2 Which phrases are incorrect? Correct them.

1 a shop what sells second-hand computer games

2 someone who looks after animals

3 the woman we saw yesterday

4 the couple who house is for sale

5 someone who is good at languages

6 the place which I was born

7 the hotel which we're staying at

8 the beach where he works at

3 Complete the sentences with a word or phrase in the box.

···
, in which , which to whom , who , whose on , when
···

1 This house Dickens lived as a child, is now a museum.

2 Our new computer system cost several thousand euros, is still not in operation.

3 The receptionist was in a bad mood, told us to wait outside.

4 He is a man the whole nation will always be deeply grateful.

5 I'll call you next week I'll have more information.

6 The fishing trade, which the whole town depends, has been badly affected by pollution.

7 The man on the left wife is wearing a red dress, is my old headmaster!

Quantifiers

Countable and uncountable nouns

- Nouns in English are either countable or uncountable. If a noun is uncountable, it does not have a plural form.
- Some nouns in English have countable and uncountable forms.
  *Colombia exports a large amount of **coffee**.* (= uncountable)
  *I've ordered three **coffees**.* (= countable: *cups of coffee*)
- Some uncountable nouns have a plural form which is different in meaning.
  *The bomb caused over $1 million worth of **damage**.*
  (= uncountable: *physical harm*)
  *The court awarded him $5,000 in **damages**.* (= plural: *financial compensation*)

Quantifiers with countable nouns

- ***Several, one or two, a couple, a few, quite a few, very few***
  A few, *a couple* and *one or two* all mean 'a small number'.
  *There are only **a few/a couple of/one or two** tickets left.*
  Several means 'more than a few'.
  *She speaks **several** languages.* (= perhaps three, four or more)
  Notice that *a few* and *quite a few* emphasise the positive.
  *I know (**quite) a few** Australian people.*
  Whereas *few* and *very few* emphasise that it is a small number.
  *There are (**very) few** people here who speak English.*
- ***many, a number of, loads of, hundreds of, dozens of***, etc.
  These are all used with plural countable nouns.
  Many and *a number of* are used in more formal situations to talk about a large, non-specific number.
  ***Many/A number of** people disagree with you.*
  Loads of, *hundreds of* and *dozens of* are mostly used informally.
- ***too many***
  Too many is used with countable nouns to mean 'more than we need or is good'.
  *I've eaten **too many** cakes.*

Quantifiers with uncountable nouns

- ***a little, very little, (quite) a bit of***
  A little and *a bit of* refer to uncountable nouns – *a bit of* tends to be used in conversation and informal situations.
  *There's still **a bit of** pudding left. Would you like it?*
  *There's **a bit of** cheese in the fridge.*
  Little/very little emphasises a small quantity.
  *There's **very little** time left.*
  Quite a bit of is used to emphasise the positive. We cannot say *quite a little*.
  *There's **quite a bit of** interest in his new book.*
- ***much, a great deal of, loads of***
  Much is used to talk about large quantities. It is used with uncountable nouns and is mainly used in questions and negatives.
  *Hurry up, there isn't **much** time!*
  A great deal of is used in formal contexts – *loads of* is informal.
  *There is **a great deal of** concern about the new proposals.*
  *He's got **loads of** money.*
- ***too much***
  Too much is used with uncountable nouns to mean 'more than we need or is good'.
  *I can't sleep. I think I drank **too much** coffee.*

Quantifiers with countable and uncountable nouns

- ***a lot of, lots of***
  A lot of is used with both countable and uncountable nouns. It is used less in formal situations. It is not usually used in negative sentences and questions.
  Lots of is used in the same way.
  ***A lot of/Lots of** people arrived late.*
- ***enough, plenty of***
  Enough is used with both countable and uncountable nouns to mean 'as much as we need'.
  Plenty of means 'more than we need'.
  *Have you got **enough** money to pay the bill?*
  *Don't worry, we've got **plenty of** time to get to the airport.*
- ***some*** and ***any***
  Some and *any* are both used with plural and uncountable nouns, and in positive and negative sentences.
  Some refers to a limited quantity or number. It can be followed by *but not all*.
  ***Some** (but not all) people like getting up early.*
  *I don't like **some** of his music (but I do like some of it).*
  Any refers to an unlimited quantity or number. With a positive verb it means 'all'.
  *You can get online at **any** cybercafé.* (= all of them, it doesn't matter which).
  Whereas with a negative verb, it means 'none'.
  *I can't think of **any** reasons to ask him to stay.* (= none)

PRACTICE 2

1 **Choose the phrase which is closest in meaning to the ones underlined.**

1 <u>Several</u> people have applied for the job.
   hundreds / loads / more than a few

2 There are <u>too many</u> people in the recording studio.
   dozens of / hundreds of / more than we need

3 We have <u>very little</u> time before the bus leaves.
   enough / not much / plenty of

4 This project has already cost us <u>a great deal of</u> money.
   a bit of / a lot of / not enough

5 You can get a free map at <u>any</u> tourist office.
   all of them / none of them / some of them

6 Don't buy any more food, we've got <u>plenty</u>.
   enough / more than enough / too much

7 He eats <u>anything</u>.
   everything / nothing / certain things

8 I don't like <u>some</u> of her recent songs.
   all / certain / most

2 **Choose the quantifier which cannot be used.**

1 There are ***a bit of / a few / quite a few / several*** things to say.

2 There is ***a bit of / a little / very little / very few*** money left.

3 There were ***a bit of / a great deal of / hundreds of / loads of*** people waiting for the team at the airport.

4 There's ***enough / much / plenty of / too much*** salt in the soup.

5 I foolishly didn't follow ***all / any / no / some*** of the advice I was given.

6 I knew some of the people in the room, but ***a few / any / many / some*** of them I'd never met before.

REMEMBER THESE WORDS

CELEBRATIONS AND PROTESTS

to address (a crowd)
a banner
a ceremony
to campaign/a campaign
to celebrate/a celebration
to cheer
to clap
to clash with
to embrace/an embrace
to gather/a gathering
to give/make a speech

to go wild
joy/joyful
a placard
to promote/a promotion
to protest/a protest against
a rebellion against
a slogan
a spectator
a victory (parade)
to wave/a wave

SPECIAL EVENTS

an anniversary
to attract people
a balloon
a bride
a bridegroom
a carnival
to charge an entrance fee
a coffin
a costume
a decoration
an engagement party
a fair
a fan
a festival
a firework

a flower arrangement
a funeral
merchandise
a mourner
a parade
a public holiday
a queue
a reception
sponsorship
a stage
a stall
a steward
to take out an ad
a wedding

PHRASES WITH TAKE

to take a seat
to take after someone
to take care of someone
to take notes
to take part

to take place
to take something seriously
to take up (a new activity)
to take your time

OTHER

an alternative lifestyle
the establishment
homelessness
hunger
a mayor

poverty
reforms
to starve
the stock market

PRACTICE

1 Match the words in the box to the categories below.

merchandise   a parade   a mourner   a steward
a funeral   a costume   a coffin   a spectator
a reception   a fair   a demonstration   a banner
a bridegroom   a balloon   a float   a victory
a placard   a ceremony

- people:
- things:
- events:

2 Choose the best answers.

1 The demonstrators were silent as the president *did / made / put* his speech.
2 The Olympics take *part / off / place* every four years.
3 The king came out onto the balcony and *cheered / clapped / waved* to the crowd.
4 Greg is terribly good at maths – he takes *up / after / a photo of* his mother.
5 I'm taking *part / a seat / place* in the annual school play.
6 Many teenagers *make a campaign / rebel / clash* against their parents.

3 Which five verbs in the box are not the same as the noun form? What are the noun forms?

campaign   celebrate   cheer   clap   decorate   gather
parade   protest   promote   queue   rebel   reform
starve   wave

STUDY TIPS

English outside the classroom (1)

1 If you are living in an English-speaking country, it is much easier to practise speaking outside the classroom, but it is still possible to do it in your own country. Tick the ideas below that are possible for you.

1 Record or film yourself doing the speaking tasks from *Cutting Edge*, using your mobile phone/laptop, etc. Plan and practise what you will say first, and ask your teacher to listen to your recording and correct mistakes.
2 Practise the pronunciation of new words at home by listening to the audio in your mini-dictionary to check the correct pronunciation.
3 Choose a short section of audio from Unit 7 and listen to it on the DVD-ROM. Practise reading it aloud yourself, then listen again and check your pronunciation. If necessary, practise it again.
4 Join an online forum about a subject you are interested in and write comments. Although you are writing, the style of English is often more like speaking.
5 Think of situations where you might have to use English (at work, speaking to tourists in your town, to foreign students at your university, etc.). Imagine the kind of thing that you might have to say, and plan and practise in your head how to say it.
6 Find a conversation exchange or English club in your local area that you can join.

2 Choose one of the ideas and try it out for a month. Then assess and compare with other students how much it has helped to improve your spoken English.

08 STUDY, PRACTICE & REMEMBER

STUDY 1

Overview of modal verbs

1 *Must/mustn't*

Must expresses necessity. There are two types of necessity.

- **Obligation**

  *I **must** go home now. I've got to be at work early tomorrow.*

  ***Mustn't** means 'obliged not to' / 'not allowed to'.*

  *You **mustn't** smoke in here! You could start a fire!*

REMEMBER!

Have to and *have got to* also express obligation. *Must* often expresses an obligation that comes from the speaker while *have to/have got to* express an obligation that comes from someone or something else.

*I **must** go home now. It's late.* (= I have decided this)

*I've **got to be** at work early tomorrow morning.*

(= my boss decided this, I have an early meeting, etc.)

The idea that something is not necessary is expressed by *don't have to*.

*You **don't have to buy** a ticket if you don't want to.*

- **Logical necessity**

  Here *must* means 'from the evidence I am sure this is true'.

  *He's not answering his phone. He **must be** in a meeting.*

  If we want to say something is logically impossible, we use *can't*.

  *Surely he **can't be** 60, he only looks about 40!*

2 *Should/shouldn't*

Should is used for obligations that are not strong – it is not necessary to do something but it is 'a good idea' or right thing.

*You **should** be in bed by now.* (= this is the right thing)

*You **shouldn't** eat so much chocolate.* (= it's not a good idea)

REMEMBER!

- *Should* can be followed by a continuous form.

  *You **shouldn't be carrying** that heavy suitcase.* (= now)

- *Ought to* has the same meaning as *should*.

  *You **ought to be** in bed by now.*

---

3 *Can*

Can expresses possibility in three ways.

- **Ability**

  *She **can** speak fluent German.* (= she is able to speak German)

  Be able to also expresses ability.

  *She's **able to** speak fluent German.*

  When the sentence needs an infinitive (e.g. after *want* or after another modal verb), use *be able to*, not *can*.

  *I want to **be able to** sing like her.*

- **Permission**

  ***Can** I interrupt for a moment?* (= is it possible to interrupt?)

- **General possibility**

  *It's very hot in summer, but it **can** be freezing in winter.*

  Notice that *can* is not used to talk about specific possibilities either in the present or in the future.

  *Look in the cupboard. It **could/may/might** be in there.*

  NOT *Look in the cupboard. It ~~can~~ be in there*

4 *Could*

Could also expresses possibility in three ways.

- Ability (as the past of can) *He **could** already walk on his first birthday.*
- Permission ***Could** I interrupt for a moment?*
- Present/future possibility *Of course, I **could** be wrong.*

5 *May*

Generally, *may (not)* expresses possibility in two ways.

- Permission (mainly in first person: formal)

  ***May** I speak to you for a moment?*

- Present/future possibility *There **may** be a storm later.*

6 *Might*

Might expresses:

- Present/future possibility *We **might** see you later. We'll see what happens.*
- Permission (rather old-fashioned) ***Might** I ask you to speak up a little?*

REMEMBER!

- The different degrees of probability expressed by modal verbs can be summarised like this.

Logically certain	must	You **must** be Annie's sister, you look just like her.
Logically possible	may/might/could	I'll call Jim, he **might/may/could** still be there.
Logically impossible	can't	That woman **can't** be your teacher, she's too young!

- These modal verbs can be followed by a continuous form to talk about things happening now.

  *Have a look outside. Someone **might/may/could be waiting** for me.*

PRACTICE 1

1 Tick sentence a or b which is closest in meaning to the first.

1 You shouldn't say anything.
   a It's not a good idea to say anything. ☐
   b It's forbidden to say anything. ☐

2 You mustn't say anything.
   a I say you're not allowed to say anything. ☐
   b It's not necessary to say anything. ☐

3 This can't be the right way!
   a I'm sure that this isn't the right way. ☐
   b Perhaps this isn't the right way. ☐

4 You don't have to tell him.
   a It's not necessary to tell him. ☐
   b It's prohibited to tell him. ☐

5 That must be Tim at the door.
   a I'm sure that's Tim at the door. ☐
   b Perhaps that's Tim at the door. ☐

6 It can snow in March.
   a It sometimes snows in March. ☐
   b Perhaps it will snow in March. ☐

7 The match could be postponed.
   a Perhaps the match was postponed. ☐
   b Perhaps the match will be postponed. ☐

2 Match the animals in the box to the information below. Then complete the gaps with a modal verb (there may be more than one possibility).

....

bat   bear   cheetah   flea   moth   mayfly
Pinta Island tortoise   tiger

....

1 It _____ run at over 100 km/h.
2 They _____ make the most of their short lives because they die within hours of being born.
3 It is one of the world's rarest land animals and _____ be extinct soon.
4 If we _____ jump as high as this creature, we would be able to jump about 150 metres in the air.
5 You _____ stay still or back away slowly if you meet this creature in the wild.
6 They make high-pitched sounds which _____ be heard by humans.
7 Some of them _____ smell a female 11 kilometres away.
8 As there is only one left, it _____ be the rarest creature in the world.

STUDY 2

Past modals

Modals sometimes have different past forms according to the meaning.

Had to

When *must* expresses obligation, the past form is *had to* and the negative is *didn't have to*.
*When I was at school, I **had to/didn't have to** wear a uniform.*

Could

The past of *can* is *could* or *was able to*, or sometimes *managed to*.
• *Could* is only used to talk about general abilities, not specific occasions.
*We **could** come and go whenever we wanted.*
(= in theory, not on any particular occasion)
• *Managed to* and *was able to* are used to talk about what you successfully did on a specific occasion.
*Although he was badly injured, he **managed to/was able to** crawl to safety.*
(= he actually did this on a particular occasion)
In the negative form, *couldn't* and *wasn't able to* can be used in all cases.
• The past form *could have* is used when it was possible for something to happen, but it didn't.
*It was stupid of you to throw it out of the window. You **could have** killed someone!*

Can't have, could (not) have, may (not) have, might (not) have, must have

These modals are the past equivalents of the modals of probability.
*You **must have been** worried when you heard what had happened.*
(= logically, it seems certain that this happened)
*They **may/might/could have got** in through the window.*
(= logically, it is possible that this happened)
*They **can't have climbed** over that wall without a ladder.*
(= logically, it seems impossible that this happened)

Should have and ought to have

The past form of *should* is *should have* + past participle.
*You **should have locked** the door before you went out.*
(= this was a good idea, but you didn't do it)
*You **shouldn't have left** the door unlocked!*
(= this wasn't a good idea, but you did it)
The past of *ought to* is *ought to have* + past participle.
*We **ought to have booked** in advance – there are no tables left.*

PRACTICE 2

1 Choose the correct past modal.

1 When I was a teenager, I *could / had to* stay out as long as I wanted, provided that I phoned home.
2 There was hardly any traffic on the road, so we *didn't have to / couldn't* rush to get to the station on time.
3 I'm sure hearing the news was a terrible shock. It *had to be / must have been* an awful experience for you.
4 David *could have / might have* left the house any time he wanted to. No one forced him to stay.
5 No wonder we're in a mess – we *should have / must have* paid more attention to the instructions.
6 We don't know what's happened to Nicola. She *may have / can have* got lost somewhere.

2 Complete the gaps with an appropriate past modal and the correct form of the verbs in brackets.

1 a You _____ (leave) your glasses at work – I saw them in the kitchen a few minutes ago.
   b You _____ (leave) your glasses at work. I haven't seen them since you got home.
2 a I _____ (study) medicine, but I decided to go travelling instead.
   b I _____ (study) medicine – my parents insisted on it.
3 a Vera and Jack _____ (get) lost – they said they'd be here by three.
   b Vera and Jack _____ (get) lost – they've been here dozens of times.
4 a Annie _____ (go) home, her car's still in the car park.
   b Annie _____ (go) home, her coat's gone.
5 a Katie _____ (buy) a lot of new clothes, as she was expected to look smart in her new job.
   b Katie _____ (buy) a lot of new clothes, she's completely changed her image!

REMEMBER THESE WORDS

MYSTERIES AND ODDITIES

an alien	proof
a coincidence	a publicity stunt
to confess	supernatural
an eye witness	suspicious
a hoax	unexplained
to investigate	unfortunate
a miracle	a tragic incident
a myth	to turn out that
a natural phenomenon	a UFO
a practical joke	to vanish

EXTREME ADJECTIVES

appalling	huge
deafening	massive
enormous	remarkable
exhausting	ridiculous
exquisite	starving
extraordinary	stunning
furious	superb
gorgeous	terrific
hilarious	tiny
horrendous	vast

OTHER

a bullet	iron bars
to commit suicide	to lock/locked
an earthquake	a prescription
an embassy	a scream
a gunshot wound	to sleepwalk
to hiccup/a hiccup	to tickle

PRACTICE

1 Replace the underlined phrases with a word/phrase in the box with the same meaning.

> a natural phenomenon   mysterious   a myth
> eye witness   UFO   practical joke

1 Do you believe that story? I think it's <u>something which a lot of people think is true but actually isn't true</u>.
2 I don't think it's <u>something that happens naturally and is not strange in any way</u>.
3 That's extraordinary. It's really <u>hard to understand what happened</u>.
4 Was that a <u>joke that you don't tell but where you actually do something to someone</u>.
5 She was the <u>person who saw it happen</u>.
6 It looked like a <u>spaceship from another planet</u>.

2 Complete the gaps with extreme adjectives.

1 The group were so far away, all we could see were some _____ figures in the far distance.
2 It was a(n) _____ moment when violence broke out between the police and the demonstrators.
3 The crowd were really _____ when the referee sent off the home team's captain.
4 We were sitting right in the front row, so at times the noise of the group was _____ .
5 The film was so _____ that many members of the audience walked out before the end.
6 Pictures of the concert were projected onto a _____ video screen, so everyone could see perfectly.
7 The march lasted for hours and after they'd been walking for such a long time everyone was _____ .
8 The evening got off to a great start with a _____ speech by the principal: the whole audience was laughing.
9 There were huge queues at the food stalls, so by the time we got to the front we were absolutely _____ .
10 All her guests agreed that Lucinda looked _____ in her wedding dress.

STUDY TIPS

Memorise new vocabulary

1 When memorising new vocabulary, surprising ideas and images are more memorable than ordinary ones, so use them to improve your vocabulary. Read the ideas below. Which do you think is most effective?

1 When you are learning new words or phrases, form a surprising mental picture to help you. For example, to remember the phrase *publicity stunt*, imagine a megaphone (a symbol of publicity) jumping across a river on a motorbike (a symbol of a stunt).
2 Record new words in a vocabulary notebook. Look at it regularly and make new sentences in your mind using the words.
3 Make ridiculous rhymes with words or phrases that you are trying to learn. (You might even try to set them to music.)
   *This is your first **exquisite** visit, is it?*
4 Go online and go to a search engine. Type in a word that you are trying to remember and see what images come up. Choose the most memorable image, print it out and write the word on the page.
5 Write new words on Post-it notes and stick them to your fridge, bedroom door, etc.
6   Personalise words that you want to remember. Use them to say something about yourself.
7 Test yourself. Research shows that testing is an effective way of remembering new information, and the harder the test, the better you will remember.

09 STUDY, PRACTICE & REMEMBER

STUDY 1

Use and non-use of articles

1 Basic rules

Indefinite articles
We use *a/an* when 'we don't know which one' because the thing:
- is one of many. *He's an artist.* (= there are many artists)
- is not unique. *I've just bought a Ferrari.*
- has not been mentioned before. *There was a new student in class.*

Definite articles
We use *the* when 'we know which one' because the thing or person:
- is unique (or unique in that context).
  The Australian prime minister. (= there is only one)
  I looked inside – the engine was in a terrible state. (= there is only one engine, in this case)
- has been mentioned before.
  The man gave me a ticket. I saw that the ticket was a single.
- is defined by the phrase which follows it.
  What's the new student's name?

No articles
We do not use an article when we talk about things in general:
- using plural or uncountable nouns. *Do you like sport?*
- with the names of people or places, but there are many exceptions (see section 3). *a book by Professor Jones*

Fixed phrases
There are many fixed phrases with and without articles. It is best to learn these individually. These include the following.
*a few   at home   at work   at the beginning   at the end
go to bed   go to the cinema/shops/station   in the world
once a week   60 kilometres an hour   the other day   the same*

2 Areas that often cause problems

Jobs
If there are many people doing a particular job, we use *a/an*.
My husband is an architect. (= there are many architects)
But if a job is specific to one person, we use *the*.
He is having talks with the French minister. (= there is only one)

Superlative
We use *the* with superlative adjectives. *She's the best person for the job.*

Last and *next*
These adjectives can be used with or without *the* but there is a change of meaning.
I saw James last night. (= the one before this one)
It's the last night of our holiday. (= a time defined by the context)
I'll see you next week. (= the one after this one)
The next time I see you, I'll be 40. (= a time defined by the context)

Institutions: *school, prison, university, church, hospital*
With words like *prison, university, church*, etc., we use no article when we are thinking about the institution, and the normal purpose we use it for.
My sister had to stay in hospital overnight.
However, if we are thinking about the building, we use *the*.
Our flat is opposite the hospital.

3 Use and non-use of definite article with phrases of time and place

Phrases of time
Some time phrases take *the*.
- dates: *the 25th of December/December the 25th*
- parts of the day: *in the afternoon, in the evening, in the morning* (but *at night, at lunchtime*)
- decades/centuries: *the 1980s, the 21st century*

Other time phrases take no article.
- years/seasons: *in 2002*
- months/days: *in August, on Friday, see you tomorrow*
- seasons can take *the*, or no article: *In the summer/In summer*

Place names
- The names of most planets, countries, continents, islands, states, provinces, towns and cities do not take an article.
  in Asia, to Sydney, from Texas, in Turkey
  Exceptions: *the Czech Republic, the Netherlands, the UK, the Arab World, the USA*
- If we talk about a region, we do not use an article.
  North-west India, Northern Europe
  But: *in the east of the country, in the south of Italy, on the coast*
- Most roads, streets, parks, bridges, shops and restaurants do not take an article. *Central Park, Harrods, Oxford Street, Tower Bridge*
- The names of theatres, cinemas, hotels, galleries and museums take *the*. *the Hermitage, the National Theatre, the Odeon, the Ritz*
- The names of particular mountains and lakes do not take an article. *Lake Victoria, Mount Everest*
- Mountain ranges, rivers, seas and canals take *the*. *the Atlantic, the (River) Danube, the Himalayas, the Panama Canal*

PRACTICE 1

1 Complete the text with *a/an* or *the*.

Chewing gum

Teachers have always tried to ban it, but [1]___ new study has revealed that people can actually benefit from chewing gum: [2]___ author of [3]___ study, Dr Andrew Scholey, claims that there is [4]___ link between chewing and memory. [5]___ link may be connected with [6]___ production of oxygen in [7]___ brain.

For [8]___ study, [9]___ group of volunteers at Northumbria University performed [10]___ number of tests designed to test their memory and concentration. [11]___ first group were allowed to chew gum: [12]___ second only pretended to chew, while [13]___ third did not chew at all. There was no difference between [14]___ three groups in terms of concentration, but in memory tests, there was [15]___ big difference: [16]___ group who had been allowed to chew performed 35 percent better than [17]___ other groups.

2 Complete the text with *a/an*, *the* or no article (ø).

The UK's hardest working man?

[1]___ hardest-working man in [2]___ UK has decided to take life [3]___ little easier. James McSporran has retired as [4]___ only police officer on [5]___ tiny island of Gigha in [6]___ north-west Scotland. However, he will continue to serve Gigha's 200 inhabitants in [7]___ number of other roles, for he is also [8]___ only postman, [9]___ ambulance man, [10]___ shopkeeper and [11]___ taxi driver for [12]___ island. [13]___ police job wasn't demanding, he told [14]___ *Times*. [15]___ people on the island are all either [16]___ relatives or [17]___ friends, so [18]___ crime is unknown!

3 Add *a* or *the* to the sentences below, where necessary.

1 My brother works as travel representative in Canada.
2 President of USA has resigned!
3 Sahara is largest desert in Africa.
4 He was last person to see victim alive.
5 I'll see you next week.
6 Weather is better in south of country.
7 I live near hospital.
8 He'll be here in morning.
9 Can I have two tickets for 9 p.m. film?
10 My dream is to retire to tropical island somewhere.

STUDY 2
Different ways of giving emphasis

1 Intensifiers

Absolutely, completely, really, so
We use these words to add emphasis to adjectives.
*Her new book is **absolutely** brilliant.*
*It's **so** annoying.*
Absolutely and *completely* are usually used only with ungradable adjectives (for example *fantastic*, *awful*, etc.) which already describe an extreme or absolute quality.
*The weather was **absolutely** perfect.* (NOT ~~absolutely good~~)
*The second half of the match was **completely** awful.*
(NOT ~~completely bad~~)

FAR
Far is used for emphasis with *too* + adjective or *too much/many* + noun.
*It's **far** too much trouble.*
We also use *far* with comparative adjectives.
*You're **far** taller than I'd expected.*

2 *So* and *such*

So is used before adjectives to intensify them. *You were **so** lucky!*
Such is used before an adjective + noun.
*We're having **such** beautiful weather!*
A/An are used after *such*. *It was **such** a long journey!*
Notice that with *much/many* + noun, we use *so*.
*We've had **so many** problems!*
*It takes **so much** time!*

3 Use of auxiliary verbs

We often add an auxiliary verb in the positive for emphasis.
*Your father **does** make me laugh.*
We also use auxiliary verbs in the positive to emphasise a contrast.
*Donna is a vegetarian, but she **does** eat fish.*
Adding *really* before the auxiliary also adds emphasis.
*I **really do** apologise for what happened.*

4 Cleft sentences

The usual word order for a sentence in English is subject + verb + object + (adverbial phrase). *I like your sense of humour (most of all).*
However, if we want to emphasise that we like his sense of humour (more than anything else about him), we can use a cleft sentence that begins with a *what* clause and the verb *be*.
What I like most (about you) is your sense of humour.
Similarly, if we want to emphasise a particular person (more than anyone else), we use a cleft sentence with *it* + *be* + *who*.
*Both my children like fashion, but **it's my son who** spends most of his money on clothes.*
If a pronoun is used, the object pronoun is more usual than the subject pronoun, though some consider this incorrect.
*It was **me** who found it.*

5 Emphatic questions

Informally, we can use the phrase *on earth* after a *wh-* question word to emphasise surprise, annoyance, or the fact that we do not know the answer to a question.
*You're over two hours late -- **where on earth** have you been?*

PRACTICE 2

1 Choose the correct words.

1 That TV programme was **absolutely / completely / so** funny.
2 Believe me, I **really / did / have** try to phone you.
3 **That / What / Which** I liked about the film was the acting.
4 **He / It / What**'s my son who's the expert on computers.
5 What **at / in / on** earth do you mean by asking me that?
6 It was **so / such / very** an uncomfortable journey that we couldn't sleep at all.
7 Your new girlfriend is **completely / really / absolutely** nice.
8 It's **far / so / such** more difficult than you think to get a good job these days.
9 That new exhibition is **very / such / absolutely** incredible.
10 I **do / so / far** believe you. You don't have to repeat yourself.

2 Complete the conversation, adding emphasis to B's replies.

1 **A:** I love camping.
   B: Me too. What I like _____ is living outdoors.
2 **A:** Is that flat expensive?
   B: Yes, it's _____ too expensive for us.
3 **A:** Why did you buy that painting?
   B: Because it's _____ incredible. I love it.
4 **A:** You're not interested in what I'm saying.
   B: I _____ want to know about your day, but I need to work.
5 **A:** I hate waiting for buses.
   B: Me too. It's _____ a waste of time.
6 **A:** Jorge threw a rock at Pedro today.
   B: What _____ _____ did he do that for?

REMEMBER THESE WORDS

GETTING NOTICED

acronyms	to make eye contact
ASAP	name-dropping
to attract attention (to yourself)	a narcissist
status	to pretend
to get noticed	to set goals
to hold your head high	status
to make an entrance	

PHRASAL VERBS

to look up to someone	to stand for (an idea)
to make something up	to stand out (from the crowd)
to pass out	to stand up for what you believe in
to see through someone	

JOB INTERVIEWS

an applicant	(to have) lots of drive
better-paid	personal qualities
a candidate	(the right) qualifications
enthusiastic	outgoing
a job seeker	talented
good people/IT skills	a weekend job

TAKING NOTES

abbreviation	main heading
bullet point	subheading
highlighting	underlining

PHRASES WITH *RIGHT* AND *WRONG*

Everything's gone wrong.	That's all right by me!
I'll be right back.	There's something/nothing wrong
It looks about right.	with it.
It's the wrong way round.	What's wrong?
Right here, right now.	You were completely right/wrong
That serves you right.	about her!

OTHER

criticism	take deep breaths
sympathy	What on earth ...?
to sympathise	a wimp

PRACTICE

1 Choose the correct meaning for the phrasal verbs in bold.

1 I'm not talking to her. We still haven't **made up**.
   a become friends again after an argument
   b told a story which is not true
2 If you don't know the meaning, **look it up**.
   a ask someone you respect
   b find it in a dictionary
3 ASAP **stands** for 'as soon as possible'.
   a is the short form of
   b believes in
4 Sit down and be quiet. I won't **stand for** this behaviour.
   a get out of my seat
   b accept

2 Complete the sentences below with a verb from A and noun from B. There may be more than one possible answer.

A make an make hold your get set take

B head high deep breaths noticed entrance
   eye contact goals

1 Before you start your presentation, _____ a few _____ _____ and try to calm down.
2 I know you lost your job but it wasn't your fault. You can still _____ your _____ _____ and be proud.
3 When she comes in the room, everyone stops talking. She knows how to _____ a great _____.
4 The best way to be successful is to _____ _____ and then work hard to achieve them.
5 Never _____ _____ _____ with an angry dog. They take it as a sign of aggression.

3 Complete the reply using a phrase with *right* or *wrong*.

1 **A:** I lost a lot of money on that horse.
   B: That serves ... *you right*.
2 **A:** I bought pizza for dinner. **B:** That's all ...
3 **A:** Why are you upset.
   B: Oh, it's such a pain. Everything's ...
4 **A:** Where are you going? **B:** Don't worry. I'll be ...
5 **A:** It's broken. **B:** No, it isn't. There's nothing ...
6 **A:** Does this look strange to you? **B:** Yes, it's the ...

4 Replace the underlined phrases with words from the box.

right qualifications   better paid
good IT skills   job candidate   outgoing

1 Let's talk to the person who wants the job.
2 Would you describe yourself as lively and easy to talk to?
3 You need to have the ability to use a computer well.
4 This job is better in terms of money than my last one.
5 I've got the correct education and training for the job.

STUDY TIPS

English outside the classroom (2)

1 Read the ways below that you can engage with English outside the classroom. Which do you do frequently, occasionally or never?

- watch films in English (with or without subtitles)
- read books in English (in the original form or graded, e.g. Penguin Readers)
- listen to songs in English
- read English magazines (choose a subject that you are interested in)
- listen to English radio stations
- make friends with English-speaking people
- play computer games in English
- meet up with classmates and talk in English

2 Which ways might you try in the future?

STUDY 1

Reporting people's exact words

1 Change of tense

When we report what someone said, the verb forms generally move one tense into the past.

*'I **believe** that what I **am doing** is right,' she said. 'I **will** continue.'*
*She said she **believed** that what she **was doing was** right, and that she **would** continue.*

direct speech	reported speech
Present simple (*I **do***)	Past simple (*I **did***)
Present continuous (*I'm doing*)	Past continuous (*I **was doing***)
Present perfect (*I **have done***)	Past perfect (*I **had done***)
Past simple (*I **did***)	Past perfect (*I **had done***)
Past continuous (*I **was doing***)	Past perfect continuous (*I **had been doing***)
Past perfect (*I **had done***)	no change possible
Past perfect continuous (*I **had been doing***)	no change possible
will	*would*
is going to	*was going to*
can	*could*
must	*had to*

The Past continuous frequently does not change in reported speech.

REMEMBER!

- The change of tense often happens because what the person said is now in the past.
  *His teachers said he **would** end up in trouble, but now he's successful.*
- If what the person says is still true/relevant now, we often don't change tenses. *'I'll be late for the meeting.'*
  *Pippa says she'**ll** be late.* (= the meeting is still in the future)
- It is possible to change tenses in such cases, but it is often done in more formal contexts.
  'Today's agreement is a historic opportunity,' the minister said.
  *The minister said that today's agreement **was** a historic opportunity.*
  (probably in a newspaper or on the news)

- If the reporting verb is in the present tense, there is no change.
  *Mum **says** I **can** borrow the car tonight.*

2 Reported questions

Because reported questions are not real questions, the word order is the same as in statements.

*'**Will you** continue to fight this case?' the journalists asked.*
*The journalists asked if **they would** continue to fight the case.*

3 Some common reporting verbs and the constructions used after them

- **say:** *He said (that) he was enjoying his new job.*
- **tell:** *He told me (that) he was enjoying his new job.*
- **answer:** *She answered that she had no intention of resigning.*
- **reply:** *She replied that she had no intention of resigning.*
- **add:** *She added that she wanted to thank her supporters.*

The verb *ask* is most commonly used to report questions, but *wonder* and *want to know* are sometimes used, too. Question words are used as conjunctions to introduce reported questions.

*The police **asked (him) where** he had been.*
*They **wanted to know what time** he had arrived home.*

With *yes/no* questions *if* or *whether* are used.

*Ben **wondered if/whether** you wanted to come round for dinner.*

REMEMBER!

Say does not take a direct object, but *tell* always does.
*He **said** (that) he'd be here about nine o'clock.*
NOT *He ~~said~~ me (that) he'd be here about nine o'clock.*
*He **told** me (that) he'd be here about nine o'clock.*
In both cases, *that* can be omitted.

4 Other changes in reported speech

- When we report what someone said, we need to show any changes in the situation (e.g. a change in speaker, time or place).
  Direct speech: *'I'll help **you** clean the car later on **today**.'*
  Reported speech the next day:
  *You said **you** would help **me** clean the car **yesterday**.*
- Here are some typical changes of time phrases in reported speech. Notice that they do not happen automatically; it depends on the situation.

direct speech	reported speech
now	
today	*that day/last Tuesday*, etc.
yesterday	*the day before/the previous day*
tomorrow	*the next day/the following day*
this week	*last week/that week*
last year	*the year before/the previous year*
next month	*the month before/the following month*
an hour ago	*an hour before/an hour earlier*

- However, we often omit the time reference if it is not important.
  'We are unable to report the weather this evening.'
  The announcer said that they were unable to report the weather.

PRACTICE 1

1 Correct the underlined mistakes.

1 The journalist <u>told</u> the prime minister <u>did he know</u> anything about the scandal.
2 The minister <u>said</u> journalists last year he <u>will</u> resign if his policy <u>is</u> not successful, but he is still in his job.
3 The manager <u>told</u> that his team had done their best <u>yesterday</u> but <u>if</u> the other side had simply played better.
4 Journalists <u>added</u> the minister when <u>will he make</u> his decision.
5 The president said he <u>is</u> speaking to other leaders later <u>this</u> day to discuss how they <u>will</u> react.

2a Who do you think said the sentences below: a journalist, a celebrity or a politician?

1 There is no truth to the rumours that we are getting divorced. Our marriage is rock solid.
2 Most of our readers will find that quite hard to believe. I find that quite hard to believe.
3 Folks, who do you trust to run the country, them or us?
4 Did you know about the missing money, minister?
5 We have just adopted our third child. Her name is HoneyBee.
6 Are you going to resign?
7 I have no intention of resigning. This mess is not my fault.

b Report what each person said using *say*, *tell*, *ask* and *add*.

The celebrity said that there was no truth to the rumours that she was getting divorced. She added that their marriage was rock solid.

STUDY 2

Verbs that summarise what people say

There are a large number of verbs that summarise what people say without reporting every word. The patterns that follow these verbs vary and have to be learned separately. With some verbs, more than one pattern is possible. Here are some of the most important.

1 Verb + *that*

explain: *He **explained (that)** it wasn't possible.*
(also: *agree, claim, complain, insist, recommend, say, suggest*)

2 Verb + object + (*that*)

tell: *She **told me (that)** she was in love.*
(also: *warn, assure, persuade*)

3 Verb + gerund

admit: *The politician **admitted lying** to the press.*
(also: *deny, suggest, recommend*)

4 Verb + preposition + gerund

confess: *My daughter **confessed to eating** all the biscuits.*
(also: *apologise for, insist on, object to*)

5 Verb + object + preposition + gerund

accuse: *Don't **accuse me of lying**!*
(also: *blame someone for, congratulate someone on*)

6 Verb + infinitive

refuse: *I **refused to meet** her after what she'd said.*
(also: *agree, decide, demand, offer, promise, threaten*)

7 Verb + object + infinitive

invite: *Did you **invite her to speak** at the conference?*
(also: *tell, ask, order, remind, warn*)

REMEMBER!
Negative gerunds and infinitives can also be used.
*I decided **not to accept** the job.*
*She blamed him for **not helping** her.*

PRACTICE 2

1 Complete the story using the correct form of the verbs.

Driven to divorce by the media

When Kay Tott got home, tired from work one evening, she just wanted to watch a video, but her husband Martyn suggested [1]_____ (watch) the news first. Now they must wish they hadn't.

The TV news bulletin said that someone in their area of north-east England [2]_____ (fail) to claim a National lottery prize of €4,334,496 and warned the winner that, if they [3]_____ (want) the money, they had better appear quickly, because the six-month period in which to claim was nearly up. The numbers were 5–8–17–25–39–41. Kay jumped up and screamed 'We've won! They're our numbers!' Martyn went silent, then admitted [4]_____ (throw) the tickets away several weeks earlier.

Kay persuaded [5]_____ (her husband/get in touch) with the lottery organisers, Camelot, and explain what had happened. Officials agreed [6]_____ (investigate) the matter, and soon rang back to tell [7]_____ (the Totts/they/have) no doubt their claim was genuine, and that it would be investigated further.

The next day, a lottery investigator came to their house and warned [8]_____ (the couple/not/inform) any newspapers about what was happening. Six weeks later, he returned to tell them that they [9]_____ (Totts/they/break) the rules which stated that lost tickets must be reported within 30 days. Camelot were refusing [10]_____ (pay out). Furious, Kay ordered [11]_____ (him/leave) their tiny flat. The next day, a desperate Martyn decided [12]_____ (inform) the media. Interest was immediate: a tabloid offered [13]_____ (put) the Totts up in a five-star hotel in return for an exclusive interview. Several TV companies invited [14]_____ (the couple/appear) on daytime TV. In an angry confrontation, a Camelot official apologised [15]_____ (cause) the couple so much disappointment, but insisted [16]_____ (they have to follow) their rules. The couple angrily accused [17]_____ (Camelot/ruin/their lives) by raising their hopes and putting them through 'torture'. They even threatened [18]_____ (sue) the company over the mental stress they had suffered. Officials, however, denied [19]_____ (make) any false promises.

In the end, the Totts got little except a brief taste of tabloid fame. Two years later, the couple divorced. Kay blames [20]_____ (the media/raise) their hopes of a millionaire lifestyle: 'Before this happened, we were quite happy. Between them, Camelot and the newspapers turned our lives into a living hell.'

2 Here are some quotes the characters in the story might have said. Rewrite them using the reporting verbs in brackets.

1 Remember to put the ticket in a safe place, love. (remind)
   Kay reminded her husband to put the ticket in a safe place.
2 Shall we have a quiet night in and watch a video? (suggest)
3 I'm sorry. I threw the ticket away the other week. (apologise)
4 We'll investigate the matter most thoroughly. (promise)
5 You mustn't even tell your family about this. (warn)
6 We won't talk about the investigation. (refuse)
7 We had no problems in our marriage before. (deny)

REMEMBER THESE WORDS

MASS MEDIA

a broadsheet	to portray (men/women, etc.)
circulation	in a negative/positive way
to control what people think	to protect your privacy
coverage	readership
a drama series	reality TV show
an episode	screentime
a foreign correspondent	a soap opera
interactive	social media
mass media	a tabloid
a media corporation	a talent show
microblogging	a target audience
to upload	top-rated

VERBS THAT SUMMARISE WHAT PEOPLE SAY

to accuse	to invite
to admit	to offer
to agree	to refuse
to apologise	to recommend
to blame	to suggest
to confess	to warn
to deny	

SPEAK AND *TALK*

actions speak louder than words	to speak your mind
to be on speaking terms	to speak up
to know what you are talking about	a talking point
	talk radio
peace talks	to talk shop
small talk	a talk show
to speak highly of someone	talking to yourself

OTHER

a forensic investigator	to undermine parental authority
graphic violence	to uphold a complaint
ratings	

PRACTICE

1 What connects the words in each group below? What are the differences between the words?

1 drama series   soap opera   talent show
they are all kinds of TV programmes
2 broadsheet   tabloid
3 circulation   readership
4 microblogging   social media
5 a foreign correspondent   an editor

2 Complete the conversations.

1 A: I'm going to clean all the windows this weekend.
   B: Actions _____ than words.
2 A: I really like her. She's very smart.
   B: She _____ _____ of you, too.
3 A: I don't want to offend anyone, so I should keep quiet.
   B: No, go on. _____ your mind.

4 A: Why don't you go and talk to her?
   B: I can't. We're not on _____ terms.
5 A: She said that you were having some problems.
   B: She doesn't know what she's _____ _____ .
6 A: I really hate parties where I don't know anyone.
   B: Me too. I hate making small _____ .

3 Match the verbs in the box for summarising what people say to phrases 1–8.

admit   warn   deny   recommend
agree   apologise   offer   accuse

1 you tell a friend that they should try a good new restaurant
2 you say that your classmate broke the computer, not you
3 you tell someone to be careful because the food is spicy
4 you tell your teacher that you didn't do your homework
5 you say sorry for something that you did
6 you say that someone is right and you think the same
7 you tell your friend you will help them move house
8 you say that you didn't break your friend's pen

STUDY TIPS

Effective revision techniques

1 How do you revise for an English exam? Make a list of things that you do.

2 Look at the list of revision techniques below. Tick the ones you find effective. Cross the ones you don't think are useful for you.

- Read the grammar summaries and word lists in the Study & Practice sections. ☐
- Study in short periods of about 20–30 minutes. Most people can't concentrate for much longer than that. ☐
- Carry your vocabulary book with you and check it regularly (e.g. when travelling on a bus). ☐
- Record yourself reading out words or grammar examples from the book. ☐
- Study with a friend and test each other. ☐
- Look at similar exam papers from the past and try to complete them in the allowed time. ☐
- Keep yourself engaged with new techniques while. For example, switch from studying the grammar summaries to recording yourself saying new words. ☐
- Make a revision plan so that you know what you are revising each day. ☐
- Revise a little and often rather than for long sessions. ☐
- As your exam comes nearer, stop trying to learn new things and focus on consolidating the things you have already studied. ☐
- Don't always study in the same place. Research shows that studying in a variety of places is more effective. ☐

3 Which techniques do you intend to use in the future?

STUDY 1

Hypothetical situations in the present

1 Hypothetical situations with *if*

- When talking about hypothetical or imaginary situations in the present/future, we go back one tense into the past.

  *I **don't have** a cat, but if I **had** one I'd call it Henry.*

  *It's **raining** now – if it **wasn't raining** we could eat outside.*

  This is sometimes called the 'unreal past'. The unreal past is often used after *if* in conditional sentences, as above. In the main clause we often use *would* or other modal verbs.

  *If I **had** more time,   I **would start** going to the gym.*

  *I **could learn** to drive.*

- In certain phrases with the unreal past, we can use *were* with *he/she/it* with the first and third person.

  *If Rachel **were** here, she'd know what to do.*

  Some people consider this too formal and old-fashioned. However, it is still common with the phrase *If I were.*

  *I'd tell her about it **if I were you.***

2 Imaginary situations with *wish* and *if only*

- We also use the unreal past after *if only* and *I wish* because they both describe imaginary situations.

  *I wish I **could** speak Spanish.*

  (= I can't speak Spanish, but I'd like to)

  *If only we **had** a map with us!*

  (= but we don't have one)

- We can also use *wish* + *would(n't)* to refer to things that you would like to happen (but you don't think they will happen).

  *I **wish** my boss **would** give me a pay rise.*

  *I **wish** + you **would(n't)*** is often used to express annoyance.

  *I **wish you'd** hurry up.*

  (= you are being very slow)

- If there is no possibility of change, we must use the Past simple. Compare:

  *I **wish** you **were** taller.*

  (= you cannot change this)

  with:

  *I **wish you'd** be more helpful.*

  (= you can change this)

- We cannot use *wish* + *would* when the subject of the two clauses is the same.

  I wish I knew the answer.

  NOT *I wish I ~~would know~~ the answer.*

- The unreal past is also used after the phrase *It's time.*

  *It's **time** people **changed** their attitude towards plastic surgery.*

PRACTICE 1

1 Complete the sentences with the correct form of the verbs in brackets.

1 Imagine if I _____ (get) a pay rise, I _____ (can buy) a new motorbike.
2 It's time Alex _____ (start) acting like an adult.
3 I wish you _____ (not interrupt) me all the time – it's really annoying.
4 The whole thing _____ (be) funny if poor Alice _____ (not be) so upset.
5 I wish I _____ (can) translate this for you, but I can't.
6 It's time you _____ (make) an effort to understand how worried I am.
7 Suppose you_____ (win) the competition, what _____ (you do) with the prize money?
8 I wish Joe _____ (hurry up).

2 Think of two things you might wish for in these situations.

1 You are at a noisy party and you have a bad headache.
   I wish/If only I was at home.
2 It's two o'clock in the morning and you can't sleep because your neighbour's car alarm is going off.
3 You are outside in shorts and a T-shirt and it starts to rain.
4 You are stuck in a traffic jam and you are going to be late for an important appointment.
5 It's Monday morning at 6.30 and your alarm clock has just gone off to get you up for work.

3 Choose the correct answers.

1 If I ***would go / will go / went*** to India I'd definitely go to the Taj Mahal.
2 I wish I ***would type / could type / can type*** as fast as you.
3 I'd read the small print at the bottom of the form very carefully if I ***am / would be / were*** you.
4 I think Elena wishes she ***was / would be / is*** back in Russia.
5 If only I ***had / would have / have*** my camera with me!
6 It's time you ***go / are going / went*** to bed, Nicky.
7 I wish we ***aren't leaving / weren't leaving / didn't leave*** Spain.
8 What if everybody ***wanted / would want / could want*** to live in the countryside?
9 If we lived in a hotter country, we ***ate / could eat / were eating*** outside all the time.
10 I wish Tom ***doesn't work / won't work / didn't work*** at night.

Hypothetical situations in the past

- When we talk hypothetically about the past with *if*, *if only* and *I wish*, the Past simple becomes the Past perfect.

  *If only / I wish I **had thought** about it more carefully!*

  (= but I didn't)

  *If you**'d told** me about the problem earlier, I would have done something about it.* (= but you didn't tell me about it)

- In conditional sentences, if the main clause also refers to the past, *would have* + past participle is used.

  *If our best player **hadn't got** injured, we **would have** won.*

REMEMBER!

As with present hypothetical situations, *might have* and *could have* are often used instead of *would have*.

*If he **hadn't been** injured, we **might/could have** won.*

- Notice that in the sentences above, both the *if* clause and the main clause refer to the past. It is also possible to have a sentence where the *if* clause refers to the past and the main clause refers to the present.

  *If we**'d set off** earlier* (past), *we**'d be** at the hotel now.* (present)

  Alternatively, the *if* clause may refer to the present, and the main clause to the past.

  *If Dan's father **wasn't** the boss* (present), *he **wouldn't have got** the job.* (past)

PRACTICE 2

1 Complete the sentences with the correct form of the verbs in brackets.

1 If you _____ (tell) me you wanted one, I _____ (buy) you a ticket.

2 I _____ (bring) you a present back from my holidays if I _____ (have) some money left.

3 We _____ (get) to the restaurant before it closed, if I _____ (not follow) to your directions.

4 If he _____ (not fail) all his exams, he _____ (have) a job by now.

5 He _____ (never do) anything so stupid, if his friends _____ (not encourage) him.

6 If I _____ (know) you were coming I _____ (wait) for you.

7 If I _____ (take) a photo of what happened, perhaps you _____ (believe) me?

8 If you _____ (listen) to what I told you, you _____ (not be) in this situation now!

2 Think of two wishes that the speakers below might make. Use *I wish/If only* to start the sentences.

1 I've lost my job and I can't afford to pay the rent.

  I wish I hadn't lost my job.

  If only I had enough money to pay the rent.

2 My family have moved to the country and I can't drive, so I'm really bored.

3 I've lost my phone and I haven't written my friends' numbers down.

4 I ate far too much lunch and I feel really sick.

5 I failed my exams because I didn't do any work.

6 I went country dancing and broke my leg!

3 Match sentence beginnings 1–10 with sentence endings a–j.

1 If Martin had run

2 We wouldn't be late

3 Igor would have been embarrassed if

4 You could have finished your dissertation by now

5 If Peter had worked harder,

6 If you'd come to the play,

7 If you'd asked Clara,

8 If you hadn't been wearing a seat belt,

9 If Kevin had spent more time practising,

10 Steve might have got promoted

a if you weren't so lazy!

b if Sue hadn't taken so much time getting ready.

c he could have caught the train.

d he'd heard you say that.

e if he were more talented.

f you might have enjoyed yourself.

g he could be in a much better job now.

h you would have hurt yourself.

i I'm sure she would have helped you.

j he could have become a professional pianist.

4 Choose the correct answers.

1 I wish we *'d bought / would have bought* better tickets. I can't see very well from here.

2 How would you have felt if someone *had treated / would treated* you like that?

3 If I *had known / known* you were coming I would have met you at the station.

4 If only I *wouldn't have lost / had not lost* my temper!

5 If you *stay / had stayed* till the end of the film, you might have enjoyed it.

6 If Catriona *done / had done* better in the interview she could have got the job.

7 We *would have been / would be* there by now if we hadn't got stuck in the traffic.

8 Our last holiday *would be / would have been* great if the weather had been better.

9 If I had seen you walking along the road I *might have given / might give* you a lift.

10 Now Henry wishes he *went / had gone* to university.

REMEMBER THESE WORDS

SCIENCE AND PROCESSES

an asteroid strike	a nuclear bomb
a catastrophe	solar energy
climate change	a surface
an earthquake	a toxic chemical
fossil fuels	wind power
a magnifying glass	a volcanic eruption

VERBS TO DESCRIBE PROCESSES AND CHANGE

to affect	to prevent
to capture	to pump
to cause an increase	to reflect
to combat	to stir
to contribute to	to turn something into
to have an impact on	something else

PHRASES WITH *LIFE*

the chance of a lifetime	a life jacket
life expectancy	a life-threatening disease
lifelike	to make life difficult
a life sentence	in real life
a lifelong (smoker/ambition, etc.)	your private life
a life guard	

OTHER

the aging population	self esteem
the long-term effects of something	the taxpayer
peer pressure	value for money

PRACTICE

1a Cover the word list then form compound nouns using a word in box A and a word in box B.

A

solar   nuclear   life   life   life   private   long-term
wind   peer   self   fossil   volcanic   toxic
magnifying   tax

B

glass   chemical   fuel   eruption   effects   guard
payer   pressure   esteem   expectancy   bomb
power   life   energy   sentence

solar energy

b Check your answers in the word list.

2 Underline the odd one out in each group below. Give reasons for your answers.

1 an asteroid strike   an earthquake
   a nuclear bomb   a volcanic eruption
2 fossil fuel   wind power
   solar energy   toxic chemicals
3 to pump   to reflect   to stir
4 to combat   to contribute to   to prevent
5 a life guard   a life jacket   a life sentence

STUDY TIPS

Improving your reading speed

1 If you want to study or work in English, it's important to read efficiently. A good reading speed is about 150–200 words a minute. Tick the ideas below that you think will improve your reading speed/efficiency. Cross out the ones that will slow it down.

- Read as much as you can in English – websites, newspapers, graded readers ... anything! ☐
- Translate each word in your head as you are reading. ☐
- Say the words to yourself as you read. ☐
- Set yourself a time to read a text and continue until you've finished. ☐
- Stop every time you find a word you don't know and keep re-reading phrases you didn't understand completely. ☐
- Ignore unknown words, unless they recur or seem to be very important to understanding the text. ☐
- Try to get a general understanding of the whole text, and summarise the main points of what you have read after you have finished the text. ☐

2 Which things in the list do/don't you do? Choose two things that you can do to improve your reading, and practise them in the next few weeks.

STUDY 1

Use of gerunds and infinitives

1 Gerunds

Grammatically, gerunds (the -ing form of the verb) are used in the same way as nouns/pronouns.
(See Unit 2, Study 2 for a comparison between the use of gerunds and nouns.)

- As the subject or object of the sentence.
  *Too much **sunbathing** is bad for your skin.*
  *I hate **being** late.*
- After a preposition.
  *She's very good **at organising** things.*
  *He acted **without thinking**.*
- Certain verbs are followed by the gerund. These include:
  admit, can't stand, consider, deny, enjoy, hate, imagine, like, dislike, love, (don't) mind, miss, practise, risk, suggest
- There are also some noun phrases which take a gerund, for example: *have difficulty, have trouble.*
  *We're **having trouble recruiting** new staff.*
- There are also a number of useful patterns with *It* + gerund.
  *It's **worth seeing** the gardens in summer.*
  *It's **no use talking** to her – she won't change her mind.*

REMEMBER!

Notice the negative form of the gerund.
*I want to achieve immortality through **not dying**.*

2 Infinitives with *to*

Infinitives are not generally used as the subject of sentences. They are most commonly used in the following constructions.

Verb + infinitive

Certain verbs are followed by the infinitive with *to*. The most important include: *afford, agree, decide, expect, hope, manage, offer, plan, pretend, promise, refuse, seem, tend, threaten, want.*
*He has **agreed to come** into the studio and do an interview.*
*She **refused to answer** any questions about her engagement.*

Adjective + infinitive

Many adjectives are followed by an infinitive with *to*.
*It's **easy to see** why she's been so successful.*
*He was the **first to suggest** a new approach.*
Three common constructions with adjective + infinitive with *to* are:

- *too* + adjective + *infinitive*
  *He's **too experienced to make** such a simple mistake.*
- *not* + adjective + *enough* + infinitive
  *Maria isn't **old enough to go** out on her own.*
- adjective + *for* + person + infinitive
  *It's **easy for people to get** information over the internet.*

Noun + infinitive

The following nouns are followed by the infinitive with *to*: *chance, decision, effort, opportunity, time.*
*Their best **chance to win** the game came in the second half.*
*They really made an **effort to make** us feel at home.*

Something / nowhere, etc. + infinitive

We often use the infinitive with *to* after words like *no one, nothing, nowhere, something, somewhere, what, where,* etc.
*There was **nowhere to buy** a newspaper at that time of night.*
*Would you like **something to eat** before you go?*

Infinitive of purpose

We use an infinitive with *to* to explain why someone does something – to express purpose.
*Helen's gone out **to buy** a newspaper.*
In more formal English, we can use *in order to*.
*Taxes have been increased **in order to reduce** inflation.*

REMEMBER!

We form the negative infinitive with *not + to +* verb
*I told you **not to do** that.*

3 Infinitives without *to*

Infinitives without *to* are used:

- after modal verbs.
  *I **can't wait** for the weekend.*
  *You **must have been waiting** for a long time.*
- after *had better* and *would rather*.
  *We**'d better go** home now.*
  *I**'d rather watch** a video than go to the cinema.*
- after *let, make* and *help*.
  *She's the kind of person who really **makes you laugh**.*
  *When I was a teenager, my parents never **let me stay out** late.*
  *Can you **help me carry** the suitcases to the car?**
  (* The infinitive with *to* is also possible here.)

PRACTICE 1

1 Are the verbs and phrases in the box followed by the gerund, the infinitive or the infinitive without *to*?

offer   enjoy   too lazy   practise   would rather
have trouble   would better   refuse   old enough
suggest   miss   let   don't mind   good at   seem
it's worth   agree   pretend

- gerund
- infinitive
- infinitive without *to*

2 Complete the sentences below with the gerund or infinitive form of the verbs in brackets (with or without *to*).

What celebrities say.

1 I would refuse _____ (go) to a club or restaurant that looked cheap or unfashionable.
2 I loathe people _____ (ignore) me.
3 When I meet new people I expect them _____ (remember) who I am.
4 I regularly spend more than an hour _____ (get) ready to go out.
5 I would make a special effort _____ (be) nice to someone if I thought they could help me in my career.
6 I sometimes make people _____ (wait) _____ (see) me in order _____ (make) them _____ (appreciate) me more.
7 I sometimes ignore people if I think they are not worth _____ (know).
8 I can't stand _____ (go) to parties where there's no one famous to talk to.
9 I sometimes tell lies about myself _____ (make) myself sound more interesting.
10 If I'm buying an outfit for an important occasion, I try _____ (find) something that will make people _____ (notice) me.
11 I would rather _____ (arrive) at a party a bit late, in order _____ (make) a big entrance.
12 I want everyone I meet _____ (like) me.

3a There are eleven mistakes in the questions below. Find the mistakes and correct them.

1 What are you planning to do this coming weekend?
2 Do you miss to be a young child?
3 What housework do you hate doing?
4 Do you think you can ever be too old to changing career?
5 Are you better at talk or listen?
6 Would you rather be watch TV or surfing the internet right now?
7 Do you tend to be more awake in the morning or evening?
8 Have you ever threatened hitting someone?
9 Would you let your 16-year-old son to stay out late at night?
10 When and where do you practise to speak English?
11 Do you have more trouble to write or to speak English?
12 Do you refuse giving money to beggars?
13 Is it easy for you to understand the news in English?
14 Is there anywhere near your house to get a good, cheap meal?

b Choose ten of the questions and write a full answer.

I'm planning to go shopping this weekend.

Different infinitive and gerund forms

1 Negative forms

Infinitives and gerunds can be used in the negative form.
*I told you **not to do** that.*
*I want to achieve immortality through **not dying**.*

2 Passive forms

Infinitives and gerunds can be used in the passive form.
*I just want **to be left** alone.* (passive infinitive with *to*)
*He'd rather not **be given** money.* (passive infinitive without *to*)
*She hates **being told** what to do.* (passive gerund)

3 Perfect forms

We use the Perfect infinitive (*to have* + past participle) when the infinitive clause refers to a time before the main clause.
*I'd like **to visit** Rome while I'm in Europe.*
*I'd like **to have visited** Rome while I was in Europe, but had no time.*
Notice the perfect infinitive form without *to*.
*I would rather **have known** the truth.*
The perfect gerund is also possible, but sounds very formal and is often avoided.
*I remember **having seen** them.* → *I remember **seeing** them.*

4 Continuous forms

We use continuous infinitives instead of the Present continuous in infinitive constructions.
*The weather seems **to be getting** better.*
*I'd rather **be lying** on a beach than working!*
The gerund is not used in the continuous form.

PRACTICE 2

1 Choose the correct verb forms.

1 Although it's probably annoying for celebrities [1]**to ask / to be asked** for their autograph in the street, the time [2]**to worry / to have worried** is when people stop [3]**asking / being asked** them!
2 The announcement asked us not [4]**to take / take** pictures during the play.
3 Harrison Ford is thought [5]**to be / to have been** one of the few movie stars [6]**to be working / to have worked** as a carpenter.
4 I'd like [7]**being seen / to have seen** the last episode. Let's hope it's going [8]**to be released / to have released** on DVD.
5 Although the food isn't particularly good at San Pedro's, loads of celebrities go there. It's the place [9]**to see / to be seen**.
6 Do you think the media should try [10]**not to interfere / not interfere** in the private lives of famous people?

2 Complete five sentences to make them true for you.

1 When I wake up in the morning I just want ...
2 I hate being told ...
3 I'd like to have learned how to ... when I was younger.
4 I once had to ask my neighbour not to ...
5 I'd rather be ... than studying English right now.
6 I'd really like to be ... right now.
7 Sometimes, I pretend to have ... when I haven't really.
8 I'm expecting to be given ... on my next birthday.

REMEMBER THESE WORDS

FAME

achieve immortality	to make a comeback
his/her career is in decline	to make your debut
celebrity-obsessed	(at the age of ...)
to change the face of	the media spotlight
(popular music)	threatening letters
daydream (about ...)	an overnight sensation
a diva	the pressure of fame
to draw huge crowds	a record deal
a household name	a reputation for ...
ill-equipped to deal with ...	splashed across the newspapers
legendary	to start out as
a living legend	

CONFIDENCE

to be comfortable in your own skin	to not lose sleep over something
to believe in yourself	self-confident
to hide behind other people	supremely confident
to lack confidence	

CELEBRITIES AND THE MEDIA

to accuse someone wrongly	to have a right to privacy
to appear in court	to have an extra-marital affair
to be a hypocrite/hypocritical	to pose for a photo
to experience paranoia	to receive compensation
to have a strong family image	a tabloid newspaper
to bully and tease someone	to take legal action
to hack into someone's phone	

OTHER

to be introduced to someone	an outfit
a gladiator	make the right impression

PRACTICE

1 Complete the conversations with the noun form of the adjectives in bold. Use a dictionary to help you if necessary.

1 A: I'm **obsessed** with Angelina Jolie.
 B: Why do you have an _____ with her?
2 A: I wish I was more **confident**.
 B: I don't think you lack _____ .
3 A: He's a **legendary** guitarist.
 B: He can't be much of a _____ – I haven't heard of him.
4 A: I want to become **immortal** through my songs.
 B: But you can't sing. Maybe you could achieve _____ in other ways.
5 A: She became **famous** when she was still a teenager.
 B: How did she achieve _____?
6 A: She's so **hypocritical**. She shouldn't accuse me of things that she does.
 B: I know. I think she's a _____ , too.
7 A: I'm feeling a bit **paranoid** today.
 B: What is causing your _____?

2 Complete the sentences with an appropriate word.

1 If you're a good public speaker you can always _____ a crowd to listen to you.
2 The story was _____ across all the newspapers.
3 Is Darren Davies really _____ a comeback? I thought he had retired for good.
4 I _____ my debut on the stage in my school play.
5 I wouldn't _____ any sleep over it. It's not a big deal.
6 Hacking into someone's phone is illegal. You should _____ legal action.
7 Did you _____ compensation after the accident?
8 As a celebrity, you constantly have to _____ for photos.
9 Perhaps you should buy a new suit for your interview. You have to _____ the right impression.

3 There are six mistakes in the text below. Find the mistakes and correct them.

My cousin Chloe

My cousin Chloe is an actress and singer. Even when she was a child it was clear that she wanted to be in the media light. 'I'm going to be a live legend,' she said. She's not a legend yet, but she does have a record dealing. I didn't think it was very good, although I didn't tell her that. She's supremely confident and very happy in her own skin. Nonetheless, I think she'll find the pressure of famous hard – it isn't easy having every detail of your life washed across the newspapers.

STUDY TIPS

English outside the classroom (3)

1 People learning English have an advantage over people in the past – the internet. Tick the things you have tried.

1 Watch videos in English on sites like YouTube or Vimeo.
2 Download podcasts (for example, from the BBC) on topics that interest you.
3 Some groups on social networks organise outings and other opportunities for people to meet and practise their English. Sign up to one of these groups.
4 Find online practice exercises that cover the grammar or vocabulary that you are studying in class.
5 Read about interesting subjects on websites like Wikipedia.
6 Go to an online corpus and type in some of the words you are learning. The results will show you how the words are used by native-English speakers and what other words collocate with them.
7 Try a language-exchange website where you help a native-English speaker learn your language, and they help you learn English.
8 Read the news from an English-language news website.
9 Listen to an English-language radio station online.

2 Which of these methods will you use in the future?

Audio script

UNIT 1 RECORDING 1

1 I've put Briar Farm for this one, because that was the name of the farm that my aunt and uncle used to own. My mum and my sister and I, we used to go there every summer for our holidays. I absolutely loved it, all the animals, and going on the tractor with my uncle and stuff like that. It was just a really special place for me.

2 There isn't really any day of the week that I don't like, but I hate mornings ... you know, getting up first thing in the morning. I'm just not a morning person at all. It's a bit of a problem at the moment because I'm a hairdresser, and I do a lot of work for TV and stuff, and normally it's fine because I work on programmes that start late, so I get up quite late. But at the moment I'm working on a film, and I have to be there really, really early. I'm getting up at about five and it's killing me! I mean the work itself is really interesting, but I just feel so horrible at that time of the morning.

3 For this one, I've written 'Kathy'. I met her when we were both working for this really awful boss, she was just the most horrible nasty woman, and it was my first job, but I think Kathy had had a few different jobs before that. Anyway, we became very close because we both hated this boss so much. We used to go out for a coffee together and compare all the awful things she'd said to us. We were really good friends for a couple of years – we even went on holiday together once – but I haven't seen her for three or four years ... I don't know why, really ... we didn't fall out or anything, but somehow we've lost touch.

4 Let me see ... I remember the house where I was born was quite small, but it had a big garden. My parents had bought the house from an old man and he'd built this amazing pond at the bottom of the garden. That's one of my earliest memories really ... I used to spend hours staring at the fish in this pond, I found them fascinating. It was probably quite dangerous, the pond, but no one seemed to worry very much. I think we lived there for about five years and then we moved in about 1993, I think it was.

5 Erm, someone I've met quite recently is Emma ... I've only known her for about six months, I met her at my exercise class as it happens, we were standing next to each other and we just started talking. It's quite a coincidence really because obviously my name's Emma too and my boyfriend's name's Johnny and her husband's called John or Johnny. We've all been out together a couple of times, and it gets really confusing!

6 Erm, can't think of anything really for this one. Oh I know, my cousin and his wife have had a baby, I think it was born about three weeks ago, a girl, I think, I don't remember its name. I'm not really into babies myself, but it looks quite sweet in the photo on Facebook.

UNIT 1 RECORDING 4

M = Maz   A = Anna

A: And everything still going well with Ben? You two still madly in love?

M: Yeah ... yeah, well, um, I need to talk to you about it some time.

A: Why, what's wrong?

M: No there's nothing wrong as such, it's just ... I mean we get on really well, and everything, but I dunno, I don't think it's like, going anywhere. I just can't see us together in a few years' time.

A: No?

M: Not really, no. I just don't think we really want the same things. I mean he's like ... perfectly happy living here ... doing the same things, seeing the same people, and well ... you know me, I've got so many plans and things I want to do.

A: And you don't think he's interested?

M: Mmm, he says he is, but sometimes I think he's just telling me what I want to hear.

A: Do you?

M: And I mean what's the point of staying together if you don't think there's any future?

A: Poor Ben ...

M: I know, I mean I do love him, and we do have a good time ... I dunno. You won't say anything to anyone, will you? Because I really haven't decided what to do.

A: No, of course not, I wouldn't dream of it. You know you can trust me ...

UNIT 1 RECORDING 5

J = Joe   A = Anna

J: So have you seen Ben and Maz at all?

A: Yes I have actually. I had coffee with Maz the other day.

J: Yeah? Everything OK?

A: Mmm. Yeah ...

J: You don't sound very sure!

A: No, well ... don't whatever you do mention this to Ben, will you?

J: No, what?

A: Only I think she's going to finish with him ...

J: You're not serious? He'll be devastated.

A: Well, you know, they *are* very different people, I mean she's always been super-ambitious, and super-dynamic, and he's like, easy-going, happy with things they way they are. At the end of the day she doesn't think they really have that much in common.

J: Poor Ben. So what exactly did she say?

A: I don't really know if I should say anything more ... you must promise you won't say a word to him.

J: No, no, I promise, but you've got to tell me the whole story now you've started!

A: Well what she told me was ...

UNIT 1 RECORDING 6

J = Joe   B = Ben

J: So everything all right mate? Maz OK?

B: Yeah, great. She's studying like crazy as usual, but no, everything's good.

J: Good ...

B: Actually, I'm planning a bit of a surprise for her.

J: Oh are you? What's that then?

B: Well you know how she loves the sun, well I'm going to book this big holiday in the sun for us both, for when she finishes her exams next summer. Two weeks on a Greek island, she's going to love it. But it's a complete surprise, so don't say a word to her.

J: Mmm ...are you sure Maz likes surprises? Don't you think you should ... erm, you know, ask her where she wants to go? I mean it's going to cost you a fortune, isn't it?

B: Oh, she'll like this, I know she will.

J: 'Cause, you know, she does have strong opinions about what she likes, doesn't she?

B: Nah mate it's cool, you don't know her like I do, she'll love it.

J: I dunno, I think it's a bit of a risk. If it was me, I'd definitely ask her before I booked it.

B: Hey, you're just not romantic like me, are you?

J: And also she might make other plans, things that she can't, like, change and then she might not be able to go ...

B: Nah, trust me, it'll be fine.

UNIT 1 RECORDING 12

1

W = Woman   M = Man

W: OK. Two. Um, right, what are the pros and cons of coming from a large family?

M: Um, I don't – I don't really know, I don't come from a large family.

W: Well imagine if you did what might be the good points?

M: Well, um, ah, lots of Christmas presents?

W: Would you say that there wouldn't be anything bad about coming from a large family?

M: Ah, if you had a small house it might be a bit cramped.

W: Anything else that you can think of?

M: No not really, no. Well ...

W: Oh, I think we're out of time.

2

W = Woman   M = Man

W: OK, your go.

M: My go. One, two, three, four, five. Right, oh, that's a good one, um, who have you fallen out with in the past?

W: Oh no, um – I did fall out with, ah, my sister quite recently, ah, we had an argument last New Year's Eve, but I can't remember what we were arguing about.

Audio script

M: Oh no, so you don't actually know why you fell out?

W: No, it was – well, we were, I think we were arguing about something that happened to us in the past that we obviously hadn't brought up before, um, so …

M: Something to do with the family maybe?

W: Yes, yeah if anything it will definitely have been to do with the family.

M: And when was it, it was at Christmas did you say?

W: No, last New Year's Eve.

M: Oh, New Year's Eve.

W: But I think 'cos, because it was New Year's Eve you're feeling quite emotional and, ah, excitable and …

M: And it was your sister?

W: Yes, but we argue quite a lot anyway. And we're friends now.

3

W = Woman   M = Man

W: What is the ideal age to get married and why?

M: Well, I don't necessarily believe that there is an ideal age to get married. Um, I mean some men feel that they need to be a little bit older before they get married and, um, a lot of women feel that they're ready to get married and vice versa as well. Um, er, let me see, er, I mean, er, in times gone by, people got married quite young, and um, er, you know, erm, I think my parents got married when they were a lot younger, er I don't know. I don't the answer to this question, I'm sorry.

UNIT 1 RECORDING 13

1 A: … and most of the people there seem very friendly, so, yeah, all that side of things is fine.

   B: Good.

   A: It's just that … well, I don't want to sound as if I'm moaning already or anything, but I've got a bit of a problem with my boss somehow. It's a bit hard to explain. When you first meet her, she seems perfectly nice, you know, good fun, and young and everything, but I don't know. She's got this way of kind of ignoring whatever I say. She doesn't actually criticise me, not openly, but she just doesn't seem to take any of my suggestions very seriously.

   B: Oh … how annoying.

   A: Yeah, well, I'm supposed to be her assistant manager, not some junior who doesn't know anything about the job.

   B: That sounds awful. Have you tried talking to anyone else about it? Or to her, even?

   A: Well, I don't know. I don't feel as if I'm really well enough established there yet.

2 A: … well, if we hurry we might just get there. Oh, no!

   B: What's the matter?

   A: Look! Look at the traffic! It's just solid. Oh I don't believe it. I mean how is anyone supposed to get around …

   B: OK, OK. Calm down, calm down!

   A: Will you stop telling me to calm down? It is SO annoying … Come on, will you!!

   B: Look, there's no point in getting upset about it. It's rush hour. There's bound to be a lot of traffic.

   A: Yes, and when we turn up an hour late, I can imagine they're gonna be really happy about it.

   B: OK, come on, we're not going to be an hour late. I tell you what, I'll give them a call and tell them we're stuck in traffic, OK?

   A: Yeah, OK, I mean there's not much else we can do is there, short of buying a private helicopter. I mean the traffic in this town is just …

3 A: Hello?

   B: Simon? It's Linda here.

   A: Oh, hi … How's it going?

   B: There's a bit of a crisis, actually. That's why I'm ringing. I don't know what to do.

   A: Oh, dear. You haven't locked yourself out again, have you?

   B: No, no, it's … it's Tony.

   A: Oh, Tony.

   B: He should have been back hours ago. I mean he's always here when I get in from work, always, and he's just not here. He's disappeared!

   A: Well, never mind. I'm sure he'll come back. He always does, doesn't he?

   B: Yeah, but, you never know what might've happened. I mean he's not used to being out on his own.

   A: Have you looked under the bed? That's where he was last time.

B: Of course I have. No, he's not in the flat. He's gone. I just don't know where.

A: Look, Linda, try not to worry about it. He's probably out with one of his girlfriends or something. Have you called him? He could be in the garden.

B: Yeah, I've looked everywhere. He's not in any of his usual places.

UNIT 2 RECORDING 2

F = Frankie   R = Rick   N = Nancy

F: Yeah, well, I guess it's all the normal stuff for a student really. Having an active social life makes me happy and my friends are important. Good friendships are always important, aren't they? Erm, what else …? Well, I guess I like my subject. I just enjoy the intellectual stimulation of philosophy, even if the tutors are a bit … crazy sometimes!
But the other side of it that I don't enjoy so much is the loneliness. All those late nights studying on my own. And sometimes, you know, I get nervous about exams. I failed my last one so … well, exam stress is definitely a problem for me. And I guess I'd like to meet more people. It's like, well, lack of confidence can hold me back a bit, sometimes.

R: Let's start with the things that make me feel bad. What I really hate is lack of sleep. It leaves me just exhausted. And because I'm so tired I fall asleep in the evening when I should be relaxing. So, yeah, not having time to relax is also a problem. The other thing that annoys me is criticism from my family, from my wife in particular. She works long hours, you know, she's a currency trader in the city, so sometimes when she comes home, her complaints can really wind me up.
But the positives definitely outweigh the negatives. I mean, watching my children grow up is the most important thing in the world to me, spending so much time with them … even if it is a bit exhausting. And I enjoy being a bit of a non-conformist. I'm the only dad around here who looks after the kids, and I like that … being a bit different …

N: Being the CEO of a big company has a lot of advantages, of course. It's my company and nobody tells me what to do. That's number one for me: I like being an employer, not an employee. You know, I don't like firing people but I do it if I have to. Then, of course, financial security makes me feel good. I earn a good salary … but I work hard, so I deserve it. My company does market research for corporate clients so, yes, I'm the face of the company. It's an important role.
So what makes me feel bad? Well, firing people, like I said … and, well personally I think the taxes in this country are too high. So, no, I don't like paying taxes, but then, who does? And I guess I worry about where society is going. I worry about anti-social behaviour on the streets. That makes me feel bad. All in all though, I'm happy with life. I work hard and that brings results.

UNIT 2 RECORDING 4

1 There are a few things that scare me but probably one of my biggest fears would be spiders, um, I just really, really hate them, um, the small ones aren't so bad but, um, when you get a, a big one like in the bath if you find it in the bath when I go in, um, that's just really, really horrible, um, and I can't really, um, I wouldn't ever want to touch one or anything like that, um, sometimes, um, I get, ah, somebody to go in before me if I think that there's a likelihood that there might be a spider in a room, um, but yeah that's my, that's probably one of my biggest fears.

2 My problem is that nearly everything makes me giggle because it depends on my mood, it depends if I've not had much sleep for example oh my goodness then I just can't hold the giggles in and the more serious it is, um, like if I'm at work or something, the worse the giggles get because I know I'm not supposed to do it. So if somebody says something that I find mildly amusing in normal life if the stakes are higher and I'm at work and it's a really important meeting, and I'm a little bit tired, then I just go to pieces, it's terrible, and somebody can just look at me the wrong way, and I've gone and I cannot stop either, and the more I try to stop the more impossible it is, and it's even happening now, brilliant.

3 I think it's fair to say that I am governed by time. I think I – I resent it but it's true and the idea of being late just – just makes me, makes me really, really stressed. I always try and get a, ah, get somewhere – well, I always try to get where I'm going at least half an hour in advance because, the idea of being late just you know there's a, there's a

chemical reaction in my body and I just can't, I can't deal with it so, um, I would say that being on time is, um, is very important to me and if I'm not gonna be on time I get incredibly, incredibly stressed out by it.

4 I think something that, ah, something that's quite new to me, um, makes me really happy, ah, I've recently become a father and, ah, seeing my – seeing my little boy when I go home is like the best thing in the world and, ah, going through the front door, often he'll hear the front door open and I can hear him wherever he is around the house kind of shouting and screaming and then he'll run down and just give me like a massive cuddle and it's just, it's just the best thing in the world and it just fills me with joy, um, seeing his little face, he's happy, I'm happy, and it's just, it's just amazing yeah, um, hearing him laugh makes me laugh and, ah, yeah it's something that's really tough but actually the main thing is it just makes me so happy all the time, so yeah my little boy.

5 I find things like crime and war and poverty and things like that very depressing, because there doesn't seem to be a solution, um, I don't think there ever will be, and that's depressing you know because nobody, well we hope nobody really wants those things to exist and yet they always do it's like illness, as soon as we've cured something, another illness pops up because that's just life so, um, yeah that makes me sad, and some of those things, um, you know we can work on and improve upon but, again you can't help feeling like people are just people and, um, unfortunately we're stuck with those things I think, it's humanity.

UNIT 3 RECORDING 1

C = Clare   L = Luke   R = Rachel

C: This was really embarrassing! I was about 17 and this guy I really liked asked me out. And it wasn't the first time I'd been on a date, but it was like the first time I'd been on a date to a restaurant, and I was really nervous and excited, even though it was only a burger restaurant! Anyway I ordered my burger, but I was so nervous and I was talking so much that I got confused and put sugar on my burger instead of salt. But I was too embarrassed to say anything, and I don't think he noticed, or if he did he was too polite to say. So I had to sit there and eat this burger covered in sugar and pretend that I was enjoying it, and it was so disgusting! We did see each other again, but I never admitted what had happened, I just felt too silly.

L: A few years ago I had this job in a hotel for a few months, a kind of temporary job. Normally I served in the bar, which was quite easy. But one day, after I'd been working at the hotel for a few weeks they had a big dinner event and a lot of the waiters were sick, I don't know why, so they were a bit desperate, and they asked *me* to wait on the tables. I hadn't done any training as a waiter, so I was very nervous. It was quite a smart event, everyone was wearing evening dress and it was all quite formal, so obviously I was feeling quite stressed. Anyway, I was serving vegetables at this table … mashed potato to be precise, and I had this big spoonful of mashed potato in my hand. Then suddenly, for no reason really, I kind of tripped and fell forward, and the mashed potato went flying off the spoon and landed on the shoulder of one of the women at the table. So there was this 60-year-old woman sitting in her best dress, with a great big piece of mashed potato on her shoulder! I felt so humiliated!

R: There's a family story about my great aunt and uncle which sounds a bit like a bad comedy sketch, but apparently it's completely true. They lived in a remote part of Wales and they were travelling to London for some reason, which was a big thing for them because they didn't travel much. Anyway, they'd been travelling for a few hours and the train stopped at some station, and in those days trains used to stop for quite a long time and people got off and bought cups of tea and stuff. So my great aunt got off – she wasn't wearing her coat or hat and it was the middle of winter, and she went into the station buffet to buy two cups of tea. But unfortunately she came back out through the wrong door onto the opposite platform and got onto another train – which was going back to Wales! Apparently she was searching for my uncle for ages before she realised what she'd done, and of course he was going absolutely mad, worrying about her! I think they stopped travelling completely after that. It was just too much for them!

UNIT 3 RECORDING 4

B = Bill

B: It was about midnight, I guess. I was coming home from a Christmas party with my friend Frank. It was very, very cold – absolutely freezing. There was thick ice everywhere and it had been snowing for several hours. Actually, maybe it was still snowing because we really couldn't see where we were going. The road we were walking down was on a really steep hill, too, so you can imagine, it was just so slippery, and we couldn't see a thing, so, well, we just kept falling over. We'd get up, and two seconds later, we fell over again. Not because we were drunk or anything, but just because it was so slippery. Anyway, for some reason, this all began to seem very funny, and we were laughing our heads off and calling to each other for help, you know. We really didn't know how we were going to get down that hill. We weren't making any progress at all. Well, eventually we realised that the only way we could move at all was if we held on to the cars that were parked in the street for support. So, that's what we did, and slowly we were managing to move along. Except suddenly this police car drew up and two police officers got out and started shouting at us. We tried to talk to them and find out what the problem was, but they wouldn't listen to us. They just pushed us in the back of the car and drove us to the nearest police station. To be honest, I can't remember much after that, but a few hours later, I woke up in a police cell, feeling absolutely terrified, not to mention freezing cold.

UNIT 3 RECORDING 5

W = Old woman

W: It all happened at about one o'clock in the morning, I would say. I had gone to bed at ten, as usual, but I had to get up to go to the bathroom. As I was getting back into bed, I heard this dreadful noise outside in the street … men shouting … so of course I went to the window to see what was going on. Anyway, I looked out and saw these two young men just outside my house. They were swaying all over the place, shouting and swearing at each other. They had obviously been drinking, you could see they were drunk – very aggressive and nasty-looking types. Then I noticed that they were doing something to the cars. It was a very clear night, with a full moon, so I could see everything. They were banging on all the car windows trying to break into them. Obviously as soon as I realised what was going on, I called the police straightaway, and thank goodness, they came more or less immediately, and arrested them before they could do any damage. It was very lucky I happened to wake up and catch them, otherwise I'm sure half the cars in the neighbourhood would have been robbed, even stolen. This is a nice neighbourhood. People have expensive cars with all sorts of expensive things in them. It was very lucky that I saw it all.

UNIT 3 RECORDING 8

Article A

A: Reporting live from outside the courthouse in Swindon is our reporter, Deborah Manning.

B: Thank you Jackie. Judge Mark Horton handed down suspended sentences of 11 months in jail each to Amanda and Michael Stacey today, following a trial in which the couple were found guilty of fraud and theft. The charges related to an incident nine months ago when Amanda found a lottery ticket on the floor of her local Coop supermarket. Amanda and her husband claimed the £30,000 prize when the ticket won. Unfortunately for them, the real owner of the ticket, Dorothy McDonagh, realised that she had lost the ticket and immediately informed the police.
At the trial it emerged that the Staceys had already spent half the money. The judge ordered them to repay the remaining £15,000 to Mrs McDonagh, along with £111 interest. He did not, however, order them to repay the £15,000 they had already spent, instead just imposing a £5 fine. Mrs McDonagh will have to take the Staceys to court to get that money and, after legal fees, it is doubtful that she would see much of it. Back to you Jackie.

Article B

A: Now, Robyn, I believe you have a further update on the Leon Walker story.

Audio script

B: That's right, Greg. Leon Walker, you'll remember, was the man from Rochester Hills in Michigan who was charged, back in 2010, with hacking into his wife's email account. He maintained his innocence but his wife Clara went on television to talk about how violated she had felt. Well, Greg, two years after Leon was charged and right before he was due to go on trial, prosecutors have unexpectedly dropped the charges against Leon. And the reason? It turns out that Clara had been reading her husband's text messages while they were still married and had admitted to this in an email. Leon described himself as 'relieved but angry'.

A: Astonishing news! Now, over to our sports desk where Jamie has some news about …

Article C

B: … and I have our science correspondent, Robert Walsh, here in the studio with me. Robert, before we catch up on all the latest developments in the world of science, can you tell me what happened to Richard Handl?

A: Yes, absolutely Don. Well, as our listeners probably remember, Richard Handl was the man who tried to set up a mini nuclear reactor in his kitchen. Using radioactive materials that he'd bought, Mr Handl attempted to split the atom and he posted the results online, along with the now-famous picture of his cooker after the experiment.

B: Yes, I remember that.

A: Of course, when the police were alerted to what Mr Handl was doing, they confiscated all his nuclear material and his computer. Mr Handl faced the prospect of up to two years in prison, so, as you say Don, what has happened to him? Well, the answer is absolutely nothing. Since they confiscated his radioactive material several months ago, neither the police nor the Swedish Radiation Authority have been in touch. So it looks like Mr Handl won't be prosecuted after all.

B: Well, that's good news for amateur scientists I guess. Now, on to this week's other science stories Rob …

UNIT 3 RECORDING 9

Conversation 1

A: Tickets, please. Thank you. Tickets, please. Your ticket, sir?

B: I'm sorry but I don't have one. The machine at the station wasn't working.

A: You need a valid ticket, sir, otherwise you'll have to pay a £50 fine.

B: **I understand that but** I couldn't buy a ticket. The machine wasn't working.

A: Where did you board the train, sir?

B: Penley South.

A: There's a ticket office at that station, sir. You could have bought your ticket there.

B: It doesn't open until eight o'clock and this train left at 7.30. Look, I want to buy a ticket, I'm happy to pay for one now, but I can't buy one if the machine is broken.

A: Well, I'm sorry sir but I'm just doing my job. You have to have a ticket before you board the train.

B: **Can I make a suggestion? Why don't I** buy a ticket now and then everyone is happy.

A: I … don't think so, sir. If you don't have a ticket I have to fine you.

B: Look, **this is ridiculous**. I'm not a criminal. I want to pay for my ticket!

A: … Well … all right sir. But just this once. Where are you travelling to?

Conversation 2

A: Wow! What a huge space.

B: Yes, beautiful. So much to explore.

C: This museum was only opened in 2010 you know. It's the largest in the country.

A: Oh! Really.

C: Yes, it houses some of the most important Roman artifacts in the world. I can show you round some of the highlights if you like.

A: Well, er, what do you think, Beth?

B: Er, OK I mean, if you've got the time.

C: Oh, sure, sure. I like to show people round. Come on, follow me. I'll take you first to … and all of those coins were found by a farmer who was digging up his field! What a lucky guy, huh?

B: Wow! How interesting.

C: So, here we are back where we started.

A: Well, thank you so much. That was really kind of you.

C: Oh, don't mention it. You know, I usually charge £30 for my tours but

you have been such good company that for you it's only £25.

A: Er, sorry, your tours?

C: Yes, my tours. I hope you thought it was worth the money.

A: Oh, right, yes … I see … err …

B: Look, **there's been a misunderstanding. We didn't realise that** you wanted to be paid.

C: Well, it's only £25. It's more of a gift really. I help you out with an informative tour and you help me out with a small gift.

B: **I don't think that's fair.** You should have told us at the start.

C: Didn't you enjoy the tour? Most of my customers are …

B: That's the thing, you see. We aren't your customers.

C: Well, look. I can see it's just a bit of a misunderstanding and I appreciate what you're saying. Let's call it £20.

B: No, **you don't understand**. We really aren't your customers. Thank you for your time but we're not going to pay you for it. Come on. I want to go back to that room with the Roman coins.

Conversation 3

A: Hello, madam.

B: Hello. We booked a table for two. The name is Pole. P – O – L – E.

A: Right … yes, right. Ms Pole. That table was for eight o'clock, wasn't it?

B: Yes, eight o'clock. That's right.

A: Well I'm afraid we had to give your table away. As you see, we're very busy and we weren't sure if you were coming so we had to give your table to someone else.

B: **What do you mean** you've given it to someone else? I booked it.

A: Well it is almost quarter to nine, madam. We get a lot of customers booking and not turning up so generally, if anyone is more than half an hour late, we give their table to someone else.

B: Oh, honestly. **It's not my fault that** we couldn't find a parking space.

A: I understand that, madam and I'm really sorry. But as you can see, we're completely full.

B: **I can see that, but** this is very unfair. **Perhaps I need to speak** to the manager.

A: Bear with me a minute, madam, and I'll see what we can do. Perhaps one of our customers who booked for 8.30 won't show up. If you just take a seat at the bar …

UNIT 4 RECORDING 5

A: Redland Staff Services

B: Hello. I'm trying to hire a new PA and I was wondering if you could help.

A: Certainly. Is the PA going to work with you?

B: Yes, that's right. I've had a few applications but I'm not sure where to go from here. I mean, can I have the applicants interviewed?

A: Certainly. We can provide a detailed report on each applicant. You can even have their personalities assessed.

B: OK …

A: And you can have their IQ tested as well if you want even more information.

B: Mmm, it all sounds good. Can you send me some information about how much it all costs.

A: Of course, let me take your email address.

UNIT 4 RECORDING 6

N = news reader   B = science correspondent

N: This week it has been reported that the Mars 500 'space mission' has 'landed' after more than 17 months. With us to discuss this fascinating experiment is our science correspondent, David Simpson. David, for those listeners who are not familiar with the Mars 500 mission could you tell us about it?

S: Well the Mars 500 mission was actually a simulated space mission in which six international volunteers – three Russians, two other Europeans and a Chinese man spent 520 days in a space capsule buried beneath a car park in a suburb of Moscow.

N: And what exactly was the point of that?

S: Well scientists wanted to study the physical and especially the psychological effects of spending that amount of time in the confinement and isolation of a space capsule, which is of course what a space crew would have to do if they travelled to Mars for example.

N: And why is that useful?

S: Well it would help in future to select the right kind of people to take part in this kind of mission. So for example, the crew's stress levels and moods were carefully monitored, and the kind of issues that created conflict.

N: And what did they find?

S: Well the data is still being analysed. However, while it has been stressed by the ESA – the European Space Agency – that overall the six men got on well and worked successfully as a team, although there were issues, certainly.

N: For example?

S: Well, you have to remember that the six men had to deal with the boredom and isolation of 17 months together, and it seems that in these highly stressful circumstances small jealousies can easily become a problem. For example the men, had a lot of chores and tasks, which they had to share out and organise themselves, and it was felt that the workload wasn't always fair, and this caused problems. There were also jealousies over who had the most contact with their family and friends 'back home', and there were also certain tensions between the different nationalities.

N: Wouldn't it have been easier if all the men had been of the same nationality?

S: Possibly, but you have to remember that any future mission to Mars will almost certainly be international, so this was one of the issues that had to be looked at.

N: So what conclusions can be drawn about the kind of people that are suitable for such a mission in future?

S: Well, as I say, the data is still being analysed, but I think there are certain obvious conclusions. The crew of any such mission would have to be extremely self-sufficient, to deal with the incredible boredom and isolation, and to be able to deal with all the unexpected problems that might arise during the mission. This is also an incredibly stressful situation and so they would have to be able to stay calm under pressure, and obviously they would need to be able to get on with each other and work as a team, yet provide leadership where necessary.

N: Does it ever happen that crews on missions like this simply don't get on?

S: Well generally the crews' frustrations tend to be directed towards the ground crew at mission control. It is common for the space crew to complain that they are not being sufficiently supported by the ground crew, but there was one case where the two crew members on a mission together didn't get on at all.

N: And what happened?

S: Well it was a Russian space mission in 1982, and the two crew members hardly spoke to each other for the whole 211 day mission, because they just got on each other's nerves, basically ... they just didn't like each other!

N: Imagine spending 211 days alone with someone you can't stand. That certainly sounds stressful! David Simpson, thank you very much. And now to ...

UNIT 5 RECORDING 2

According to recent research, over 60% of new couples in the USA now meet online. But it's perhaps surprising that any of those relationships ever get started in the first place because over 80% of people lie in their online profile. Clearly, the temptation to exaggerate is just too great for most people. The most common lie that men tell is about their job. They exaggerate the importance of their job or they lie about the industry that they work in. The most common lie is claiming to work in finance or the film industry. The men hope, presumably, that women will fall hopelessly in love with them on the first date and not care when they find out that he isn't really a film director but actually drives a taxi. Men also tend to claim that they have a PA when in fact they don't. Apart from their career, men are most likely to lie about their height, and body shape, choosing, for example, to describe themselves as 'athletic' or 'muscular' rather than 'average build'.

The top two lies that women tell in their online profile concern their age, and body shape. Women typically take four years off their true age and present themselves as slimmer than they actually are. They also tend to use a photo that is one and a half years old compared to men, who use a photo that is six months old.

So if you want to know whether a profile that you are reading is mostly lies, keep an eye out for three things. Firstly, the number of times that the word 'I' is used. The less often someone uses it, the more likely they are to be lying.

Apparently this reflects a desire to distance ourselves from our lies. Secondly, shorter profiles. These can be a sign that someone is being 'economical with the truth'. People write shorter profiles when they want to avoid telling a lot of lies that they will have to remember later. The less information there is to remember, the easier it will be on the first meeting. And thirdly, keep an eye out for negative statements. People who are lying tend to prefer them to positive statements. For example, a liar will describe himself or herself as 'not boring' or 'not sad', rather than 'exciting' and 'happy'.

Some people say, however, that it is necessary to lie a little bit in your online profile. Perhaps it's even expected because if you tell the truth, people will believe that you are older, less attractive (and less successful) than you actually are. Most online daters know that they have to take what they read with a pinch of salt. Telling little white lies online can also have a positive benefit, by encouraging you to live up to the standards that you set in your profile.

It's best not to stretch the truth too far, however. One online dater called Karen posted her story on the web. She went to a restaurant expecting to meet a 29-year-old investment banker who enjoyed 'surfing, swimming and going to the gym'. 'The person who walked through the door', she wrote, 'was about 40 and wearing a supermarket uniform. He'd clearly used a photo that was over ten years old. In those last ten years he definitely hadn't been to the gym.'

UNIT 5 RECORDING 3

R = reporter   J = Josh

R: So, Josh, **could you tell me what you were looking for**, before the date I mean?

J: Oh, well, I guess I was hoping that she'd be the one for me, you know? A mix between Beyonce and Eva Peron. Ursula wasn't that!

R: **Wasn't your first impression of Ursula good?**

J: Oh no, it was really good. Excellent. She looked great. I've got no idea what she thought of me though!

R: That's always the problem, isn't it. OK, so, **who did she remind you of?**

J: Well, no one in particular really but if I had to choose one person it would be my sister.

R: OK, and, er, oh yes, **what did you talk about?** You know, what topics.

J: Um, I think we talked about films and books and that sort of stuff. You know, cultural stuff. But, er, to be honest, most of the time I was so busy trying to eat my lobster that I wasn't listening to what she was saying.

R: Oh! That doesn't sound very good.

J: I know. Lobster probably wasn't the best choice really.

R: So did you have any awkward moments?

J: Well, at one point a piece of my lobster flew off my plate and landed on her dress. But luckily I don't think she noticed.

R: **You don't think she noticed?**

J: Oh no! Did she?

R: You'll have to read the magazine to find out! Now, um, **how similar are you and Ursula?**

J: Well, I think we're actually quite similar. We both get stressed out on first dates.

R: OK, and finally, **what marks out of ten would you give Ursula?**

J: Oh, I hate that question. I'd have to say seven. Possibly seven and a half.

R: OK, well, thanks, that's ... oh! Sorry, I forgot. One last question.

J: Sure, no problem.

R: **I wanted to ask if you'd** want to meet Ursula again?

J: Oh yes, definitely, but just as friends I think.

R: Great. Well, thanks very much. I hope ...

UNIT 5 RECORDING 6

1 At my fantasy dinner party I would have to invite Lady Gaga, um, I think she'd be a really fun guest to have at a dinner party, um, it would probably be a fancy dress dinner party and then I could ask her all about her clothes and where she finds them all, um, we could talk about her music and fashion and things like that, and I'd also get her to sing some songs at my dinner party as well.

2 I've always wanted to meet Eddie Murphy actually, that would be the person that I would choose, um, for my dinner party if I could. And the reason is because I just find him absolutely hilarious and I'd want to ask him what it is about him that makes him funny. What does he think it is

Audio script

because some people just are funny, other people aren't. And I'm really interested to know what that magical ingredient is and if you can teach it or if he's always been funny which probably he has. And what does he prefer like to, um, to do most, um, stand up in front of an audience or movies and TV or interviews, I'd be interested to know the answer, um, to that question.

3   Ah, if I could choose, um, someone to invite I think it would be, ah, Mother Theresa, um, I think it's someone that's always, ah, fascinated me, um, having – having travelled, ah, quite a lot and seen what you see in, um, in countries that aren't your own and the poverty and the illness I think it's, um, quite amazing that someone gave up their whole life to, ah, to try and address that problem. And, ah, it's someone that's really fascinated me for quite a long time. I'd ask her why she chose to, um, to give up her life and, ah, and help others, um ... I think that she'd be, um, just so fascinating to talk to, um, and it's someone I really admire so I'd kind of like to say thank you for – for the inspiration that she's given me.

4   I'd love to meet Marilyn Monroe, so I would definitely invite her, and the first reason would be because to have somebody that beautiful and amazing in a room would just be phenomenal and a one off, and I then could ask her questions like what colour lipstick is the best red that you can get, and all those girlie questions that you could ask but then I'd ask her stuff about her movie career and whether, um, she felt like she'd ever been in love and, um, who those people would be that she really felt she loved. And I think I'd ask her if she hadn't have been, um, if she hadn't have died when she did what she would have liked to have gone on to do after.

5   I would choose any king or queen from history but probably, um, I think the most interesting person to have at my dinner party would be Queen Elizabeth the First because there would be so much to ask her about and she's such a fascinating, um, figure, um, first of all I'd like to ask her how she managed to be such a powerful queen for so long when being a woman in those days was difficult enough; and, um, how she maintained her power, um, over all those years, um, and of course I'd like to ask her about her day to day life and all those domestic details like, was she able to brush her teeth or, or was she bald under her wig or – you know so many interesting details which I think would be, it would be amazing to find out the truth about them and, um, and how she really felt about being Queen of England, um, and what that meant to her ...

6   Um, if I could invite anybody I wanted to a dinner party, er, I think I would invite David Beckham. Because not only is he extremely good looking, um, but also I think he'd have some really good stories to tell about places he'd been and people he'd met and, um, you know, the World Cup and what it feels like, just what it feels like to be as famous as he is, really. And what his life's like, I suppose. Yeah he'd be really good.

UNIT 5 RECORDING 7

Conversation 1

Hello? Hello? Sorry? Yes, that's right, this is Stephen Lloyd, yes, thanks for getting back to me ... yeah, um, I left a message earlier about the furniture that you're supposed to be delivering to me at the end of this week ... and I wondered if ... sorry? ... no, no it's just that I'm on a train and I keep losing you ... we, we keep going into tunnels ... I said I keep losing you whenever we go into a tunnel ... could you speak up a bit, please? No, your voice is very faint ... yeah, yeah, that's better yeah ... yeah, I can hear you perfectly, yeah ... sorry, you said that you'll be delivering the furniture on Friday, is that right? About what time? Sorry? No, your voice has gone very faint ... I can hardly hear you ... sorry, you're breaking up ... shall I ... shall I ring you back? Look, I'm going to call you back. OK? Hello? Hello?

Conversation 2

A: Hello, thank you for phoning Gas Line. You have three options: if you want to enquire about new Gas Products, Press 1. If you have an enquiry about an outstanding bill, Press 2.
    Thank you. We're now going to connect you to one of our sales team.
B: Hello, welcome to Gas Line. My name's Andy, how can I help you?
C: Hello, yes, I'm calling about my bill.
C: Have you got your customer reference number, please?
B: Um ... yeah, it's V290 636K,
C: OK, just get your file up on the screen. Can I just confirm your name and postcode, please?

B: Yes, it's Christine Ford, and the postcode is MN8 6DK.
C: OK, that's fine and how can we help you this morning?
B: Well, you sent me a bill which I think I paid three weeks ago, but you've sent me a letter which says that unless I pay it within seven days, you'll ...
C: Sorry to stop you there. I'll have to put you through to another department as we don't actually deal with invoices which are more than three weeks old. If you'll just bear with me ...
B: Yes, but ...
D: Hello, Customer Service Department.
B: Yes, it's about a letter you sent me. The customer reference is V290 636K, and I sent you ...
D: Can you just confirm your name and postcode for me, please?
B: I've just given all this information to another young man. Do I have to go through all this again? It's MN8 6DK and my name is Christine Ford. Now about this bill you say I haven't paid, now I know I made the payment at least ...
D: Sorry is that M for Michael, N for Nigel ...

Conversation 3

A: Yes, hello, Linda Bates speaking.
B: Hi, it's Jane Markham from Adonis Travel. It's regarding your flights to Istanbul next week. I've just got a couple of queries ...
A: Oh, yes. Hello. Oh sorry, just a second ... No! Not there! Where I told you by the bookcase ... Sorry ...
B: Yes, I just wanted to know if you'd mind taking a flight a bit later than the one we discussed ...
C: Mum? Mum? Have you seen my trainers anywhere?
A: Please, don't interrupt me when I'm on the phone, yes sorry, you were saying ...
B: No, don't worry ... am I calling at a bad time? I'll call back later if it's easier for you.
A: Do you mind, it's just that there are some delivery men, and ... will you be careful with that please? Sorry ...
B: No problem ... when would be a good time to call?
A: Oh, if you give it about an hour things will have settled down a bit ... thanks.
B: OK, I'll speak to you later.
A: OK, thanks. Bye.
B: Bye.

UNIT 6 RECORDING 1

1
The Mesopotamians were probably the first people to invent writing – in about 3,200BC, although it is believed that it was also invented separately in several different places – by the Ancient Chinese and then later by the tribes who lived in modern day Mexico.

2
By the middle of 16th century, Arab and European astronomers had discovered a great deal about how our solar system works. However at this point, Europeans still hadn't travelled to many parts of their own planet. Columbus had only arrived in the Americas in 1492, Australia wasn't discovered by Europeans until the 17th century, and Antarctica wasn't explored until the 18th and 19th centuries!

3
By the middle of the 19th century, we had made big advances in science and engineering. In 1860 the first combustion engine was invented, which led to the invention of the motor car. However, we still hadn't discovered that bacteria cause diseases, and didn't realise that we needed to wash our hands in order to prevent the spread of germs! It wasn't until the work of the Frenchman Louis Pasteur was published in the 1860s that this idea was put forward, and even then many scientists initially dismissed his ideas as ridiculous!

4
Today, at the beginning of the 21st century we have made the most extraordinary technological advances. We have invented the aeroplane, landed on the moon, invented computers and the worldwide web as well as countless other amazing pieces of technology. However, bizarrely, we haven't yet discovered a cure for the common cold. A scientific break through has recently been made at Cambridge University though, which means that a cure may be found in the next decade or so!

5

Most experts believe that within twenty years or so we will have sent a manned mission to Mars – the US Senate has recently passed a law allowing this to happen! Doctors, also believe that we will have found a cure for many forms of cancer and other diseases by then. However, most experts agree that we probably won't have learnt how to control the weather. We will probably have learnt how to modify it in small ways, indeed this has already been done. The Chinese government managed to delay rainfall at the opening ceremony of the Beijing Olympics in 2008, by firing rockets into the sky. But it is extremely unlikely that we will have learnt how to control or prevent extreme weather events like storms or hurricanes. Indeed, many scientists believe that it would be dangerous even to try.

UNIT 6 RECORDING 3

1   Um, the achievement that I would like to nominate, um, it's been the subject of the programme, would be, um, the invention of the internet, um, it was a man called Tim Berners Lee amongst other people who actually invented the internet and I think it was an amazing achievement because it's opened up so much of the world, um, in terms of knowledge and communication and technology, um, think it's been one of the most important, ah, inventions in, certainly in recent years, but has also changed, changed the way we communicate as a – as a race.

2   Ah my, ah, nomination, um, would be, ah, Neil Armstrong, ah, the first man to walk on the moon. Um, I just think it's, it's something that even now we look back at and think wow how – how did that happen? How did he do that, how did NASA do that, um, technology then was so, um, you know it was –we've got so much more technology now and it still feels like it's an amazing event and something really quite difficult to achieve, um – I think it was, I think it's a life-changing event as well for the, for the whole world, um, I think looking back from the Moon at the Earth put a lot of things into perspective, so yeah Neil Armstrong and NASA.

3   Um, I would have to nominate, um, William Shakespeare, um, not only is, um, he a giant in the, ah, the literary world but, um, he's also touched everyone's lives ah whether they know it or not throughout history, um, and, um, I think his plays can be reinvented for every generation and he speaks timeless truths to everybody and, um, his works are produced and studied in countries all over the world, he is probably, um, the most, um, widely read, um, author of – of literature that the world has ever seen, and for that reason I would like to nominate him for, for my short programme.

4   Well if you're talking about top fifty human achievements, I dare say places are very limited but I'd like to include Felix Baumgartner the guy who went up in a balloon into space and jumped with a parachute, I mean this guy pushed his personal boundaries literally, literally to the edges of the Earth and, I think that's really courageous I mean you could ask has the – has the world changed at all by him jumping out of that and back down to Earth, but I think in a subtle way it probably has because it's a, it's an example, it's a role model of somebody who wanted to really test their metal and their courage and did it, and I think the effects of that'll filter down to us all for, well for years to come really.

5   I'd like to talk about The Beatles, ah, for my subject, ah, they, ah, they revolutionised ah music as we know it today, and without them there wouldn't be ah pop music, um, they globalised music and, um – ah, their songs will endure, ah, timelessly, um, everybody can name a – a Beatles tune or five and, ah, I think that their – their influence is still being felt in the music industry today, ah, without them pop music wouldn't have grown in the way it did. And, um, I think that we – we are all indebted to – to what they did to, ah, change the face of music in the world today.

UNIT 7 RECORDING 2

Harriet

Quite a few of my friends had absolutely huge [...], which cost thousands and thousands of pounds, with, like a mega-expensive dress, a massive cake, loads of flower arrangements everywhere and literally hundreds of guests, loads of their parents' friends. I mean one of my friends didn't even know some of the guests at her own [...] I mean how crazy is that? She had hardly any time to talk to her own friends, because she was so busy being

polite to people she didn't know! And then you hear all these stories about people getting really stressed beforehand, when it's supposed to be, like a joyful occasion! Another of my friends fell out with her future mother-in-law over the arrangements ... Apparently, the mother-in law nearly didn't come to the [...] though luckily they made it up before the big day, but it's ridiculous, isn't it? Anyway, as I say, I'd been to several of these and it was all far too impersonal, there was far too much fuss. So anyway, Freddie and I decided we wanted something completely different, so we've just invited close family and a few old friends to the ceremony and the reception, and we're saving the money my parents gave us to spend on our new flat. We'll have a nice party a couple of weeks later to celebrate with all our friends and it'll be fantastic, no stress, none of my mother's friends, heaven.

Bethany

[...] is basically a day that most people spend with their families. They have a big family gathering either at home or in a restaurant, a special meal with special dishes, and everyone eats far too much food ... and then no-one can move so they all sit around and watch TV. There are always several big football matches on TV, and there's also a big parade that you can also watch on TV, with like amazing floats ... and costumes ... and balloons ... and fireworks, so that's kinda fun to watch if you've got nothing better to do. But basically it's a pretty lazy day after you've finished eating. And surprisingly it's not particularly commercial. Very few people exchange presents or cards, you might take a small gift if you're invited to someone's house for a meal, you know, some flowers or a little candy for the kids, but really it's all quite low key ... it's really nice in that way.

Dan

I guess I'm a bit of a [...] freak really, I go to more or less any [...] I can ... sometimes I manage to get work as a steward, in return for like a free ticket. It's always really exciting when you arrive, there's this amazing buzz that you get from being surrounded by thousands and thousands of people, you know, all of them there like to enjoy themselves. I love the feeling when you wake up and gradually everyone comes out of their tents, and slowly the place comes to life and there's this build up of excitement as the bands are about to start playing, first the small bands on several different stages, building up to the headline act at the end of the evening on the main stage. Some [...] are friendlier than others but there's usually a great atmosphere, you can get talking to anyone really. The party really starts about midnight after the bands have finished, and I often stay up most of the night, I never get enough sleep! What else? These days I would say the facilities in most places are pretty good, there are usually enough toilets – though there are always massive queues – and there are plenty of stalls to buy food and drink – though none of it's cheap – and of course there's always loads of merchandise on sale, band T-shirts and stuff ... I always spend far too much money! There's one thing that always annoys me though. There's never enough water, you know not enough taps, for getting water to wash or drink, and you always have to walk miles to find a tap. Apart from that I don't have many complaints. I just wish I had more time ... to see more bands!

UNIT 7 RECORDING 4

1   Do you normally take your time getting up in the morning?
2   Do you know anyone who's really good at taking photos? Who?
3   If someone asks you to 'take a seat', do you stand up or sit down?
4   If you took up a new sport or interest, what would it be?
5   Do you ever have to take care of small children? Who?
6   Which sports do you play? Do you take them seriously?
7   When you arrive home, what's the first thing you take off?
8   Who do you take after more in terms of appearance, your mother or your father?
9   Have you ever taken part in a concert? What was it?
10 How long did it take you to get here today?
11 Have any important historical events ever taken place in your town?
12 Have you taken any notes during this lesson? What about?

UNIT 7 RECORDING 5

1

A: Oh, Bella, you've finished. You must be hungry. Go on, have some more. Have the last piece.

B: Oh, no thank you. **It was very nice but I'm really full.**

A: Oh, go on. I insist. Have the last bit.

Audio script

B: **No, really. I couldn't manage any more.**
A: OK. Maybe I'll finish it then.

2

A: Anyway, while I was waiting ... Oh no! I'm so sorry, Bella. I'll get a cloth.
B: **Oh, don't worry, Sally.** I can wash it when I get home.
A: It was really stupid of me.
B: **It doesn't matter. These things happen.**

3

A: Hi Bella. It's been a while hasn't it? How have you been?
B: Oh, hi there. I'm fine, thanks. How are you?
A: Oh, good, good. You know, same old same old.
B: So ... wow ... it's been a long time. **When was the last time we met?**
A: Oh at that party at Jake's house I think.
B: Oh, that's right. **And how's everything going?** You know, job, home life ...?
A: Yes, everything's fine, thanks. We've just moved house and ...

4

B: That man is really annoying!
A: Who, James? My new boyfriend?
B: Is he your new boyfriend? **Oh sorry, I didn't realise. I hope I didn't offend you.**
A: No, not at all. His laugh is very annoying.
B: James! Could you turn it down a bit?
C: Sorry Penny.

5

A: So, anyway, by the time I found out where he was I was going crazy with worry. I mean, he's no ordinary cat, as you know. He's got such a sweet personality. Anyway ...
B: Sally, sorry to interrupt you but **I think there's someone at the door.**
A: Oh, don't worry. I'll hold. I'm sure you want to know what happened in the end!
B: Well yes, but I know you're really busy so **I don't want to keep you. I'll call you if I get a chance next week.**
A: Oh, OK Bella. Sure.
B: Speak soon. Bye!

UNIT 8 RECORDING 1

1

Do fish sleep? The answer is yes ... and no. Fish don't close their eyes and dream like humans, and some of them, such as sharks, have to keep moving or they die. But fish do seem to be less active, physically and mentally, at certain times and this seems to perform the same function as sleep in humans.

2

Why don't polar bears' feet freeze? Polar bears are probably the best insulated animals on land. They have about 10 cm of fat beneath their thick fur. Their feet are covered in fur too, as well as a thick layer of dead skin which protects them when they come into contact with the ice. That's why their feet don't freeze.

3

Can a loud sound kill you? Yes, it can. Sound becomes painful at around 130 decibels – a jet engine around 20 or 30 metres away makes this kind of sound. At around 170 decibels your eardrums burst and a sound of 200 decibels will probably kill you.

4

Can humans catch diseases from plants? Humans can't catch diseases caused by viruses or bacteria from plants however they can have an allergic reaction to them. Every summer millions of people suffer from hay fever and this is caused by plants.

5

Why do chilli peppers taste hot? They taste hot because of a chemical in them called capsaicin. This chemical tricks your body into thinking it is being burned, even when it is actually not. The capsaicin doesn't harm you – it is all in your mind. Because of its unusual qualities, capsaicin is used by the police in some countries in a special form called pepper spray. It causes temporary blindness but doesn't do any long-term damage.

UNIT 8 RECORDING 2

A few days before the Great Exhibition in Paris was due to start, two English ladies, Clara Redwood and her twenty-year-old daughter Eleanor, arrived in the city on their way back to London from India, where they were escaping the latest outbreak of the plague.

Neither woman could speak much French and it was very difficult to find a hotel room but after searching for some time they eventually managed to book the last two rooms available at one of the most famous hotels in Paris. After arriving at the hotel both women signed the register, and were shown up to their rooms. The mother was given room 342, a particularly luxurious room decorated with beautiful red velvet curtains.

Almost immediately however, the mother fell ill and they had to call the hotel's doctor. He examined Mrs Redwood carefully, then called the hotel manager and spoke urgently to him in French. Eleanor didn't understand what they were saying, but after a few minutes, the doctor explained in English that he couldn't leave Mrs Redwood because she was too ill, so he gave Eleanor a prescription and asked her to go and fetch the medicine her mother needed, which was available only at his surgery on the other side of Paris.

The doctor lent Eleanor his own carriage to travel in, but the journey was frustratingly slow, and it was four hours before Eleanor finally returned with the medicine. She rushed into the hotel foyer and asked the manager anxiously how her mother was. The manager stared at her blankly. 'What are you talking about, Madame?' he asked. 'I know nothing of your mother. You arrived here alone.' The hotel doctor also denied ever meeting her mother, and when Eleanor insisted on seeing the hotel register, only the young woman's signature was there.

Eleanor managed to persuade them to take her back to room 342, but her mother had vanished and the room was empty. Even more mysteriously, the decorations appeared to have been completely replaced, and the beautiful red velvet curtains had disappeared.

The distraught girl rushed to the British Embassy to tell her story, but officials refused to believe her. Eleanor became ever more frantic with worry, and when she returned to Britain she was declared insane and put in a mental hospital. However, the girl continued to insist that her story was true, and doctors never found any other evidence that she was mentally ill. Eventually she was released, but her mother's body was never found.

UNIT 8 RECORDING 3

So what is the explanation for this strange disappearance? Many experts in historical mysteries believe that Mrs Redwood might have brought the plague back with her from India. If this news had become widely known, it would certainly have ruined the Great Exhibition, so the hotel manager might have conspired with the doctor to keep the terrible news a secret. They certainly must have conspired together in some way or other. However, the British Embassy let the young woman down disgracefully, they should have investigated her story more fully at the very least. On the other hand, surely the hotel staff can't have disposed of the body and redecorated room 342 in just four hours? Perhaps after all Eleanor was insane and she made the whole story up. But in that case, what did happen to her mother, and why was she never traced again, dead or alive?

UNIT 8 RECORDING 6

1 Twenty-five years ago you couldn't send emails and texts. So now you can contact somebody really urgently and get a quick response, but twenty-five years ago you couldn't.
2 Something I could do then that I can still do now is speak Italian. We lived in Milan for four years when I was young and I became fluent then.
3 Well, I'm the mother of um teenage children and something I didn't have to do ten years ago, which I have to do now is supervise children's homework and I must say it's one of the most frustrating tasks I could ever have imagined.
4 Yesterday at work I had to talk to somebody because there'd been a complaint about them. I didn't want to do it because I really like that person, but, well, it's part of my job, so I had to do it.
5 Um, I should have posted a letter this afternoon and I remember walking right past the post office and just forgot all about it.

UNIT 9 RECORDING 4

1 A: I'm absolutely exhausted. Let's stay in and watch a film.
   B: Oh, you're so boring these days. I want to go out.
2 A: I really like living here because it's so near the centre of town.
   B: That's true, but it gets really noisy at night.
3 A: Thanks for everything, we've had such a nice evening!
   B: You're welcome. Come again soon!
4 A: I suppose you want to see Liz.
   B: No, actually it was you I wanted to see.
5 A: Why on earth are we inside on such a beautiful day?
   B: Well, it was you who wanted to spend the day at a museum.
6 A: Ouch! This tooth is so painful.
   B: You know you really need to go to the dentist's.
7 A: What's all this broken glass! What on earth have you been doing?
   B: Don't blame me! It wasn't me who broke it!
8 A: Your friend was really lovely. I do hope you'll invite him again.
   B: Yes, I will. I think he really enjoyed the evening as well.
9 A: Come on, let's go to that new club.
   B: Look, I really do think it's time we went home. It's nearly three.
10 A: I really think you ought to apologise to her.
   B: Why on earth should I apologise? It wasn't me who started the trouble.

UNIT 9 RECORDING 5

Hello. My name's Rebecca Wade and I'm going to talk today about how to give a presentation. All of my ideas, incidentally, are available in my book 'How to Give Incredible Presentations'. Now, when I say presentation, I don't just mean standing on a stage talking to lots of people. We all have to make presentations these days, often to colleagues or classmates, and the audience may be just a few people rather than a few hundred. And success in life often depends on being able to communicate your ideas effectively to a group of people. So the advice I'm going to give is true for all these situations. And why do we need this advice? Well, according to some studies, most people's number one fear in life is public speaking. This means that standing in front of a room full of people, for some of us at least, is scarier even than death. But it doesn't need to be, if you follow these simple tips.

First, let's start with a few important points. These are the things you should try not to do. Firstly, never read out your presentation. There is nothing more boring for an audience than listening to someone reading out notes. It makes for a monotonous intonation in your voice and your audience will quickly realise that they could get the same information in half the time just by reading your script.

And secondly, try not to move around too much or talk too fast, especially at the beginning of a presentation. Keep your head and hands still. It takes an audience a bit of time to get used to your voice and if you are dancing around at the front of the room, trying to be energetic, it can be very distracting.

And the last point is this. Nothing is more annoying for an audience than to be kept waiting, particularly at the end of a presentation when everyone is probably desperate for a coffee, try to make sure you start and finish on time. So, be nice to them and they'll be nice to you.

UNIT 9 RECORDING 6

So we've looked at the things you shouldn't do, now let's look at the things you should do. In terms of planning your presentation, try to remember this simple rule: less is more. Fewer slides are better than a lot of slides. If you have thirty slides for a 30-minute talk, that's too many. Your audience will suffer from information overload and they won't be able to pay attention to you as you speak. In fact, this is the classic mistake that presenters make – they spend so long preparing a set of fancy, colourful, animated slides that they forget to think about what they are actually going to say and how they are going to say it. Generally one slide for every two minutes of your talk is plenty. Remember also that fewer words on a slide is better than more words. And as the saying goes, a picture is worth a thousand words.

Secondly, it's a good idea to think carefully about the first few lines of your presentation. These are often the most difficult because your stress levels are highest when you begin speaking, so if you can get through these lines, the rest usually follows quite smoothly.

And lastly, in terms of planning, try to practise your presentation at least once before you give it. Find a friend who is willing to sit and listen and then ask for their honest opinion.

And what about delivering your presentation? What tips can help? Well, many presenters have key words on cards that they can hold and look at while they talk. That way, if they forget what they want to say, which is a big fear for many people, the cards will remind them.

The second tip that really helps a lot of presenters is to remember to make eye contact with people in the audience as early as possible. This really helps to build rapport and understanding.

And thirdly, don't forget to include some interaction. Ask your audience for their opinion near the start of the talk. Sometimes it helps if you ask a question and then give your audience some time to discuss the answer with the person they are sitting next to.

So, that's about all I have time for right now. If you want to learn more about my ideas, please visit my website.

UNIT 9 RECORDING 7

A = Amy   L = Lisa
A: How's work? Are you still feeling fed up?
L: Yeah, especially with this new boss, I absolutely hate every minute of it. I just want to do something different ... a job where I get out of the office and meet new people, and talk about something I'm actually interested in.
A: Like what?
L: I dunno, but there must be something better than this ... Any suggestions?
A: This might sound a bit strange, but have you ever thought about becoming an estate agent? I think it would be really good idea. You know how much you love looking round other people's houses and you're always watching property programmes on TV and stuff.
L: Yeah, actually I have thought about it before, but I've no idea if I'm qualified to do it or not.
A: I'm sure a lot of it's personality, and you've definitely got the right kind of personality for that job ... confident, and good at persuading people ... you ought to look into it, you know.
L: Yeah, perhaps you're right ... I ought to ... I don't know where to start though.
A: You could look online I suppose, there must be websites giving information about that sort of thing. Or why not go into an estate agent's and just ask? I'm sure they like people who show initiative.
L: Mmm it would be good if I knew someone who could give me some advice, you know, so that I know what they're looking for.
A: Mmm, I know what you mean. Hang on, I know what you should do ... remember my friend Alex? His mum used to be an estate agent. I'm sure she'd give you some advice. Why don't you have a chat with her? She's really, really nice.
L: Do you think she'd mind?
A: Course not. Go on, give her a call, why not? I'll text Alex and get her number.
L: Well, OK then ... yeah ... thanks.

UNIT 9 RECORDING 8

L = Lisa   J = Jenny
J: Hello, Jenny Harrison speaking.
L: Oh hello Mrs Harrison, you don't know me but my name's Lisa Allen. Your son Alex gave me your number, I hope you don't mind me calling you.
J: Not at all, Alex said you were going to call. What can I do for you?
L: Well, I'd like some advice about careers, basically. The thing is I'm working as a PA at the moment, but I'm really looking for a career change, and erm ... well ... I'm interested in becoming an estate agent, and I just wondered if you've got any advice about what I should do? I mean, are there qualifications that I need, or can I just apply? I don't know.
J: Mm, well you certainly need qualifications if you want to progress in the job, so you should definitely look into that – I can tell you which websites to look at. But to be honest, the most important thing is personality, you do need to be very outgoing and confident, and obviously you need to be interested in everything to do with houses!

Audio script

L: Oh well I'm certainly all of those things ...

J: ... and obviously it's essential to have good computer skills, and these days you need good digital photography skills, so if you're not very good with a camera, I would recommend taking a course.

L: No actually I can do both of those things.

J: Well that's good ... mmm ... You know what I would advise? I would suggest that you try to get a weekend job with a local estate agent's showing people round houses. A lot of estate agents have extra staff just for the weekend, because they're so busy then. I think that would be really useful, that way you can see whether you really like it, and obviously it would give you a bit of experience.

L: That's a really good idea, I hadn't thought of that. Thank you. How do you think I should apply?

J: If I were you, I'd just write to all the estate agent's in the area with your CV, telling them a bit about yourself and what you want to do, I'm sure if you try hard enough, you'll find something.

L: That's great thank you, I really appreciate your advice.

J: You're welcome, and good luck, I hope you find something.

L: Thanks.

UNIT 10 RECORDING 1

P = Presenter   M = Monica   E = Ewan   F = Fred
H = Hannah   D = Damien   L = Lisa

P: And now it's time for *Quiz the Expert*. Our expert this week is Monica Jessop. Monica will be familiar to some of our listeners. She has worked at a number of top UK universities.
Good to have you on the programme Monica.

M: Thanks Doug.

P: So Monica, our first question comes from a caller in South Wales. Hello Ewan.

E: Yes, hello.

P: What's your question for our expert, Ewan?

E: OK, well, a question I've always wanted to ask is: who actually controls the media?

M: Well Ewan, the simple answer is: it depends. In some countries the government controls the media. In other countries it's private individuals or companies who own it. What we call mass media nowadays also includes the internet and you could argue that we all own that because we can all set up a website. However there are certainly some very large media corporations that own and control a lot of what we see and hear. In the US around 25 years ago there were 50 major media corporations. Now there are just six.

P: Does that answer your question Ewan?

E: Yes ... I think it does, thanks.

P: Great stuff. Now on to Fred from Bristol.

F: Thanks Doug. Monica, I'm interested in your opinion. Does the media reflect what we think or does the media control what we think? I mean, you know, do we just think about the things that the media wants us to think about?

M: Ah, the eternal question, Fred. It used to be said that the most powerful person in the country was the newspaper editor because he, and it always was a 'he', decided what went on the front page and so decided what was important and what wasn't. However, the internet has had an impact. Now, anyone can create news. With the camera in our smartphones we can record a high-definition video of an event, upload it to the internet and hey presto, people all over the world can see. Big media corporations are being cut out. Sites like globalvoicesonline.org are bringing the news directly from the people who are experiencing it, inside war zones for example. So in answer to your question, while the media does still control what we think to some extent, people are now able to use the media to reflect what they think.

P: That's a fascinating idea. I must check it out. Thanks for that question Fred.   Now we have Damian in Leeds. Hi Damian, What's your question?

D: Oh, yes, er you mentioned how the internet has changed news, Monica. How else has the internet changed things? How has it affected the world of media?

M: Well, of course it's introduced a lot of new words to our language. Who had heard of 'microblogging' before the internet? But more importantly, I believe the internet has made media more interactive. Media used to be a one-way process – they spoke and we listened. Now its much more like a dialogue. Every article has reader comments below it, every concert is reviewed and discussed on Twitter. Unfortunately, I think the internet has also made us all more separate from each other. We're all watching and listening to different things. Young adults now probably don't even remember the time when everyone watched the same thing on television and then talked about it the next day at work or college. In 1986 the top-rated TV show in the UK got 30 million viewers – that's half the population. Twenty-five years later the top-rated show got less than half that number. As a society we just don't share the same experiences any more. We watch and listen to different things.

P: OK, thanks Monica, and thanks Damian for that question. We've got to move on, we've only got time for one more question, I think, which is from Lisa in Edinburgh.

L: Hi, Monica.

M: Hi Lisa. What's your question?

L: Well, you mentioned newspapers earlier. They're having a hard time of things. Will we still read newspapers in the future?

M: Most countries have seen a drop in newspaper circulation in the last few years, particularly broadsheets. They're finding it much harder to survive and many have gone out of business. It's not just the loss of readers that is a problem. In the US newspapers make almost 90% of their money from advertising. When circulation drops, fewer people want to advertise in the newspaper and they won't pay as much to advertise.

P: OK, thanks Monica. Fascinating as always to talk to you and thanks for taking part in *Quiz the Expert*. Now it's time for travel news. Gary, over to you ...

UNIT 10 RECORDING 4

1   The weather forecast said it was going to be nice today.
2   The police officer told us there was nothing to worry about.
3   Our teacher said the test was going to be easy.
4   Clare told me she was staying in tonight.
5   Jonnie said the money was his.
6   She said she couldn't afford to come out for a meal with us.
7   Rick said he would be home early.
8   Alex told me she'd passed the exam.

UNIT 11 RECORDING 3

Case 1

Miss K, a 15-year-old secondary school student wants to have plastic surgery to change the shape of her nose. Although no-one at her private girls' school has bullied her about it, she feels that peer pressure to look attractive is very strong and she says the issue is affecting her self-esteem, and making her depressed. It is Miss K's ambition to become a corporate lawyer, and she believes that her nose will also affect her career prospects. Her wealthy parents don't believe that her nose is such a serious problem, and feel that she should wait until she is at least 21, as she may feel differently about it by then. However, they have said that they will pay for the surgery if doctors agree that it is in their daughter's best interests.

Case 2

A six-year-old boy, S, has been diagnosed by doctors with attention deficit disorder (ADHD) and prescribed a new drug which he will probably have to take until he is an adult. The drug is not thought to lead to dependency, but the long-term effects are not fully known. His mother, who is separated from his father, and who has custody of their three children, is keen to try the drug. She says his problem is badly affecting his life both at school and at home. He is distracted at school, is already falling behind other children in his schoolwork, and his. teachers are unsympathetic. At home, his bad behaviour causes constant stress, and his mother says that the only thing that keeps him calm is playing computer games. His father, who lives 100 kilometres away, is against him taking the drug. He says that his son is just a normal boy who needs to move to a more disciplined school with a calmer working environment, and that he needs to play outside more instead of staying indoors and playing computer games.

Case 3

Dr Z, a prominent National Health Service specialist, has created a big stir in the media by publicly questioning whether he should treat a patient who is a heavy smoker. The woman, Mrs X, who is in her early sixties, has a life-threatening illness that requires expensive surgery and medication. She has been a lifelong smoker and says that she cannot give up. Dr Z says that treating her 'does not represent value for money for the taxpayer', as she is shortening her life expectancy considerably by smoking. However opponents of Doctor Z point out that Mrs X, who is a retired school secretary, was a taxpayer all her working life. Furthermore her illness is not directly linked to smoking, and she is currently in good enough general health to undergo surgery and treatment. But, as the aging population grows, and healthcare gets more and more expensive for the state, the case is causing huge public debate.

UNIT 11 RECORDING 6

N = newsreader   R = reporter

N: Two recent opinion polls have given new life to the debate on animal testing. So, Sasha, what else do the polls show?
R: Well, they show that the majority of people feel that medical research on animals is justified in some circumstances. Only around one in five people believe that it is never acceptable under any circumstances.
N: Well that seems quite clear. What else does the poll show?
R: Well, the problems start when you ask what sorts of experiments are justified. Three quarters of people, for instance, think that experiments on monkeys and other primates should not be allowed. And more than four out of five people think that experiments which cause severe suffering or pain should be banned. However, just over half the people polled also said that experiments on new medicines should be allowed. The problem of course, is what if that experiment on a new medicine causes severe pain to the animal.
N: I see. What do people feel about testing cosmetics on animals?
R: Well that's very clear. The vast majority of people, over 90%, are against testing cosmetics on animals.
N: So how would you summarise the polls overall?
R: Generally speaking, it's a mixed picture. But the results certainly show that more and more people are concerned about animal testing.
N: OK. Well, thank you for that brief round up, Sasha. On to other news ...

UNIT 12 RECORDING 2

1

An unnamed entertainer has today taken out an injunction to prevent the news media from publishing details of an extra-marital affair that he had with a colleague last year. The entertainer, a married father of three is described as 'a household name with a strong image as a family man. He says in a statement released by his lawyers that he and his family have a right to privacy and that he has taken legal action to prevent his children from being bullied and teased at school.

2

The singer Charlotte Morland appeared in court today to describe the suffering that phone hacking by tabloid newspapers has caused her and her family. Repeated hacking into her private voicemail messages meant that details of her mother's mental illness were published in a number of newspapers, eventually causing her mother to have a breakdown. Miss Morland described the 'paranoia' she experienced as she read newspaper stories about information that she had only revealed to close friends and family members, and how she had wrongly accused friends of selling stories to journalists.

UNIT 12 RECORDING 3

P = Presenter   B = Becky   C = Carl
L = Lesley   G = Gemma   R = Robert

P: And today, we have heard news of an 'unnamed entertainer' let's call him X, who has taken out an injunction to prevent the media from reporting his extra-marital affair, in order, X claims, to protect his children from play ground bullying. Also this week stories about the hacking of celebrities' phones continue to emerge, especially the sad story of Charlotte Morland and her mother.

So today we're asking you: is the way that the media behaves towards celebrities acceptable? Should the law protect the privacy of the famous and their families, or should celebrities shut up and just accept that this is the price they pay for fame and publicity? Tell us what you think. First, over to Becky in Somerset. Hello Becky and welcome to the show, tell me, what's your reaction to the stories we've heard this week?
B: Hello Andrew. Well I think it's right that the law protects famous people and their families and allows them to have a normal life. I mean, this X, whoever he is, his children are innocent, aren't they? They deserve to have the right to a normal life, like other children. It isn't really any of our business what X does or doesn't do. It's his wife's business, not ours. So I think what's happened is right.
P: You don't think that if people choose to be in the public eye, then they should just put up with this kind of thing if it happens?
B: Well, their children don't choose to be famous, do they? And they're the ones who are going to suffer here.
P: Fair enough Becky, thanks for your views. Over to Carl in Liverpool now. Carl, Do you agree with Becky?
C: No I disagree 100% ... if what I've read is right ... this is someone who appears on family TV shows, who has his photograph in magazines with his wife and children, who makes a lot of money out of being in adverts looking like the perfect family man ... and then he goes and has an affair. I mean it's really hypocritical isn't it? If he wants to make money out of being seen as a family man, then he should behave like one. And if he doesn't, then I think we have the right to know about it.
P: OK, then, strong views there from Carl in Liverpool, Lesley in Bristol, I believe you agree with Carl, can you tell us briefly why?
L: Hi, Andrew. Yes, I just want to say that if X doesn't want his children to be upset, he should think about that before he starts having an affair. That's the same for anyone isn't it? If you don't want your kids to suffer, you don't do things like that. So if they do get teased at school then it's his own fault, he can't blame the media.
P: Thank you Lesley. And here's a text here from Carol in Derbyshire, agreeing with Carl and Lesley. She says simply 'X is not taking legal action to protect his children, it's to protect HIMSELF!!!' Thank you for that Carol, it's an opinion expressed in many other texts and emails that we've received from our listeners. OK, now over to Gemma in Cardiff. Gemma, you want to talk about the Charlotte Morland story?
G: That's right. I just want to say how disgusted I am to hear what this newspaper did to Charlotte Morland and her mother. I think what happened to her mother is a disgrace, and it really makes me feel ashamed to be British. I just can't believe that this kind of thing is allowed to happen.
P: Well of course if the journalist who is accused of hacking is found guilty, he could be sent to prison, and we also know that the Morland family are likely to receive several hundred thousand pounds in compensation. But presumably you don't think that makes up for the suffering they have been through?
G: No I don't think so. I don't think anything can compensate for that kind of trauma.
P: Well thank you, Gemma, we've received a large number of texts and emails making the same point as Gemma, so thank you very much for those too. But Robert in London, you want to make a different point about this story?
R: Good morning Andrew, yes I do. The fact of the matter is that tabloid newspapers only publish stories if they think that people want to read them. So they must know that stories like this one sell newspapers. And the people texting you saying how terrible they think the newspapers are – well they're probably the same people who read the stories about Charlotte Morland and her mother. So isn't it we the public who are the real hypocrites, not the journalists?
P: Very interesting point there Robert, thank you for calling. So what do you think? Call, text or email us and share your thoughts. And now some music from ...

Audio script

UNIT 12 RECORDING 5

E = Eliza   H = Harriet   J = James

1

E: If I had to be famous I would like to be famous for being a painter, um, I think it would be nice to be famous for being a painter because, um, I really enjoy painting and, it would be nice to be famous but – but mainly because I really enjoy painting ...

H: Challenge, repetition!

2

J: I think it must actually be more difficult because I don't think you would know who were genuine friends and who just wanted to be friends with you because you were famous. I think that, ah, being famous brings its, its own problems, I think suddenly everyone wants to be your friend, and therefore forging any sort of, ah, real friendship with someone, ah, must be really difficult, let alone forming a relationship with someone of the opposite sex that you might want to, um, marry or be, ah, be a partner with.

E: Well done, that's 30 seconds.

J: Wow.

3

H: I would love to appear on a reality TV programme, especially if it was one where you could learn to dance really well I think learning to dance would be amazing and what a great opportunity. Um ...

J: Challenge, sorry you hesitated there.

Verb list

VERB	PAST SIMPLE	PAST PARTICIPLE
be	was/were	been
beat	beat	beaten
become	became	become
begin	began	begun
bend	bent	bent
bite	bit	bitten
blow	blew	blown
break	broke	broken
bring	brought	brought
build	built	built
burn	burned/burnt	burned/burnt
burst	burst	burst
buy	bought	bought
can	could	been able
catch	caught	caught
choose	chose	chosen
come	came	come
cost	cost	cost
cut	cut	cut
dig	dug	dug
do	did	done
draw	drew	drawn
dream	dreamed/dreamt	dreamed/dreamt
drink	drank	drunk
drive	drove	driven
eat	ate	eaten
fall	fell	fallen
feed	fed	fed
feel	felt	felt
fight	fought	fought
find	found	found
fly	flew	flown
forget	forgot	forgotten
forgive	forgave	forgiven
freeze	froze	frozen
get	got	got
give	gave	given
go	went	gone/been
grow	grew	grown
hang	hung	hanged/hung
have	had	had
hear	heard	heard
hide	hid	hidden
hit	hit	hit
hold	held	held
hurt	hurt	hurt
keep	kept	kept
kneel	knelt	knelt
know	knew	known
lay	laid	laid
lead	led	led
learn	learned/learnt	learned/learnt

VERB	PAST SIMPLE	PAST PARTICIPLE
leave	left	left
lend	lent	lent
let	let	let
lie	lay	lain
light	lit	lit
lose	lost	lost
make	made	made
mean	meant	meant
meet	met	met
must	had to	had to
pay	paid	paid
put	put	put
read	read	read
ride	rode	ridden
ring	rang	rung
rise	rose	risen
run	ran	run
say	said	said
see	saw	seen
sell	sold	sold
send	sent	sent
set	set	set
shake	shook	shaken
shine	shone	shone
shoot	shot	shot
show	showed	shown
shut	shut	shut
sing	sang	sung
sink	sank	sunk
sit	sat	sat
sleep	slept	slept
slide	slid	slid
smell	smelled/smelt	smelled/smelt
speak	spoke	spoken
spend	spent	spent
spill	spilled/spilt	spilled/spilt
spoil	spoiled/spoilt	spoiled/spoilt
stand	stood	stood
steal	stole	stolen
stick	stuck	stuck
swim	swam	swum
take	took	taken
teach	taught	taught
tear	tore	torn
tell	told	told
think	thought	thought
throw	threw	thrown
understand	understood	understood
wake	woke	woken
wear	wore	worn
win	won	won
write	wrote	written

Pearson Education Limited
Edinburgh Gate
Harlow
Essex CM20 2JE
England
and Associated Companies throughout the world.

www.pearsonelt.com

First published 2013
ISBN: 978-1-4479-3698-5

Set in Bliss Light 10.5pt/12pt
Printed in Slovakia by Neografia

Acknowledgements
*The publishers and authors would like to thank the following people and
institutions for their feedback and comments during the development of
the material:*

Stephanie Dimond-Bayir, Bell Educational Services, Cambridge, UK;
Amanda French, Languages International, Auckland, New Zealand;
Elizabeth Gregson, Università degli Studi di Trento, Italy; Fiona
Johnston, International House, London, UK; Hanna Malgorzata
Dobrzańska-Watanabe, The Maria Curie-Sklodowska University
(UMCS) of Lublin, Poland; Denise Metzger, Navitas English, Sydney,
Australia; David Petrie, International House Coimbra, Portugal; Wayne
Rimmer, International House, Moscow, Russia; Nathalie Vermeire, City
of Bristol College, University of Bath, UK; Damian Williams, Tailor-
Made English, Rio de Janeiro, Brazil

Text acknowledgements
*We are grateful to the following for permission to reproduce copyright
material:*
Extract 5. adapted from 'We may have 750 friends online, but we're
lonely', The Times, 03/12/2011 (Andy Jones), copyright © *The Times*,
2011, www.nisyndication.com; Extract 7. from *The People's Century:
From the Start of the Nuclear Age to the Close of the Century, Volume
2*, BBC Books (Godfrey Hodgeson 1996) pp.190, 193–194, Reproduced
by permission of The Random House Group Limited; Extract 7. from
*People's 20th Century: From the Dawn of the Century to the Start of
the Cold War*, BBC Books (Godfrey Hodgson 1995) p.159, Reproduced
by permission of The Random House Group Limited; Extract 8. from
Reader's Digest Book of Strange Stories Amazing Facts, 2nd edition,
Readers Digest (1984), Reproduced by permission of Reader's Digest
Association Inc.; Extract 11. adapted from 'Inspiration and Chai Regrets
of the Dying' by Bronnie Ware, http://www.inspirationandchai.com/
Regrets-of-the-Dying.html, Following on from this article, Bronnie
Ware has released a full-length book, titled *The Top Five Regrets of the
Dying – A Life Transformed by the Dearly Departing*. It is a memoir
of Bronnie's own life and how it was changed by the regrets of dying
people. It is published in English by Hay House and has been sold for
translation into more than 25 other languages.

Photo acknowledgements
*The Publisher would like to thank the following for their kind
permission to reproduce their photographs:*

(Key: b-bottom; c-centre; l-left; r-right; t-top)

Alamy Images: ACE STOCK LIMITED 106/4, Classic Image 76tl,
corfield 106/3, betty finney 22 (litter), Malcolm S Firth. BA(Hons)
ARPS 56t, Neil Ginger 57tl, GlowImages 111t, INTERFOTO 58cr,
Juice Images 26tl, NASA Archive 59c, NASA Photo 59r, North Wind
Picture Archives 58cl, Archives du 7e Art / Photos 12 15, Brad Rickerby
42tl, Ian Thraves 72tl, Ruth Tomlinson / Robert Harding Picture Library
Lt 70 (float), Ivan Vdovin 57tr, Lisa F. Young 107/6; **Bridgeman Art
Library Ltd:** Self Portrait with Bandaged Ear and Pipe, 1889 (oil on
canvas), Gogh, Vincent van (1853-90) / Private Collection 76tr; Corbis:
Rick Gomez / Bridge 19t, William Gottlieb / Retro 44, Mark Stevenson
/ Stocktrek Images 85l, Eadweard Muybridge 104-105t, Tom Odulate
/ cultura 45r, Schnoerrer / dpa 8tl, George Tiedemann / Historical 611,
Underwood & Underwood 56b, 58r; ESA: 41; **Fotolia.com:** 25b, Yuri
Arcurs 54, auremar 78, elavuk81 113, flas100 104b, fovito 23 (spider),
Hirurg 33c, hues 63, PatrykKosmider 66b, 70 (fireworks), MO:SES
84t, Karen Roach 6 (A), StudioAraminta 102b, Unclesam 118; **Getty
Images:** 90, VegarAbelsnes Photography / The Image Bank 77r, LUIS
ACOSTA / AFP 8b, James Balog / Stone 106/1, Martin Barraud / Stone
22 (traffic), Thomas Barwick / Iconica 42tr, Thomas Barwick / Stone
20br, Vincent Besnault / Photodisc 114, Michael Betts / Photographer's
Choice RF 124l, ERproductions Ltd / Blend Images 42bl, John Bryson
/ Time Life Pictures 100b, Peter Cade / The Image Bank 20bl, Dario
Cantatore / Getty Images Entertainment 7, Ed Darack / Science Faction
84b, Stuart Dee 58l, Krzysztof Dydynski / Lonely Planet Images 72tr,
Tony Esparza / CBS Photo Archive via Getty Image 102t, Tom Fullum /
E+ 511, Adam Gault / Digital Vision 26b, 34, Glowimages 116t, Jo Hale
/ Getty Images Entertainment 120r, Pando Hall / Photographer's Choice
RF 51r, Lewis W. Hine / George Eastman House / Archive Photos 82t,
Dave Hogan / Getty Images Entertainment 9t, STAN HONDA / AFP
69r, Anwar Hussein / WireImage 100t, Asia Images Group 36b, 45l,
ImagesBazaar / the Agency Collection 94, Imagno / Hulton Archive 24l,
Jupiterimages / Comstock Images 42cl, Keystone-France / Gamma-
Keystone via Getty Images 68l, Howard Kingsnorth / Photographer's
Choice 26c, Howard Kingsnorth / Riser 23 (man laughing), Jan Kruger
/ Getty Images Sport 70 (mugs), Fred W. McDarrah / Premium Archive
68r, Medioimages / Photodisc 43c, Michael Wildsmith / Taxi 6 (C),
K. Miller Photographs / Flickr 42cr, Abel Mitja Varela / the Agency
Collection 99, Dave Nagel / Taxi 73tr, Gabe Palmer / Workbook Stock
14, Popperfoto 59l, Zachary Scott 86t, Reg Speller / Fox Photos /
Hulton Archive 77l, SSPL via Getty Images 65tr, 65b, SSPL via Getty
Images / Science Museum 57tc, Stock Montage / Archive Photos 38
(A), Stephen Swintek / Stone 26tr, John Tlumacki / The Boston Globe
via Getty Images 69l, Penny Tweedie / Stone 125, uniquely india 86b,
92cl, Universal Images Group 39 (B), Charles von Urban / Museum of
the City of New York / Archive Photos / Archive Photos 82b, Westend61
6 (D), Zero Creatives / Cultura 6bl, 10; **Pearson Education Ltd:** Jon
Barlow. Pearson Education Ltd 42br, 50, Tim Draper (c) Rough Guides
76b, 85r, Imagemore Co., Ltd 106/5, itanistock 43t, Dave Pattison.
Alamy 73tl, Jules Selmes 6 (B); **Press Association Images:** Andrew
Milligan / PA Wire 124r, Karl Schnoerrer / DPA 8tr; **Rex Features:**
120cr, 130, Image Source 46b, 48-49, TB / TS / Keystone USA 120l,
Moviestore Collection 83, 116b, 120c, PhotosportInt 64, Roger-Viollet
61r, SNAP 120cl, RICHARD YOUNG 60 (Bob Dylan); **Science
Photo Library Ltd:** PASIEKA 106/2; **Shutterstock.com:** 3103 30cl,
Alenavlad 18r, Ambient Ideas 19b, Andresr 92r, AraBus 96, 117, Sergey
Ash 30c, Binkski 57b, BlueOrange Studio 20t, Joy Brown 70 (balloon),
Cienpies Design 46t, Andrea Danti 36t, 126, GoranDjukanovic 66t,
AndreyEremin 30l, Paul Fleet 70 (present), Benjamin Albiach Galan
38 (C), Goodluz 92cr, JorgHackemann 112, haveseen 92l, iofoto 23
(woman and beach), Brian A Jackson 23 (newspaper), Kittisak 30cr,
Michal Kowalski 102c, Bernd LeitnerFotodesign 16r, lendy16 6 (F),
Andrew Lever 16l, LittleRambo 52b, lsantilli 25tl, Paul Maguire
53, malost 79 (prickly pear), McCarthy's PhotoWorks 70 (mask),
mexrix 79 (chilli), michaeljung 43b, OcskayBence 25tr, Oligo 30r,
outdoorsman 79 (polar bears), photomak 22 (scared), Pina 111b, rebvt
65tl, karen roach 6 (E), serg_dibrova 79 (fish), Steve Collender 76cr,
SergiyTelesh 22 (candles), Tribalium 33b, Suzanne Tucker 111c, Marco
Uliana 18l, vgm 39 (D), wavebreakmedia 91; **swns.com:** 33t; **The
Kobal Collection:** 9b, REKALL PRODUCTIONS 40; Veer/Corbis:
jgroupstudios 70 (cake), mitarart 60-61 (pyramids)

All other images © Pearson Education

Cover image: *Front:* **Fotolia.com:** Beboy

Illustrated by: Gregory Baldwin pp.28–9; Natalie Dion (Anna
Goodson Agency) p.75, p.99; Grems (Anna Goodson Agency) p.52,
In-house p.14, p.34, p.54, p.94, p.114; Andrew Lyons (Handsome
Frank) p.80; Julian Mosedale p31, p.40, p.62, p.88; Juice Creative p.41,
pp.96–7, p.107, p.108; Peskimo (Synergy Art) p.12